Viewpoints

on English

as a Second Language

Edited by
Marina Burt
Heidi Dulay
Mary Finocchiaro

In Honor of JAMES E. ALATIS

REGENTS PUBLISHING COMPANY, INC.

Published by
Regents Publishing Company, Inc.
2 Park Avenue
New York, N.Y. 10016

Printed in the United States of America

ISBN 0-88345-298-7

This volume was prepared in honor of Dr. James E. Alatis to celebrate his tenth anniversary as Executive Secretary of TESOL (Teachers of English to Speakers of Other Languages)—August 1, 1966 to August 1, 1976.

Dr. James E. Alatis
Executive Secretary, TESOL
Dean, School of Languages and Linguistics
Georgetown University

It is not a simple matter to prepare a dedication which would do honor to James Alatis. The problem does not lie in the fact that there is not enough to say. Quite the contrary. There is just too much. Which facet of Jim's character and person do we focus upon—the scholar; the administrator; the friend; the family man; or Jim Alatis, the guiding force of the TESOL organization?

Since this book was first conceived to symbolize the gratitude of the TESOL profession for Jim's ten years of uninterrupted tenure as Executive Secretary of the organization, it might be well to start from there. It may be important, in this regard, to point out to those who have joined our professional ranks only in the last few years that Jim was not just one of a succession of executive secretaries. He was the *first* executive secretary of the TESOL organization, and has stayed with it through every childhood disease and growing pain. Another historical note may be in order at this time. The founding members of TESOL were drawn from the most disparate theoretical schools of linguistics and hyphenated linguistics. They came from the National Association for Foreign Student Affairs, the Modern Language Association, the National Council of Teachers of English, and the Speech Association—all well-established organizations. None of the organizations, however, was able to devote full time to the needs of non- or limited English speakers, many of whom had lived in the United States for decades without being fully integrated into American life.

Organizations like the MLA and NCTE had made valiant efforts to bring together materials and other teaching aids. By the early 1960s, however, it had become painfully obvious that more, much more, was urgently needed to help respond to a situation of such complexity that many schools in the Southwest, in Florida, and in New York were virtually at a standstill. What was needed was a group of professional educators who recognized that nearly every program developed for speakers of languages other than English had led to failure and, more importantly, that this diverse group would make a valuable contribution to American life if given the opportunity of educational equality, an equality to be sought through many channels.

And so, TESOL was born—an association whose primary concern was the teaching of English to speakers of other languages and dialects, an association which would help set standards for teacher training and which would formulate guidelines for action and for the preparation of appropriate materials, in collaboration not only with other associations but also with all members of the communities involved.

When the time came to select an executive secretary for the new organization, Jim was urged by all those from the founding organizations who knew of his boundless energy, his willingness to work long hours to achieve a goal, and above all, his ability to weld together groups with seemingly different philosophies, to take the helm of a then rudderless ship and to steer that ship to a safe haven.

No one could have done a more magnificent job. From an organization whose members numbered a mere 375 a decade ago, TESOL can now boast of a national association of near 7,000 members and of 27 state and international affiliates. TESOL's members teach at every level of the educational system, specializing in areas that range from teaching English in bilingual education programs to teaching English for special purposes in overseas programs in remote corners of the world.

While the founding organizations continue to maintain a separate existence, there has been a close collaboration in programs, publications, and conferences between members of TESOL and members of the MLA, ACTFL, and other groups in the United States. Nor are the United States the sole boundaries within which TESOL operates. In addition to the formally established overseas affiliates, TESOL is represented in numerous overseas organizations as, for example, FIPLV (Fédération Internationale de Professeurs de Langues Vivantes); IATEFL (International Association of Teachers of English as a Foreign Language); and IALA (International Association of Applied Linguistics).

Let us look for a moment at a few of TESOL's organizational accomplishments under Jim Alatis's leadership. Procedures have been established to amend the constitution to respond to the evolving needs of an ever-growing membership; special interest groups have been set up to prepare programs relevant to them and to present these programs at the Annual Convention; by-laws have been written which ensure the widest possible geographic and academic distribution of members of the Executive Committee; a Journal and a Newsletter are distributed regularly, and numerous other books and monographs are published as well; position papers on matters of the utmost importance to TESOL members are prepared and distributed regularly; the Annual Convention, which attracts about three thousand members each year, is a stimulating event which all members look forward to with undisguised eagerness.

While, of course, Jim is assisted by members of various committees—Executive, Program, Publications, and so on—we think it would be appropriate to say that little happens in TESOL which has not passed through his hands. And this is exactly what has made the Organization thrive. Jim's initiative and intervention, when sought, have given TESOL the continuity, coherence, and cohesion that any group needs if it is to grow and prosper.

Jim's appointment in 1973 as Dean of Georgetown University's School of Languages and Linguistics is a tribute to his scholarship and professional leadership. The Georgetown University Round Table Conferences and conference proceedings have won international recognition under his chairmanship and editorship; and he regularly receives numerous invitations to speak on the most minute aspects of our multifaceted discipline. In addition, despite a near superhuman work schedule, Dean Alatis finds time to maintain his native language and culture by teaching two courses in Greek each semester.

Those of us who have worked intimately with Jim recognize additional qualities which are not always obvious to outsiders. He is a devoted husband; a loving, warm, caring parent; and a superb friend. He makes time for his own family and his "extended" family. He is never too busy to do a favor for a friend, or a friend of a friend. He is never too tired to right a wrong that may have been done to even a casual acquaintance. The doors to his office, to his home, and especially to his heart are open wide to his staff, to his students, and to the members of the TESOL profession.

Although it is not customary to compile a *Festschrift* for one as young as Jim Alatis, who is in the prime of his professional career, the magnitude and scope of his accomplishments deserve commensurate recognition. When one thinks of true professionalism in TESOL, the first name which comes to mind is that of James E. Alatis, to whom these *Viewpoints* are dedicated with affection and gratitude.

Marina Burt, Heidi Dulay, Mary Finocchiaro

Table of Contents

III. SOCIO-POLITICAL DIMENSIONS

Introduction

This volume was designed to accomplish two seemingly divergent goals: 1) to stimulate those who have been in the English as a Second Language (ESL) field and know it well, and 2) to inform those who are new to the profession about basic concepts and issues in ESL today. Consequently, the 21 "viewpoints" in this volume are those of leading practitioners and scholars who have drawn upon their extensive experience in teaching and research to summarize an important aspect of the field or to advance a new and perhaps controversial idea. This volume is intended to offer the reader a cohesive framework of broad issues, as well as to place into perspective recent specific innovations and suggestions.

The last decade has seen intense activity and change in ESL, to the point where some declare a state of "revolution"; others bemoan the lack of a theory that will answer all questions; and yet others take refuge in an eclecticism that sometimes smoothes the jagged edges of conflicting beliefs. It seemed necessary, therefore, to gather together respected people in the field—some of whom have been in the profession more than a generation and have seen movements come and go, others for whom this "movement" is the first—and ask them to share their viewpoints on areas of common interest and current controversy.

Three areas were chosen. The first, "Instructional Perspectives," is the common ground—the eventual meeting place of almost everyone in the field. The "perspectives" are by necessity broad, so as to be useful to the profession regardless of specialization. For example, there are few among us who have not wondered what causes some students to learn languages faster than others; or what it is about some teachers that contributes to their effectiveness in a language classroom. Although the state of knowledge in the field is not such that there are comprehensive answers to these questions, what is known is substantial and may be especially useful to beginning teachers and to researchers in need of testable hypotheses. Both John Carroll, who discusses the successful learner, and Betty Robinett, who discusses the effective teacher, focus on personality traits that may be cultivated, albeit with some effort. Current theory and research, along with years of classroom practice, converge in their cogent treatments of these central topics.

Two current issues in curriculum which have occupied much space in journal pages and conferences are presented by Robert Lado and Valerian Postovsky. Lado argues for the inclusion of reading activities from the very beginning of a second language curriculum, contrary to the traditional sequencing of the four language skills. Postovsky, in a coincidentally complementary position, suggests we postpone speaking until the learner has had sufficient listening time—at least several weeks. These suggestions are the result of diligent efforts to draw from existing pedagogical research, implications for improved ESL instruction.

To suggest that ESL teaching become more "natural" or more sensitive to the "communicative needs" of learners has become axiomatic and perhaps almost hackneyed. J. Donald Bowen and Paul Pimsleur et al. have, however, given fresh and additional meaning to these terms. Both microanalyze native speaker speech, Bowen focusing on natural pronunciation, Pimsleur et al. on speech rate. They then suggest how teachers might improve a learner's ability to understand the everyday conversation of native speakers and to produce its informal features. On the other hand, Kenneth Johnson focuses on the teaching of standard English as a second dialect (ESD). He discusses some of the important differences between teaching a second dialect and teaching a second language—what is to be learned, motivational factors, and teacher expectations of students.

William Mackey and Reinhold Freudenstein present techniques for teacher training. They report on the now widespread practice of recording and analyzing teacher-student interaction in the language classroom. Freudenstein suggests refinements in observational techniques and categories in an attempt to make more productive observations of teacher-student behaviors. Mackey describes a specific device that can be used for the efficient and easy recording of such interactions.

The other two sections in this volume focus on areas which have received much attention in the last ten years: 1) empirical investigations into the roles of cognition and affect in the learning process (the domain of psycholinguistics) and 2) the sociopolitical and educational contexts of second language learning. These dimensions have deepened and expanded our notions of the learning process and have become indispensable to anyone concerned with the language education of those who speak a language other than English.

No longer content with wholesale borrowing of theories from the source disciplines of psychology and linguistics, scholars interested in second language acquisition have spent long hours analyzing the speech and environments of second language learners in an effort to gain more insight into the complex process of becoming bilingual. The second section in this volume, "Psycholinguistic Insights," begins with three articles that reflect the results of such research. Heidi Dulay and Marina Burt focus on the creative aspects of children's acquisition of a second syntax. They suggest ways in which the learner's cognitive and affective apparatus function 1) to select from available primary linguistic data that which will be attended to and processed and 2) to regulate environmental pressures such as frequency and perceptual saliency during the learning process. Eduardo Hernández-Chávez breaks important ground in his pioneering analysis of aspects of a child's developing semantic system. He demonstrates that major semantic relations develop in the second language independently of those the child already knows in the first language. This perhaps unexpected finding parallels that found for children's developing L2 *syntax,* namely, that there is virtually no product transfer of first language syntactic structures onto the second language.

Switching to adults, Stephen Krashen suggests that both unconscious and conscious processing take place in adult second language acquisition. In addition to a creative construction process similar to that described for children, it is suggested that adults also learn rules with conscious effort, and that they can therewith voluntarily control and modify their linguistic output under certain conditions.

Within the same general theoretical framework of active and creative learning, Wilga Rivers and Bernice Melvin draw on information processing research to argue that memory too, is a dynamic process in which the language learner's past experiences and future goals determine what and how new information is "stored." Memory is not a bag in the brain "into which we can stuff things to be withdrawn as we require them"; it is a multifaceted and complex process of perception and organization.

Attitudes, motivation, and personality comprise the affective side of the psycholinguistic coin. Intimately integrated with cognition, attitudinal, motivational, and personality factors have long been considered important stimulants (or depressants) to a student's efforts to learn a language. To provide a general background for future empirical research in this area, as well as for the formulation of theoretical and pedagogical principles, is the purpose of the last three papers in this section.

Maureen O'Brien presents an overview of the major psychological schools and relates them to current research trends and teaching practices. Renzo Titone suggests the incorporation of all the facets of an individual's personality into theory construction in language acquisition. And John Oller presents inconsistencies among various major findings in attitude research of the past decade in order to highlight the need for more productive research methods in this highly elusive area of psycholinguistics.

The last section of the volume presents social and political contexts within which the learning and teaching of English as a second or foreign language often take place. An understanding of these contexts is a prerequisite for maximally effective ESL programs.

The problems and conditions of increasing migration have touched millions—immigrants and hosts alike—in numerous countries throughout the world. Mary Finocchiaro and Lars Ekstrand discuss some of the most pressing problems. They discuss the need for "receiving" communities to have much more information about those who plan to settle there, so that fears due to ignorance do not cause unnecessary hostilities. Conversely, "sending" communities should obtain and make available accurate information about receiving communities to those planning to emigrate. Educational planning cannot be effective if insufficient information is available, as instructional programs must be tailored to particular needs of diverse students.

Focusing on the United States, Patricia Nakano provides an invaluable analysis of the legal history, the opinions, and the educational aftermath of the *Lau* vs. *Nichols* decision of the United States Supreme Court. This landmark decision of 1974 is the first Supreme Court ruling to mandate the formulation and implementation of special educational policies and programs for students with limited English speaking proficiency in the United States. It has already had a resounding impact on school districts across the nation, who are now giving much more thought and effort to providing subject matter instruction in languages other than English, as well as English second language instruction. Nakano clarifies confusions surrounding the "OCR/Lau Remedies" (guidelines for implementing the *Lau* decision) that have resulted from a misunderstanding of the definition and scope of "ESL" and "bilingual education," stressing that ESL is an *integral part* of bilingual education, not at odds with it. She summarizes some of the ways in which the decision is actually implemented in school districts with the technical assistance of the national Lau Centers.

Most educators who have given serious thought to educational approaches that will benefit students who are still in the process of learning English agree that offering these students subject matter instruction in their dominant language while they are learning English is educationally sound. And beyond this rationale of survival—of at least keeping up with monolingual English-speaking peers in the development of concepts and skills—lies the attractive prospect of graduating high school students who possess the additional assets of being bilingual and biliterate. The last three papers, therefore, comprise an effort to provide information about bilingual education—its history, its philosophy, and its implementation.

José Vázquez points out that a century ago bilingual education was initiated by German Americans in the United States as an alternative to the unsatisfactory education given their children by the public school system. He argues that if the enrichment aspects of bilingual education are neglected—namely, giving students more sophisticated linguistic and cultural knowledge and skills—we cannot expect it to become an integral part of American education. In addition to general educational goals, bilingual education has as a major objective the continuing development of a student's home language. Albar Peña argues that the benefits of using the home language as a medium of instruction cannot be realized unless its usage becomes a stable instructional practice.

The implementation of some of these ideas is reported by Alfonso Ramírez, who traces the ten-year development of a bilingual program in Texas. The accomplishments of this program, including the creation of widely used Spanish-English curriculum materials and demonstrable student gains in various areas of the curriculum, should encourage those who are in the process of planning educational programs to meet the needs of non-English-speaking children in the United States.

An underlying aim of this volume has been to capture the depth and scope of what it means to know something about English as a second language. The "viewpoints" presented here comprise an effort to make available current knowledge about the process of language learning, the profession of language teaching, and the many social and political contexts in which English is learned and taught. As James Alatis has often said:

TESOL is *not* a method, *nor* a movement. It is either the *field*, or the professional *organization*, both of which are in a state of dynamic, relevant, ever-changing development.*

* * *

We would like to convey our sincere appreciation to Penelope Alatis and Carol LeClair for their invaluable assistance in obtaining background data on Jim; to Jacqueline Flamm and Julio Andújar, whose support at Regents made this publication possible, to Eve Dulay for her tireless efforts in typing the manuscript during her spare time, and finally, to the contributors who have, with us, contributed all royalties for this volume to the TESOL organization.

M.B., H.D., M.F.

---

* J.E. Alatis, "The Compatibility of TESOL and Bilingual Education." In J.E. Alatis and K. Twaddell (eds.), *English as a Second Language in Bilingual Education*, (Washington, D.C.: TESOL, 1976) p. 7. Also in M.K. Burt and H.C. Dulay (eds.), *New Directions in Second Language Learning, Teaching and Bilingual Education*, (Washington, D.C.: TESOL, 1975), p. 5.

INSTRUCTIONAL
PERSPECTIVES

Characteristics of Successful Second Language Learners

John B. Carroll

Successful language learners are those who master a second language to the point of using it comfortably and effectively for whatever purpose or purposes they may have in mind. These purposes are varied: some learners are interested mainly in reading materials written in the second language; others may want only to understand the speech they hear in foreign language films or TV broadcasts; and still others are interested only in conducting commercial correspondence in the second language. For most second language learners, however, the ability to speak the language fluently, and to understand it when spoken by native speakers, is the kind of competence that is most valued and desired, with reading and writing being important secondary goals.

Even among those who attain fluency in speaking and understanding a second language, there is no one type of successful language learner, nor is there any one way of achieving success. Some people seem to have a "gift" for language learning, and make rapid progress under almost any circumstances. Others seem to require much more time and exposure to the second language, and attain their goals only after long and patient effort. Some people can learn quite successfully in formal school environments, while others find that learning occurs best if they can place themselves in a family or a community where they must communicate in the second language in order to survive in everyday living.

1

Successful second language learning, then, depends on an elaborate interaction of the characteristics and motivations of the learner and the circumstances in which the learning takes place. It also depends on the particular strategies employed by the learner to achieve the desired degree of success, and it is with these strategies that this article will be most concerned. For it is through the adoption of appropriate learning sets and strategies that learners can often be successful even when the talents they bring to the task are only moderate, or indeed only minimal.

The "Ear for Language"

Talent in learning languages does play some part in achievement, and it has to be considered here if only to suggest how a learner can surmount the obstacles presented by limitations in talent.

Besides the basic amount of human intelligence that is required to learn almost anything, there are several kinds of ability, according to research, that are especially relevant to the learning of second languages by persons who are beyond the age of primary language acquisition, and that constitute what is often called an "ear for languages."

One of these, which I have called phonetic coding ability, is the ability to listen to second language sounds or words, to identify them as distinctive, and then to store them in memory so that they can later be recalled accurately on an appropriate occasion. A person with a high degree of this ability finds it easy to imitate accurately a second language utterance of, for example, 10 to 15 syllables, even without knowing the language. But persons without high degrees of this ability can still be successful if they will direct their attention to hearing the particular sounds and learning about the speech movements necessary to produce them. Endowing these second language sounds and words with any associations that can be mustered, and carefully practicing their pronunciation over a period of time and on different occasions, will eventually make them easily recalled and produced.

An ability that is useful to many learners is what I have called grammatical sensitivity. This is the ability to understand the grammatical functions of different kinds of language elements (words, particles, suffixes, etc.) and the rules governing their

2

use. Possession of this ability may depend somewhat on the amount of formal grammatical training the learner may have had in the native language. Persons with above average amounts of this ability, however it may have been acquired, are those who are likely to be successful in formal second language courses that emphasize grammatical analysis. Persons with limited sensitivity to grammar may be better off in courses that de-emphasize grammar and concentrate on exposing the learner to large amounts of the second language in actual use. Nevertheless, many of them will find it profitable to note carefully, and to try to correct, the errors they make in producing second-language utterances. Others, as they use the language more and more, may find it more satisfactory simply to wait until a natural correction process takes over, somewhat the way children learn to speak their native language in increasing conformity with adult norms.

A third ability that is specially relevant to second language learning success is inductive reasoning ability—the ability to infer, from the way in which different words and grammatical constructions are used in the second language, the rules governing the use of those words and constructions. Persons with high degrees of this ability will almost automatically come to recognize the distinctions in meanings between closely related second-language words and the differences in meaning that are conveyed by closely similar grammatical constructions. Persons who have difficulty in recognizing these distinctions will need to have them pointed out, either in formal instructions by teachers or through the corrections and suggestions that native speakers will offer in the course of everyday conversation. Regardless of their levels of inductive reasoning ability, successful language learners need to be alert to possible distinctions conveyed by different second-language forms, actively seeking out examples that illustrate these distinctions.

Motivation

Psychologists have long debated whether motivation is necessary for learning; they have not been able to agree on an answer. Some kinds of learning—for example, the accumulation of certain memories for experiences—occur even when the learner appears to have no motivation for that learning, and some aspects of second language skills can be learned even with little motivation. Nevertheless, it is universally agreed that motivation always helps, particularly when one is learning a complex and difficult skill. Mastery of a second language is certainly that, at least for most people. Successful second language learners are nearly always highly motivated to learn the language, and they persist in spite of the frustrations that almost inevitably accompany that learning. This means that they are able to tolerate and accept the difficulties and frustrations, particularly those encountered in the early stages when the second language may seem strange-sounding and irrational, and when they are almost totally unable to communicate in it because of their lack of mastery.

Contrary to some widely-circulated myths, the key to success is to understand that second language learning is a rather difficult task, which demands much time, patience, and effort. It also requires a tolerance for ambiguity and for seeming irrationality. The successful language learner takes the attitude that the right and rational way of expressing ideas in the second language is the way of the native speakers of the language.

There is a subtle aspect of motivation which seems to be related to personality. The most successful language learners tend to be those who enthusiastically look forward to communicating with speakers of the second language and expect to like, or at least to find interest in, their ideas, experiences, attitudes, and customs. Open, outgoing, friendly people are more likely to have this kind of motivation than persons who have closed minds and rely only on their own ideas and ways of doing things. Some successful language learners may even be persons who are dissatisfied with their own milieu or culture.

Strategies for Second Language Learning

Successful second language learners are likely to be those who can adopt good strategies for coping with the difficulties of their task.

Strategy for learning is partly a matter of attitude. Already mentioned are attitudes concerning the fact that second language learning is often difficult and frustrating. Successful learners are those who can recognize and accept this fact. They can often be helped to accept it if they realize that the difficulties occur more in the early stages of learning, and that after the initial difficulties are overcome, the learning process becomes easier and even enjoyable.

Successful strategy is also a matter of consciously adopting certain habits in approaching the learning task. One such habit is that of fixing attention on each detail as it comes, long enough to understand and assimilate it, at least minimally, before going on to the next. This may even involve consciously ignoring, or being careless about, matters other than the one at hand. Related to this is the habit of recognizing a detail that has been studied and partially learned previously, and deliberately focusing on it to perfect one's mastery of it.

A most important strategy to adopt is that of always attempting to convert passive knowledge into active, productive knowledge. Passive knowledge might be, for example, recognizing the meaning of a second-language word or grammatical construction, while active knowledge would be the ability to recall the second language word, or to use the grammatical structure in a new sentence. Repeated recall of active knowledge will cause that knowledge to become more accessible and automatic. The mistake that many unsuccessful learners make is to allow their knowledge and skill to remain passive. In a classroom situation, good learners will be trying to answer every question for themselves, even when not directly called upon by the teacher.

Another important strategy is to use constantly one's knowledge in a live communication situation, even if the situation is imaginary. Words and sentences heard on a tape, or seen printed on a page, are tools for communication in the second language; one can anticipate their eventual use by pretending to be using them in an imagined situation.

Curiosity about the new language and active searching for opportunities to use it are characteristics of successful language learners. Making one's own lists of words and idioms, and notes about the grammar, are behaviors often observed in good second language learners. Good learners spend as much time as they can in second language activities outside class—seeing films, reading books and magazines, and conversing with speakers of the language.

5

In active use of the language, whether in the classroom or outside it, good language learners are not afraid of making errors, and actively seek information on the correctness and appropriateness of their efforts in the second language. They realize that, through the influence of their native language patterns, or through false analogies and comparisons in the second language, errors are natural. In fact, it has been observed that successful language learners try to talk more, and actually make more errors as a consequence, than the less successful learners. Successful learners learn from their errors. Willingness to try using the language, and to make errors, is somewhat connected with the learner's personality—not necessarily with what is commonly called "extraversion," but with a kind of self-control and confidence whereby the learner can attempt self-expression without feeling self-conscious or threatened by making errors and being corrected. In some cultures classroom errors are extremely embarrassing. Learners with such backgrounds must overcome this attitude and recognize that errors are normal and even helpful in a language learning situation.

More needs to be said about the successful learner's approach to the second language itself. Even though the language being learned sounds initially very strange and foreign, and its vocabulary and grammar seem formidable, difficult, and even irrational, the successful language learner realizes that to a native speaker of the language it is entirely familiar and sensible. Even things that seem irrational, such as—to native English speakers—the use of supplementary or redundant negatives in certain Romance languages, have their own internal logic in the perceptions of native speakers of those languages. The successful language learner, therefore, tries to "get inside" that internal logic and understand the special strategies that native speakers have for communicating their ideas and feelings. By "getting inside" the second language in this way, successful language learners will feel that they are thinking in that language, and they become more and more bilingual.

References

Carroll, J.B. 1973. Implications of aptitude test research and psycholinguistic theory for foreign language teaching. *International Journal of Psycholinguistics*, 2:5–14.

————. 1974. Learning theory for the classroom teacher. In G.A. Jarvis (ed.), *The challenge of communication: ACTFL Review of Foreign Language Education*, Skokie, Ill.: National Textbook Co., 6:113–149.

Gardner, R.C. and Lambert, W.E. 1972. *Attitude and motivation in second-language learning.* Rowley, Mass.: Newbury House.

Naiman, N., Fröhlich, M., and Stern, H.H. *The good language learner.* Toronto: Modern Language Centre, Ontario Institute for Studies in Education, forthcoming.

Why Not Start Reading Earlier?

Robert Lado

1. Your Name Please?

What do you do when you meet a person and do not get the name? You can ask for a repeat, of course, protesting that you did not hear. What do you do if you do not "hear" it the second time? You cannot ask for another repetition; that would be rude. So what do you do? You can ask, "How do you spell it?" And, surprisingly, you may hear it right when it is spelled. Why? The fit of the spelling and the pronunciation of names in the U.S. is worse than that of English writing to speech. Then how can the spelling of the name be an aid in hearing it? And better than having it spelled is seeing the name written on a calling card. There is usually little doubt then, and we believe that the name will be remembered better that way.

2. Anti-Graphic Preconceptions

Yet in language teaching we have strong preconceptions against letting students see the written words at the beginning. And these negative preconceptions are taken as valid, self-evident truths. Many of us, probably most, accept as fact that showing the written forms in the initial stages will distort the students' pronunciation; that the native language sound value of the letters will be transferred with negative effect; that the students will not listen to the spoken form when they can see the written

8

one instead, and they will introduce spelling pronunciation errors in their speech; that they will not learn to hear the foreign language unless they struggle with speech itself from the beginning without the crutch of writing; that reading intonation is different from speaking intonation and therefore the students will transfer their reading intonation to their speech, not the other way around; that even after six weeks of exclusively oral work, as soon as writing is introduced, their pronunciation deteriorates; and so forth.

Different but equally strong preconceptions exist concerning reading by preschool children: Will it hurt their eyes to engage in early reading? Will it warp their personality development? Will they be bored in school later? Never mind the fact that learning to hear and speak the native language does not hurt their ears and tongue or warp their personality, but actually helps to develop them. Still, the reservations persist: the written form is not language, it is an imperfect representation of it; let the children learn the language first—meaning speech—and then reading becomes only a matter of decoding the written representation into sounds.

Who says these things? Almost everybody does. In the Audio-Lingual methods there is an initial period devoted to listening and speaking without reading and writing, to force the students to hear and pronounce correctly, without the interference of writing. The Audio-Visual methods do not introduce writing in the initial period. The Direct methods begin with spoken utterances and demonstration of their meaning, without written representation. Even some recent innovative methods such as Lozanov's Suggestopedia (1971) begin with oral work without the support of writing. Only Grammar-Translation methodology starts and continues with written forms, and in that view speaking and listening are not objectives; the objective of G-T is translating as a form of reading and writing. Programmed learning is usually bound to written forms by its format. And within the linguistic methods, the Spoken Language Series adapted from the ASTP (Army Specialized Training Program) uses a modified spelling as a "guide to listening" plus the ordinary spelling representation. In the Oral Approach, a phonemic alphabet was used to teach pronunciation, and conventional spelling was presented after the students had mastered the pronunciation of the material. Those who believe that the written representation should be withheld or delayed at the beginning find themselves in good company. The question is whether the preconceived notions about reading are as true as they are taken to be.

3. Rationale

We know that unfamiliar sounds and sequences of sounds are elusive to the ear. In listening to an unfamiliar name when we are looking at its written form, we can make an approximate guess as to its syllables and vowels and consonants and focus our attention on those features. Thus the written representation might function as a rough guide to listening if the letters are familiar to the students. On the other hand, if the students see the written form without the opportunity to hear it, they may be expected to pronounce it with the sound values of their native languages and may produce unintelligible or very poor speech.

If they learn the written form at the same time as the spoken one, both of them will be part of the students' language competence so that when they see the written form again they will recall the spoken image as well as the meaning. Thus seeing the written forms will function as language use whenever these elicit meanings and sounds in inner speech, or inner listening, especially when the visual forms can be processed at a speed approximating that of speaking.

With preschool children, learning to read words and sentences is also a form of functional language use. Such reading should contribute significantly to the oral language development of children. And it should contribute to the permanence of bilingual competence in speaking as well as in reading since it constitutes additional bi-sensory experience in the use of the language. In situations where one of the languages dominates in the environment, bilingual reading might well supply the essential contact with both languages for the maintenance of functional bilingual competence.

In addition to the above potential supportive effects from the early introduction of the written forms, there are of course more direct potential advantages in the development of the skills of reading and writing. Söderbergh (1971) reports that her daughter had mastered Swedish spelling, which is comparable in diffi-

10

culty to that of English, by age seven without any formal teaching of it. Early reading should also improve school performance since reading is essential to success in academic work. And early introduction of the written form in EFL should accelerate development of skill in reading on the part of our students which is a major desideratum in learning a foreign language. A foreign graduate student reading 25 to 50 words a minute can hardly compete with native-speaking graduate students who read on the average between 300 and 350 words per minute. Yet that may be precisely what is happening in many cases today. The average reading speed with comprehension among non-native speakers of English in our colleges and universities is considerably lower than that of natives.

4. Where is the Evidence?

The above are speculative thoughts; they are more or less plausible hypotheses, but hypotheses nevertheless. We cannot risk a substantive change on that basis alone. We have already instituted too many practices on the basis of untested hypotheses; even the exclusion of writing at the beginning is the result of accepting a plausible hypothesis as fact. Is there any evidence in support of the immediate, simultaneous presentation of the written forms from the beginning, and of the teaching of early reading?

Hawkins (1971), Lipton (1969), Lado *et al.* (1968), Lado (1972), Couts (1972), Fink (1971), and others have reported experiments comparing completely oral presentation versus combined graphic and oral presentation in French, German, Spanish, and English, and they found the combined presentation superior in retention and not inferior in pronunciation. Hawkins worked with high school students; Lipton experimented with superior elementary school students in French; Lado worked with college students in Spanish; Couts worked with high school students in French; and Fink worked with college students in German. Several others of my students used English with high school and college students for research papers. One student, Rhea Gibble, made a three-way comparison of aural only, aural plus phonetic transcription, and aural with ordinary writing in German. The phonetic transcription variant was as weak as aural only with

11

those subjects who were not familiar with the phonetic alphabet and received only an initial explanation of it for purposes of the experiment. Phonetic transcription was stronger with linguistics students, who were familiar with the phonetic alphabet used. But all variants were weaker than aural plus ordinary spelling. The number of subjects was only 24, divided into four groups of six each. Nevertheless, this hints strongly that familiarity with the writing system may be at least a partial explanation of its value as supportive mediation for language learning.

Please note that I am not advocating a return to the Grammar-Translation practice of deciphering a written text as partial reading through translation. Teaching English as translation decoding is an anachronism in the 1970s. I am talking about psycholinguistic processing of the written form as reinforcement of speaking and listening at the beginning stage, and reading skill as a major objective in its own right beyond that; and when I say reading skill I mean processing language for meaning using its written form as source at normal speed, ranging between 100 and 200 to 300 words per minute, if we use the speed of speaking and listening as a yardstick.

With reference to early reading, that is, reading by children of preschool age in monolingual and bilingual situations, the evidence is accumulating in ways that cannot easily be disregarded or dismissed. Doman (1964) reports the successful teaching of reading to brain-injured children from age two. Fowler (1967) succeeded in teaching early reading to approximately 80% of the students at the University of Chicago Preschool. Söderbergh (1971) gave us a detailed linguistic description of the successful teaching of reading in Swedish to her daughter at age two and a half, using the Doman approach. Lado (1972) reports teaching early reading to a deaf child in preschool as an aid to her language and intellectual development. He also proposes (1975) the teaching of bilingual reading simultaneously in the preschool years. Andersson (1976) persuasively defends the bilingual child's "right to read" in two languages and is conducting an informal Preschool Biliteracy Project in a cooperative arrangement with parents. Kay C. Past (1975), in a master's thesis under Andersson, reports the successful achievement of biliteracy in English and Spanish by her daughter Marianne at the age of four. Dolores Durkin (1966, 1974-75) published two longitudinal studies of children who learned to read early, and Brzienski (1967) published supportive findings from the Denver study which taught early reading in kindergarten with the aid of TV and the involvement of parents.

Of course the evidence is only partial and limited to specific circumstances. We cannot generalize it to all situations and to all students. We need to know if average children under average teaching conditions will learn to read in their preschool years. We need to know if children of different language backgrounds will benefit from simultaneous exposure to the written forms. We need to know if spelling will be improved for average students as a result of early reading instruction. Postovsky (1974) reports that delay in oral responses improved learning when combined with writing of the utterances. Was it the overt suppression of speaking or the mediation of writing that produced the results? Certainly in writing one encodes the utterances covertly in inner speech.

5. Why Not Start Reading Earlier?

The rationale of simultaneous and early reading and the evidence already on hand point toward an affirmative response to our query concerning an earlier start in reading. It is not extravagant at this time to propose a principle for the presentation of new language material via written and auditory channels simultaneously. Of course, we cannot predict at this juncture how universal the principle might turn out to be. Will it apply to logographic writing systems such as that of Chinese as well as to alphabetic writing? Will it apply to unfamiliar alphabets such as those of Korean, Arabic, or the Cyrillic writing of Russian? Will it apply equally or at all to illiterates?

It certainly seems to have some substance in early reading and, surprisingly, in early bilingual reading. Children exposed to two languages in functional bilingual situations become bilingual on their own. Why couldn't they become biliterate in parallel reading circumstances?

Why not accept the concept that efficient reading is a form of processing natural language at normal speed for receptive communication and make this a part of our professional thinking, instead of considering reading and handling written forms as something extraneous to language that has to wait until the "language" has been mastered? Isn't reading like listening? In fact, can we read silently without experiencing some sort of inner hearing that functions mentally in parallel with listening comprehension?

We have argued that all the languages of the world have first developed as spoken systems of communication, and that only very late in the development of human culture does writing appear. From this we have argued for the teaching of the spoken language as the real language from which reading and writing will later develop. But is any one of the major languages of the world not fully as rich in its written tradition as in its oral one? And does not the development of writing represent such a momentous advance that we count the beginning of history from it, considering previous ages as prehistory?

With the development of writing, civilizations experience an explosion in knowledge. The members of literate societies who are efficient readers could not function if they were suddenly deprived of this form of language use; the civilization itself would grind to a halt and collapse.

At this stage in our professional knowledge it seems that reading should begin when language teaching begins. The pre-reading oral period no longer seems justified. The negative effect of exposure to the written form has been exaggerated, at least when the auditory form is presented simultaneously. The amount of learning seems to increase with the use of written support. Reading for information is unquestionably a highly valuable skill in a foreign language. Adequate speed in reading with good comprehension is a responsibility of any educationally-based course in EFL. Children can learn to read earlier than they now do, enjoy the process, and obviously benefit from the result. Then why not start reading earlier? Why not begin reading at the beginning?

References

Andersson, Theodore. 1976. The bilingual child's 'right to read.' *Georgetown University Papers on Languages and Linguistics*, no. 12.
Andrews, A., Bélisle, L., Fancy, R., Lortie, R., and Racle, G. 1972.

Report of the Canadian team on their stay at the Institute of Suggestology in Sophia. Mimeographed private circulation.

Bancfort, W. J. 1972. Foreign language teaching in Bulgaria. *The Canadian Modern Language Review*, 28:9–13.

Brzienski, Joseph E. 1967. *Summary report of the effectiveness of teaching reading in kindergarten.* Denver: The Denver Public Schools.

Couts, Gilbert D. 1972. The Effect of Oral, Orthographic, and Combined Presentation on the Memorization and Pronunciation of Basic French Dialogs. Ph.D. dissertation, Georgetown University.

Curran, Charles A. 1972. *Counseling-learning: a whole person model for education.* New York: Grune and Stratton.

Doman, Glenn. 1964. *How to teach your baby to read: the gentle revolution.* New York: Random House.

Durkin, Dolores. 1966. The achievement of preschool readers—two longitudinal studies. *Reading Research Quarterly*, 1, 4.

————. 1974–75. A six-year study of children who learned to read in school at the age of four. *Reading Research Quarterly*, 10, 1.

Fink, Stefan. 1971. A Comparison of Three Strategies for Dialog Memorization in German Involving Graphic Stimuli, Auditory Stimuli, and a Combination of the Two. Master's thesis, Georgetown University.

Fowler, William. 1967. A developmental learning strategy for early reading in a laboratory nursery school. ERIC ED 031 289 PS 001921.

Gattegno, Caleb. 1963, 1972. *Teaching foreign languages in schools: the silent way.* Second ed., New York, N.Y.: Educational Solutions.

Georgetown University Papers on Languages and Linguistics, No. 13. Papers on Early Reading by Theodore Andersson, Ragnhild Söderbergh, Robert Lado, and Bibliography by William Higgins presented to the Special Interest Group on Early Reading at the 1976 Georgetown University Annual Round Table.

Gibble, Rhea. 1972. Unpublished term paper.

Hawkins, Lee. 1971. Immediate versus delayed presentation of foreign language script. *Modern Language Journal*, 55:280–290.

Lado, Robert. 1972. Evidence for an expanded role for reading in foreign language learning. *Foreign Language Annals*, 5: 187–192.

————. 1972. Early reading by a child with severe hearing loss as an aid to linguistic and intellectual development. *Languages and Linguistics Working Papers 6*, Washington, D.C.: Georgetown University Press.

————. 1975. Early bilingual reading. In *Introduction to Bilingual Education.* Ortega, Luis (ed.). New York: Anaya Las Américas.

Lado, Robert, Kahn, B. Baldwin, and Lobo, F. 1968. The effects of reading and listening on vocabulary expansion. *The Florida FL Reporter.* Fall.

15

Lipton, Gladys C. 1969. To read or not to read: an experiment on the FLES level. *Foreign Language Annals*, 3:241–246.

Lozanov, George. 1971. *Suggestology*. Sofia, Bulgaria: Nauka Press (in Bulgarian). See Bancroft (1972) and Andrews, *et al.* (1972).

Past, Kay E. C. 1975. Reading in Two Languages for Age Two: A Case Study. The University of Texas at Austin. Master's thesis. Theodore Andersson, Mentor.

Postovsky, Valerian A. 1974. Effects of delay in oral practice at the beginning of second language learning. *Modern Language Journal*, 58, no. 5–6.

Söderbergh, Ragnhild. 1971. *Reading in early childhood*. A Linguistic Study of a Swedish Preschool Child's Gradual Acquisition of Reading Ability. Stockholm: Almqvist & Wiksell. Reprinted 1976 by Georgetown University Press, Washington, D.C.

Why Not Start Speaking Later?*

Valerian A. Postovsky

What do we learn when we learn to speak a language? The answer to this complex question may vary (as it has for centuries) depending on a set of fundamental assumptions one makes on what language is and how it is acquired. The views will range from the "verbal habits" of the empiricists to the "innateness hypothesis" of the nativists and the Whorfian concept of "linguistic relativity." The philosophical discussion of the issue, however, is quite outside the scope of this article; here let us limit the subject to a simple pragmatic observation: when we learn to speak, we learn to decode sequentially ordered vocal messages into meaning, and to encode thought into sequentially ordered vocal messages.

Is "learning by doing" an efficient way to learn a foreign language? The answer to this question is *yes*, provided we have a clear notion of what "doing" is in different phases of the learning process. In the initial phase of learning, I suggest "doing" is developing an auditory receptive ability to comprehend the spoken language. At this stage the learner develops some covert processing strategies to transform foreign auditory input into meaning. The process serves to imprint the integrated structure of language in human memory on the level of recognition.

---

* The views and opinions expressed in this article are not necessarily those of the Defense Language Institute or the Department of Defense.

When new linguistic patterns have been thus perceived, frequent reactivation of these patterns on the recognition level will make them more and more retrievable, and as linguistic features of a foreign language become retrievable, spontaneous vocal responses follow. At this stage of development the learner is ready for oral practice, and the proposition that "one learns to speak a foreign language by speaking it" makes sense.

Admittedly, that is, at best, an oversimplified model of the second language acquisition process. Research in this complex field is just beginning to generate some useful data, and at this point in time has produced more questions than answers. But, nevertheless, the picture that is emerging tends to substantiate the theoretical position outlined above, and suggests that emphasis on aural comprehension training and relaxation of the requirement for oral production in the initial phase of learning tend to foster development of linguistic competence and produce better results than those obtained through early intensive oral practice. For example, in a study on the effects of delay in oral practice (Postovsky, 1970, 1974), it was found that students who were learning Russian intensively in a six-hour-per-day program, with initial delay in oral practice, achieved better results than the students who were exposed to massive oral practice from the very beginning of the course. The delay in oral practice in the experimental condition was realized by replacing oral drill in the first month of instruction with writing practice from spoken input. Students' performance was measured at two different levels of achievement—six- and twelve-week grading periods—by standardized tests designed to provide a separate measure for each of the basic skills—listening, speaking, reading, and writing. Test results clearly indicated that the experimental condition induced a greater amount of learning; the experimental subjects outperformed the control subjects on all criterion measures, including speaking. In oral production experimental students were found to be superior to control students in both pronunciation and control of grammar.

The study in delayed oral practice approach was replicated and further advanced by Judith Olmsted Gary (1975), who experimented with elementary school children learning Spanish as a second language. Her 22-week experiment contained an experimental condition in which oral practice was totally absent for the

18

first 14 weeks and for the first half of each lesson thereafter, and a control condition in which children from the start were required to speak immediately upon hearing the model utterance. Comprehension in the experimental condition was assessed by requiring a nonverbal gross motor response, such as nodding or pointing to objects; in the control condition, subjects were required to repeat commands and questions after the teacher as well as to respond to them physically. Upon completion of the study Olmsted Gary found superiority of the experimental subjects in listening comprehension with no significant difference between groups in oral production, although the rate of learning between the 14th and 22nd weeks appeared to favor the experimental condition, suggesting, perhaps, a latency effect in the transfer of learning.

Several other researchers, using different modes of nonvocal response in development of listening comprehension, have reported similar findings. Notable among them are: Asher (1965, 1969, 1972), Winitz and Reeds (1973, 1975), Sittler (1975), and Ingram, Nord, and Dragt (1974). These researchers and others have clearly demonstrated that development of linguistic competence is enhanced when massive practice in listening comprehension precedes oral practice. Their data also suggest high positive transfer of learning from aural comprehension to speaking as well as to other language skills.

These results should not be surprising given what we know about the language acquisition process in natural situations. In child language, the overt speech development begins with production of one-word sentences usually between 12 to 18 months of life, although children clearly demonstrate comprehension of far more complex sentences at an earlier age. This sequence of events is not limited to the first language alone. In a recent study, Susan Ervin-Tripp (1974) described English-speaking children age 4 to 9 who were enrolled in Swiss schools where the language of instruction was French. She noted these children did not volunteer production of foreign utterances for a prolonged period of time—some remained silent for many months —but when they did finally speak, their speech output progressed at an accelerated rate. She concluded that in this respect the second language acquisition process must be much like the first. The covert receptive processes apparently pave the way for subsequent production.

19

Olmsted Gary (1975, p. 90) cites Sorenson, an anthropologist who has studied Colombian and Brazilian Indian cultures. In these cultures "a strong social value is placed on the ability to communicate fluently in foreign languages. . . ." As a consequence, members of these cultures do not use a language overtly until they know it well. "Rather, adults and adolescents first receptively familiarize themselves with the pronunciation and syntax of new languages. When the new languages are finally spoken, they are spoken with great fluency." What appears to be a common feature in all natural language learning environments is this latent period, the nonvocal phase on the learning continuum which typically precedes free production. Latent learning, after all, is a well-established notion in developmental psychology.

In contrast to these natural learning environments, we have a foreign language classroom in which listening comprehension has been traditionally treated as a passive skill; the emphasis of instruction, therefore, is almost exclusively on the overt linguistic behavior, the common assumption being that if speaking ability is developed, listening comprehension will follow. Nothing, however, can be further from the truth since we know that expressive language depends on receptive processes for its development.

Let us, then, review the "dynamics" of listening comprehension and identify some critical characteristics of the latent period or the prevocal phase. Since language originally developed to fill the need to communicate, we must assume that transfer of meaning is one of the most important operating contingencies in the language learning process. Students from the very first day should be exposed to meaningful utterances, and respond to them, although initially their response need not be vocal. Furthermore, the language materials used for listening comprehension exercises should include some unfamiliar but "contextually interpretable" lexical and/or structural elements. Students should be challenged to guess at the meaning of these elements, since at this point there is the development of covert, heuristic devices (or processing strategies) in the student's brain to transform foreign utterances into meaning.

Since processing of auditory input is essential and intrinsic to language learning, then we must ensure that the input which students are processing is authentic, because students learn essentially what they hear. In a comprehension-oriented approach, this requirement is easily satisfied, but in a foreign language classroom, where the goal of instruction is to make each student as vocally active as time permits—as in a pattern drill, or dialogue recitation—students process (or hear) much of their own output which is neither authentic in form, nor meaningful in content.

Premature emphasis on oral production tends to increase the complexity of the learning task and to cause some undesirable side effects. First, when a requirement to produce a foreign sentence exists prior to the establishment of a processing strategy for such production, students will tend to process the sentence through the only channel available to them, that of their native language (Cook, 1965; Ervin-Tripp, 1970). This is where we have interference in a very real sense, and this is why the learning task becomes so difficult. Second, training for oral production too early in the course may focus students' attention on the complexity of surface structure and away from the contextual meaning of the message. Comprehension of foreign utterances in this case could become more difficult because the student may be forced into a serial mode of processing a message when the process is likely to be hierarchical in nature. This leads us to the third and, perhaps, the most significant side effect, that of the short-term memory overload. Since most of the foreign language material learned by the student needs to be habituated before it becomes automatically retrievable, the student initially holds this material in the short-term memory for immediate recall. But the rate of presentation of new material is always greater than the rate of habituation; the student's short-term memory, therefore, early in the course reaches a point of saturation, thereby causing considerable inhibition of the learning process.

The priority of aural comprehension in the language acquisition process has never been seriously challenged as a principle on theoretical grounds. On the practical level, however, this principle has received only a very superficial interpretation. Usually, it is applied in reference to a single utterance or a short passage, i.e., comprehension of a particular segment of speech is believed to be necessary before production of that same segment. Training in production, furthermore, is believed to be an

21

important motivational factor in a foreign language classroom. The two most frequent questions posed by foreign language teachers are: "How do we maintain students' interest and motivation to learn, if we do not allow them to speak?" and "How do we teach aural comprehension without teaching production?"

Let us address both of these questions simultaneously. First, delay in oral practice does not mean *prohibition* of students' attempts to *express themselves* in a foreign language. Throughout the latent period there may be *spontaneous* vocal responses, different among students, but all displaying an inclination to use language creatively. Such student-initiated speech is anticipated, but *not forced*. Second, in a comprehension-oriented course students should understand that oral practice is not totally eliminated but merely shifted to the second phase of instruction, where it is more productive. And, third, when students experience the rapid rate of learning the skill to understand a foreign language, their motivation is enhanced rather than frustrated. Listening is *not* a passive skill; it requires full participation and the undivided attention of the learner. And when the nature of the skill is understood, the process becomes exciting.

We must remember, however, that mere exposure of students to the sounds of a foreign language is not sufficient. As suggested earlier, a successful aural comprehension course must satisfy at least three essential conditions: (1) the language material presented to the students must convey meaning from the very first hour of instruction; (2) a provision must be made for a student response which will verify comprehension of each utterance or a short passage immediately after delivery; and (3) students must be challenged to problem-solve and guess at the meaning of unfamiliar elements in a foreign utterance on the basis of context and other cues in the given linguistic environment.

There are several techniques used for development of listening comprehension that satisfy these principal conditions. One which we found to be very effective is the audio-visual TV program developed at the Defense Language Institute (DLI) to teach Russian (Postovsky, 1975). The technique is based on Winitz's model which he initially used for teaching language-delayed children and later adapted to teaching German as a foreign language (Winitz and Reeds, 1973, 1975). The system is based on synchronized presentation of language material and pictorial events. The student hears the utterance and then sees the picture, thus forming a direct association between the symbol and the referent. The TV screen is divided into four equal sections by vertical and horizontal lines crossing in the center of the screen. This arrangement makes it possible to project from one to four pictures simultaneously, leading the student into a multiple-choice selection procedure. Each unit of the program consists of one hundred frames with the total running time ranging from 24 to 30 minutes. The student is thus exposed to a problem-solving situation every 15 to 20 seconds throughout the exercise. This technique has proven to be a very useful tool for presenting language material of a concrete nature, i.e., vocabulary and grammatical concepts which lend themselves to pictorial representation.

The development of receptive skills is made relatively easy by the advances made in educational technology. Television, films, film strips, viewgraphs, and even computers can be programmed to teach comprehension. Since language learning is essentially a process of human interaction, one does not need to use sophisticated hardware excessively, but only as an aid. In fact, one can do well by simply using a tape recorder or a conventional language laboratory.

Paul Parent (1976) in his recent article, entitled "Why Listening and Reading Must Come Before Speaking and Writing," suggests that students learn through careful *observation* of correct usage of the language in context by those who speak it fluently. He asks: "How can this take place in a normal classroom setting?" and goes on to say:

By way of example, let us assume we have a neat little story or report to use.
Listening. 1. First of all we record it on a tape which becomes the source of our listening comprehension exercise. 2. Before we play it for the students the first time, we give them several cues, . . . to enable them 'to latch on to something' upon this initial contact. These cues *could* consist of a few key vocabulary words which give them a general idea of the content. 3. We play the tape once. 4. We ask students to tell us in English, or in the foreign language if they can at this level, what they think

23

the general idea is. 5. We give them additional words or expressions making sure they know their meaning, and tell them that a brief multiple-choice quiz, as a classroom activity, will follow the next hearing of the tape. 6. We play the tape a second time. 7. Then we give them maybe five multiple-choice questions (aural or written depending on level and ability)—three choices, A-B-C, will be plenty. 8. We check their answers in class and discuss their responses. Finally we give them a few more specific detailed cues and announce another *brief* multiple-choice quiz which will be teacher-graded (and 'will count') after the third and final playing of the tape. 9. The tape is played a third time. 10. A brief multiple-choice quiz is given for teacher-grading.

He further suggests that the same tape coupled with the printed text may be used for reading comprehension, where students will fill in some details which they may have missed during listening.

Techniques for developing listening comprehension vary according to the mode of student responses. They range from Asher's (1965) "strategy of total physical response," where students listen to commands in a foreign language and immediately obey with physical action, to Gauthier's (1963) "Tan-Gau" method, introduced in Canada in the late fifties for teaching French to English-speaking students, where the teacher speaks French and the students respond in English until, individually, they reach the state of "speaking readiness." George Landis (1971) called this approach "alternating lingual communication" or "A.L.C." for short. He has also developed a phonetic transcription system based on Pitman shorthand, called "phoneticriture," which solves the problem of graphic interference and has potential value as a useful means for student response in the prevocal phase of instruction, and as a graphic aid to sound discrimination and auditory perception.

What is the optimum length of delay in oral practice? Obviously, the length will vary with individual students; if emphasis on listening comprehension is maintained, transition to speaking will be gradual without any clear lines of demarcation. The same is true, as Parent (1976) suggests, of the reading and writing skills. The conventional writing system and silent reading (for adult students particularly) can be introduced early in the course, especially in languages where spoken and written forms are fairly congruent. In the experimental Russian program mentioned earlier, the Cyrillic alphabet was introduced from the beginning and reading comprehension exercises (silent reading) were conducted throughout the prevocal phase of instruction.

What is important in the proposed system is not the explicit division of a foreign language course into phases—intrinsic interaction of language skills will fuse the borderlines—but creation of a learning environment where the target language is not treated as an abstract subject matter divorced from reality, but rather as a viable system of communication which conveys meaningful information. By exposing students to massive listening practice, we are setting in motion the process which leads to development of full linguistic competence. As Simon Belasco (1967, p. 86) candidly observed, "the key to achieving proficiency in speaking is achieving proficiency in listening comprehension."

References

Asher, James J. 1965. The strategy of the total physical response: an application to learning Japanese. *IRAL, 3,* 4.

———. 1969. The total physical response approach to second language learning. *Modern Language Journal, 53,* 1:3–7.

———. 1972. Children's first language as a model for second language learning. *Modern Language Journal, 56,* 3:133–139.

Belasco, Simon. 1967. The plateau; or the case for comprehension: the "concept" approach. *The Modern Language Journal, 51,* 2.

Cook, H. R. 1965. Pre-Speech Auditory Training: Its Contribution to Second Language Teaching and Motivation for Continuous Broadcasting. Unpublished doctoral dissertation, Indiana University.

Ervin-Tripp, Susan. 1970. Structure and process in language acquisition. *GURT 21st Annual Roundtable,* Monograph, Georgetown University, 23.

———. 1974. Is second language learning like the first? *TESOL Quarterly, 8,* 2:111–128.

Gauthier, Robert. 1963. *Tan-Gau—A Natural Method for Learning a Second Language. Teacher's Guide to Accompany the Tan-Gau Method.* Toronto: W. J. Gage Limited.

Ingram, Frank, Nord, James, and Dragt, Donald. 1974. Developing a Programmed Workbook for Listening Comprehension of Russian. Paper delivered at the Soviet-American conference on the Russian language at Amherst.

Landis, George B. 1971. Personal communication.

Olmsted Gary, Judith. 1975. Delayed oral practice in initial stages of second language learning. In M. K. Burt and H. C. Dulay (eds.) *New Directions in Second Language Learning, Teaching, and Bilingual Education*, Washington, D.C.: TESOL.

Parent, P. Paul. 1976. Why listening and reading must come before speaking and writing. *Modern Language Journal* (in press).

Postovsky, Valerian A. 1970. The Effects of Delay in Oral Practice at the Beginning of Second Language Learning. Unpublished doctoral dissertation, University of California, Berkeley.

―――. 1974. Effects of delay in oral practice at the beginning of second language learning. *Modern Language Journal, 58*:5–6.

―――. 1975. The priority of aural comprehensiion in the language acquisition process. *Proceedings of the Fourth International Congress of Applied Linguistics*, Stuttgart.

Sittler, Edward V. 1975. Teoretische und didaktische aspecte des projekts audio-immersion. Paper presented at the 4th AILA World Congress, Stuttgart.

Winitz, Harris and Reeds, James A. 1973. Rapid acquisition of a foreign language (German) by the avoidance of speaking. *IRAL, 11/4*:295–317.

―――. 1975. *Comprehension and problem solving as strategies for language training*. The Hague: Mouton & Co., Paris: N.V., Publishers.

Speech Rate and Listening Comprehension

Paul Pimsleur
Charles Hancock
Patricia Furey

Listening is the least understood of the four language skills, and consequently the least well taught. Until recently, teachers have assumed that listening comprehension would develop of itself if we taught our students to speak. Now we are coming to realize that listening is not a mere adjunct to speaking, but an independent skill that must be taught explicitly, through systematic, well-planned classroom activities.

Rivers (1966, 1968), Asher (1969, 1974), and others have made us aware that listening is not a passive skill but an active one. To understand foreign utterances, a person must use knowledge of the phonology, syntax, and lexicon of the language, applying these simultaneously and at a high rate of speed.

Teachers are also finding that vexing motivation problems can be alleviated by devoting more class time to the skill of listening. Students who are not "academically inclined," and those "turned off" by language study, find listening less stressful and less embarrassing than speaking. Because they enjoy listening activities, they tend to stay with the program longer. Moreover, listening is a skill, like reading, in which one can realistically hope to acquire a fair degree of proficiency in two years of study. Proficiency in speaking generally takes much longer.

The growing interest in teaching listening has created a demand for stimulating, culturally authentic recorded material. Radio broadcasts, assuming one can obtain them, can fill some of the need. However, radio broadcasts are well beyond the comprehension of most students—for an interesting reason. Often, it is not the ideas, the vocabulary, nor the grammar which impede understanding. Students may "know" these elements and yet be unable to understand what they hear. Furthermore, difficulties like these can be prepared for in advance, by "pre-listening" instruction. What cannot be prepared for is the sheer flow of words. When the language is spoken at normal speed, the foreign words reach the listener's ear so rapidly that they soon pile up. The short-term memory overloads, and the listener simply "tunes out." It is important to be able to control this factor in order to teach listening more effectively.

Purpose

The purpose of this study is to provide information about one of the key factors affecting comprehension, namely *rate of speech*; to examine the speech of French and American radio news announcers; and to draw certain conclusions that may be helpful to teachers. Methods of teaching listening comprehension will not be discussed as this topic is beyond the scope of this paper and has been treated extensively in Rivers (1975).

Radio news broadcasts were chosen for a number of reasons. First, they are readily available. Second, news announcers speak primarily to communicate information, rather than to persuade or entertain, which might cause them to distort their speech. Furthermore, they speak at a rate which students and teachers might wish to emulate: slowly enough to be readily understood, yet rapidly enough to avoid boring the listener.

Radio announcers do not speak impromptu. They read a prepared text which they are likely to have rehearsed at least briefly beforehand. Therefore, the rates of speech reported here should properly be called "oral reading rates." One might prefer to study spontaneous speech rates, but these are a great deal more difficult to define, record, and measure.

Procedure

Fifteen French and fifteen American news announcers, all male, were recorded while speaking on the air during regular news broadcasts on major networks. The Americans were heard on ABC, CBS, or NBC; the French on ORTF (now defunct). After obtaining recordings of each announcer on several different days and splicing them together, we selected at random two one-minute samples of each announcer, and transcribed all he said in that time.

A decision was then required as to what to count. In previous research, phonemes, morphemes, syllables, words, and sentences have all been the focus of study. Given our purpose of providing information that teachers can apply, the choice seemed to lie between syllables-per-minute (SPM) and words-per-minute (WPM).

The simplest measure, WPM, has been criticized on the grounds that "words vary in length from the simple *a* to the classic *antidisestablishmentarianism*" (Carroll, 1967). Furthermore, different prose passages may contain words of different lengths. Carroll found that word-length ranged among six American authors from Ernest Hemingway's terse 1.20 syllables per word to Henry James' erudite 1.73 syllables per word.

We have found that radio news scripts, unlike literary passages, maintain a constant word-length. The rate of 1.7 syllables per word varies little from one broadcast to another, or even, surprisingly enough, from French to English. Since WPM can be converted to SPM quite accurately by multiplying by 1.7, we shall discuss our findings solely in terms of WPM.

Findings

Our recordings revealed that French radio announcers speak at an average rate of 182 WPM, and American announcers at an average rate of 177 WPM. The difference is not statistically significant, from which we conclude that French and American news announcers deliver their information at approximately the same rate of speed—about 180 WPM. This is somewhat faster than the 165 to 175 WPM cited in previous studies as the average rate of spontaneous American speech.

29

While French and American announcers speak at about the same average rate, their variability is decidedly different. In this regard, we asked two questions. How much do different announcers vary from each other within each language? And how much does each announcer's delivery vary from one occasion to another? In answer to both questions, we found that French announcers vary a great deal more than American announcers do.

The standard deviation of French announcers is 32.4 WPM. They frequently speak as slowly as 159 WPM, or as rapidly as 205 WPM, and it is not uncommon to find one French news announcer saying 50 words more than another in a one-minute period. This may amount to four sentences, a sizeable difference.

American announcers, on the other hand, have a standard deviation of only 7.5 WPM. They are apt to vary from each other by only a few words—perhaps one sentence—which is surprisingly little.

French announcers also fluctuate more than Americans from one occasion to another. The average difference between samples of the same speaker taken at different times is nearly twice as large among French announcers as among American: 28.7 as compared with 15 WPM.

It might be tempting to see in these findings a corroboration of the well-known French individuality, except that a more pertinent explanation presents itself. Carroll (1967) offers data showing that the standard deviation of college students reading prose passages aloud is about 20 WPM. This is much closer to our French findings than to the American, and suggests the proper interpretation to be that American announcers are remarkably uniform in their delivery, rather than the French being remarkably diverse.

Standard Speech Rates

Combining data from this and previous studies, we can propose a set of standards for teaching purposes. They reflect the variability of French announcers rather than the uniformity of American announcers.

```
┌─────────────────────────────────────────────────┐
│              Standard Speech Rates                │
│                                                   │
│              FAST = above 220 WPM                 │
│                                                   │
│     MODERATELY FAST = 190 to 220 WPM              │
│                                                   │
│           AVERAGE = 160 to 190 WPM                │
│                                                   │
│     MODERATELY SLOW = 130 to 160 WPM              │
│                                                   │
│              SLOW = below 130 WPM                 │
└─────────────────────────────────────────────────┘
```

As may be seen in the Table, the *average* rate of speech is between 160 and 190 WPM. Speech between 190 and 220 WPM is *moderately fast*; speech above 220 WPM is *fast*. Similarly, speech between 130 and 160 WPM is *moderately slow*, and speech below 130 WPM is *slow*. According to these standards, the "normal" range lies between 130 and 220 WPM.

While teachers will probably wish to remain within this range for most purposes, it should be remembered that communication can and frequently does occur outside these limits. Very rapid speech was measured in a study by Pimsleur, Stockwell, and Comrey (1962), in which 410 American college students were asked to read a passage of English prose aloud "as rapidly as possible while still remaining intelligible." Their average rate proved to be about 310 WPM. According to evidence cited by Carroll and Cramer (1968), continuous comprehension is possible at speeds as high as 475 WPM, and isolated words can be comprehended even at 700 WPM.

Some notion of how slowly a person can speak and still retain the listener's attention may be gained by studying the delivery of noted political figures addressing large audiences on solemn occasions. In a work on French listening comprehension that inclu les recordings of public figures (Pimsleur, 1974), former French President Pompidou is heard addressing a convention at 108 WPM; André Malraux intones a funeral oration at 111 WPM; and General de Gaulle delivers his final address to the French nation at the super-slow rate of 70 WPM. While such rates as these may be appropriate for highly formal occasions, they would probably become tedious as regular classroom fare.

31

Applications

The information given here on rates of speech may be applied in a number of ways. First of all, it can be used in adjusting the speed of recorded material one wishes to present—radio broadcasts, speeches, interviews, and the like—to suit the comprehension level of one's students. There are two ways of changing the speed of recordings: speech expansion and temporal spacing.

Speech expansion, and its opposite, *speech compression*, are done by means of electronic devices which can slow down a recording or speed it up without distortion. These devices are used for such special purposes as accelerating readings for the blind and fitting radio programs to exact time specifications. They are not generally available to teachers. However, it may be worth checking local radio stations, and the Speech Department of a university, to see if they have one and are willing to re-record your tapes at the rate of speech you specify.

Temporal spacing can be done by teachers themselves. The process consists of inserting pauses into recorded speech in such a way as to lengthen natural grammatical junctures. This may be done by connecting two tape recorders together, one for playing the original tape and the other for making the copy. While recording the copy, one starts and stops the original at pre-determined points between "thought-groups." The second recorder runs continuously. The result is a "spaced" copy. A number of experiments, both in the psychological laboratory and in the classroom, attest to the effectiveness of temporal spacing for teaching listening comprehension (Johnson and Friedman, 1971; Huberman and Medish, 1974). For example, a high school near Albany, New York has routinely produced "spaced" versions of daily Spanish news broadcasts for the past several years. They begin by providing frequent, lengthy pauses at the beginning of the year, then gradually diminish them in both frequency and length. By the end of the year, students are able to comprehend Spanish news broadcasts at normal speed.

What about teachers' control over their own unrecorded speech? Here, there seem to be two views. Some teachers begin speaking slowly in first year classes, intending to speed up gradually as their students progress. Other teachers speak at a more or less normal rate from the start, feeling that students will soon adjust to this. We side strongly with the latter group, having observed time and again the resistance, both conscious and unconscious, with which students meet any attempt on the teacher's part to talk faster than they are used to. We have also seen that efforts to speak slowly often lead to unnatural intonation and to self-consciousness on the teacher's part. We therefore recommend that teachers speak at a normal rate from the start—but that they train themselves to pause more frequently than they would in normal conversation, always at natural juncture points between thought-groups.

As a matter of professional curiosity, teachers may wish to check their own rate of speech, and to compare this with the rates presented in this article. It is probably inadvisable, however, for any but a few accomplished "actors" to attempt any considerable modification in their natural speech patterns.

In presenting standard rates of speech, we are mindful that speed of speech is only one factor that affects comprehension. Other factors such as motivation, context, grammatical complexity, and familiarity of vocabulary may be as important or more so. As research progresses it seems likely that a pedagogic theory will emerge in which control of several key factors will make us far more efficient than we presently are at teaching students to understand a foreign language. We believe the chief factors to control are rate of speech, rate of pausing, and syntactic and semantic familiarity. Listening comprehension, virtually unexplored until recently, is the last of the fundamental language skills to receive serious attention, and the one in which we hope to see great progress in the coming years.

References

Asher, J.J. 1969. The total physical response approach to second language learning. *Modern Language Journal,* 53, 1:3–17.

Asher, J.J., Kusudo, J.A., and de la Torre, R. 1974. Learning a second language through commands: the second field test. *Modern Language Journal,* 58, 1–2:24–32.

Carroll, J.B. 1967. Problems of measuring speech rate. ERIC Document ED 011338.

Carroll, J.B. and Cramer, H.L. 1968. The intelligibility of time-compressed speech. ERIC Document ED 021851.

Huberman, G. and Medish, V. 1974. A multi-channel approach to language teaching. *Foreign Language Annals, 7,* 6:674–680.

Johnson, R.L. and Friedman, H.L. 1971. Some temporal factors in the listening behavior of second language students. In P. Pimsleur and T.L. Quinn (eds.) *The psychology of second language learning.* Cambridge, Mass.: Cambridge University Press.

Pimsleur, P., Stockwell, R.P., and Comrey, A.J. 1962. Foreign language learning ability. *Journal of Educational Psychology, 53,* 1:15–26.

Pimsleur, P. 1974. *Le pont sonore: une méthode pour comprendre le français parlé.* Chicago: Rand McNally.

Rivers, W.M. 1966. Listening comprehension. *Modern Language Journal, 50,* 4:196–204.

———. 1968. *Teaching foreign language skills.* Chicago: University of Chicago Press.

———. 1976. *A practical guide to the teaching of french.* New York: Oxford University Press.

Characteristics of an Effective Second Language Teacher

Betty Wallace Robinett

Much thinking has gone into what constitutes minimum standards for teacher preparation, and it is obvious that teacher training programs are posited on the assumption that graduates of such programs will be *acceptable* teachers. The *TESOL Training Program Directory 1974-76*,[1] which includes all American and Canadian programs leading to a degree or certificate in English as a second language, lists required courses, thus implicitly defining the essential content of such training programs. A perusal of this directory reveals a surprising unanimity of opinion as to what constitutes minimum standards for teacher preparation in ESL.

However, there has been little straightforward discussion of what constitutes an *effective* second language teacher; and delineating the characteristics of such a teacher is not easy because teaching reflects, in many ways, the individual characteristics of the teacher. Although the ideas presented here will in no way disavow such individuality, some generalizations will be attempted. Readers should keep in mind that the views presented here are highly personal. In addition, all references to second language teaching will be in the context of English as a second language, since this is where all my experience has been. I hope that the comments may be applicable to all second language teachers, but others will have to judge whether or not that assumption can be made.

---

[1] Charles H. Blatchford, ed. (Washington, D.C.: TESOL, 1975).

In making generalizations about teachers, personal qualities must be distinguished from professional competence, which refers to knowledge of subject matter and of teaching techniques. Personal qualities tend to interact with teaching techniques to produce individual teaching styles. Thus, we can say that what one teacher may use successfully in the classroom may not 'work' for another.

I disagree with the statement "Teachers are born, not made." If I did not, I would deny my life's work. Teachers are 'made' in the sense that they must acquire knowledge of a specific subject before they can teach it to others. It is how they impart this knowledge that makes them effective or ineffective. On the other hand, it may be that qualities like patience, tolerance, sensitivity, and warmth are innate. I happen to believe that they can be nurtured, developed, brought to the surface, even created—if teachers are *really* interested in their students, if they really want students to learn, and if they are willing to try everything in their power to help their students.

One quality which comes to mind when I think about effective teaching is inspiration, the ability of teachers to use the inspiration that comes to them and, in turn, to inspire others. Inspiration permeates the thoughts and actions of effective teachers. It is the quality which maintains freshness and spontaneity in the classroom; it attracts and interests students. Effective teachers confidently expect inspiration; they listen and look for it in everything they do, both in preparation for and in carrying out their teaching tasks. They acknowledge it as the source of new and exciting ideas.

Inspiration takes many shapes. It arises primarily from a love of teaching. As a professor at the University of Minnesota, who was about to retire, recently commented, "A good teacher has to like teaching and like students. You have to have the knack of putting yourself in the student's position."[2]

Effective teachers draw inspiration from many homely activities: listening for timely ideas from every source which can be translated into classroom use; watching television with the idea

---

[2] Remarks made by Professor R. A. Baker which were quoted in *The Paper* (June 1976), a publication of the University of Minnesota Medical School.

of alerting students to especially attractive opportunities for practicing listening comprehension; reading with an eye for articles useful for discussion; clipping cartoons (or other written or pictured material) for display on bulletin boards. Finally, effective teachers listen to students' problems and use inspiration to help them find solutions.

A recent essay extolling the qualities of one particularly effective teacher describes what that author believes to be memorable about a teacher.

> When we look back on our schooling, we remember teachers rather than courses—we remember their manner and method, their enthusiasm and intellectual excitement, and their capacity to arouse our delight in, or our curiosity about, the subject taught (Hook, 1976).

One of the dictionary definitions of *enthusiasm* is "an activity that inspires a lively interest."[3] Inspiration, then is an integral part of enthusiasm. Enthusiasm inspires students; and, conversely, inspiration results in enthusiastic teachers.

Where does this enthusiasm come from? I think it derives from two sources: first, a genuine interest in the subject matter (akin to Hook's "intellectual excitement"); second, the satisfaction gained from watching students learn something (in the present context, learning a second language).

More easily described than personal qualities is the professional competence required of an effective teacher both in subject matter and in teaching techniques. Both kinds of competence are essential. One without the other results in a teacher who may be knowledgeable but boring on the one hand, or exciting but uninformed on the other. The teacher who combines knowledge with excitement is the one who holds students' attention.

In the domain of professional competence, the first thing a teacher must possess is a knowledge of the subject matter to be taught. In the case of an ESL teacher this is more than just a knowledge of the English language. It includes a linguistic awareness of such questions as what constitutes language; how lan-

---

[3] *The American Heritage Dictionary of the English Language* (Boston, Mass.: Houghton Mifflin Company, 1969).

guage operates; how speech and writing are related; how languages compare and contrast; how language reflects the culture of its speakers; how language changes; how a particular language varies from speaker to speaker and from region to region; how language is learned; how language influences people.

Why is such knowledge important? First of all, few people know much about language unless they specifically investigate it. Folk knowledge tends to perpetuate untruths or half-truths about language such as the following: "There is one correct way of saying something"; "Language is habit formation"; "Questions always rise at the end"; "There are three (six, nine) tenses in English."

Also, many persons labor under the delusion that being a native speaker of a language qualifies a person to teach it. All that is needed to convince anyone of the fallacy of this is to ask native speakers of English who are linguistically naïve (that is, without linguistic training) how questions are formed, how and when the definite article is used, or how many vowel *sounds* there are in English.

Beginning with this broad view of language, teachers must then focus attention on language-specific information. They must be thoroughly familiar with the phonological, morphological, syntactic, and lexical systems of English. No detailed listing of linguistic items is necessary here since there is undoubtedly rather widespread agreement on what is necessary and since this has also been touched upon elsewhere (Robinett, 1969); but proficiency in the subject matter of the English language may be tested by posing questions like those below, which effective teachers should be able to answer.

Phonology: What is the relationship between vowel quality and the stress system? What is the significance of rising and falling intonation on tag questions? What kinds of consonant clusters does English permit?

Morphology: What are the inflectional affixes of English? How do these differ from derivational affixes? What part does functional load play in the relative importance of these two kinds of affixes?

Syntax: What is the difference between tense and aspect in the English verb system? What is a declarative question? What are some of the possible syntactic changes which occur when sentences are combined?

Lexicon: What do we mean when we ask, "What does this mean?" What are some of the ways in which lexical items may be classified?

As essential as the above knowledge is, it is most useful to the student when combined with effective teaching techniques. Teachers must have, or must develop, that particular knack of imparting knowledge which is the hallmark of effective teaching. The professional qualities which seem to inspire learning are what we shall now concern ourselves with.

Recently the Office of Education (HEW) issued guidelines for compliance with the 1974 Supreme Court decision in the case of *Lau* v. *Nichols*. That decision requires school districts to provide equal educational opportunities for students from non-English-speaking backgrounds. The guidelines specifically state that, at the elementary level, "an ESL program does not consider the affective nor cognitive development of the students," and therefore is unsuitable.

I take issue with this statement and welcome the opportunity to set the record straight on what the profession believes ESL programs and teachers should do. What may be happening in poorly supervised ESL programs or in programs where untrained teachers are employed is not the issue here. The *profession* has standards which have always included the affective and cognitive development of students at all levels. The guidelines for ESL teachers published in 1975 by TESOL (Teachers of English to Speakers of Other Languages) identifies many specific competencies pertaining to the ability to do just that.[4]

Furthermore, many years ago as a very young teacher-trainer, I wrote an editorial for *Language Learning* (Wallace 1949) showing my concern for matters in the affective domain. I was, even then, very much aware of what Stevick (1976) refers to as

---

[4] *Guidelines for the Certification and Preparation of Teachers of English to Speakers of Other Languages in the United States* (Washington, D.C.: TESOL, 1975).

the students' need for "security," "identification," and "self-esteem"; these are similar to the features which Yorio (1976) includes in his affective variables as "playing a significant role in second language acquisition." The following remarks made in that editorial, while written in the framework of teaching pronunciation, are illustrative of the concern for the student which ESL teachers have always had. This concern is basic to effective ESL teaching at all levels.

> Unless the student feels very much at home with his teacher and with fellow students, he will not be able to achieve the freedom necessary for learning to produce sounds that are strange to him.

> To achieve this free and wholesome atmosphere it is necessary for the teacher . . . to give each student a feeling of satisfaction in attaining some goal, however small, during each class hour; to prevent the student from being embarrassed in any way; to be as patient as possible with the student's mistakes; to encourage those who are having great difficulty; and to avoid controversial discussions which involve personal or subjective opinions (e.g., anything arising out of a disagreeable or deprecating reference to a person's cultural or linguistic problems).

Another variable which Yorio mentions is "self-consciousness." Let us see what that 1949 editorial had to say about that.

> Many students can be corrected time and again without embarrassing them, but others must be handled carefully. Age and professional position seem to be directly correlated to this point of diminishing returns. The older and more educated a person is, the more careful a teacher must be to observe signs of self-consciousness.

The variable which Yorio refers to as "ego permeability" may be equated with Stevick's "self-esteem." I prefer to think of "challenge level." What was said about this?

> Some [students] can throw themselves into the experience of language learning and forget their self-restraint or pride; others find this difficult and often impossible. The teacher, in each case, needs to discover the utmost capacity of the student in this regard and hold the student responsible for that capacity. This will provide a goal for each individual which will not be beyond his reach.

If students find themselves in a non-threatening classroom operated by a sensitive teacher, they will feel secure. If they are allowed to express their own ideas without biased value judgments imposed either by the teacher or other students, they will have gained a sense of identification and self-esteem. Thus, the three very essential human needs which Stevick identifies will have been fulfilled.

The qualities implied by the above remarks are those of tolerance, patience, warmth, sensitivity, and open-mindedness. To these I would like to add flexibility.

Effective teachers are flexible in mind and in action. They are open to whatever change may be necessary because of the acquisition of further knowledge about language and language learning; for what may seem patently true today may not be so in the future, as more information about language is uncovered. Witness what has happened in linguistic inquiry since 1960!

As one example of what is taking place, let me cite the article by Robin Lakoff (1975) entitled "Linguistic Theory and the Real World." In this article Lakoff raises questions which could certainly affect the way in which ESL teachers present grammatical material or the way in which grammar items are sequenced in instructional materials. She suggests that a speaker's conceptual system probably encodes information in broad categories which may possibly be universally applicable. Categorizations which seem to be important in communicative systems are based on such matters as whether or not the information being communicated is new or old to the hearer, whether the subject under discussion is or is not unique, whether what is being discussed is good or bad. She points out that it is assignment to one or the other of these categories that determines lexical or syntactic choice. As an example of a syntactic choice which is at least partially based on these categories, she cites the definite/indefinite article choice (*I saw a/the man in a/the red coat this morning*); as an example of a lexical choice based on the good/bad categorization, she offers *The SLA admit/takes credit for the murders.*

Lakoff points out that theoretical and applied linguists (many of whom have a profound interest in ESL) should be and actually are drawing closer because the search for truth about language is more and more encompassing what happens in communicative situations—the real world.

A flexible mind is also reflected in the ability to say to students, "I don't know," which, of course, should be immediately followed with, "But I'll certainly try to find out." The ability to unself-consciously admit ignorance is the sign of a mature teacher.

Flexibility in action is shown by variety in classroom activities. Some routine is necessary for the sake of stability and security, both on the part of teachers and students, but flexibility within the routine makes for excitement and retention of interest.

Flexibility plays a role in teachers' ability to use textbooks intelligently. Teachers who lack the solid linguistic competence described above often are overly dependent upon textbooks; they become "text-bound" and inflexible. The effective use of texts depends upon the confidence teachers have in their own subject-matter competence. It has been my experience that the less confidence teachers have, the more closely they follow the text. There are some who think that if instructional materials are well-designed any teacher can use them effectively. While not disallowing the importance of soundly written instructional materials, I do not believe that they necessarily ensure good teaching. In this regard let me reiterate what I have said elsewhere about such teachers (Robinett, 1969).

> When they are forced to deviate from the text because of something that arises from the classroom situation, they often make egregious errors in judgment in terms of linguistic information and language teaching methodology. The *effective* use of materials depends upon the teacher's knowing the principles behind the textbook design: i.e. the reasons for presenting items in certain ways, the reasons for selecting certain items and omitting others, and the reasons for a given sequence of items. Only with this kind of background will the teacher ever be flexible, self-reliant, and capable of reacting intelligently to problems for which the text provides no ready answer.

The ability to be flexible in the language teaching-learning situation immediately brings to mind Earl W. Stevick, who has made outstanding contributions to the language teaching profession. His most recent publication (1976) comments on how his ideas have changed since he first entered the profession. His statements reflect the ideas of many in the profession, and anyone interested in a discussion of the many approaches and/or methods which are presently or have been in use in second language teaching will find his book, *Memory, Meaning, and*

Method, very enlightening.

One of the most important contributions that Stevick has made to the profession is a clear delineation of what comprises effective teaching materials. He says (1971) that they should have "strength," "lightness," and "transparency." The first two qualities pertain to the affective domain: "strength" refers to the relevancy of the materials to the needs of the students, their authenticity in terms of linguistic form and content, and their usefulness; "lightness" pertains to the ease or difficulty of reproducing the items, the length of attention span necessary for the completion of an item. "Transparency," on the other hand, belongs with the cognitive aspects of language. Stevick explains transparency as the ability of the text to make clear how teachers may use the materials and the extent to which students know what they are doing and why they are doing it. Although Stevick uses these terms to refer to instructional materials, I think they may also apply to effective teachers.

Teachers who have *strength* know the subject matter and know how to make the instructional material useful and relevant to students. Teachers who have the quality of *lightness* are sensitive to the individual differences of students and select materials for them which are not too difficult, but not so easy as to be boring and unchallenging. Teachers who use *transparency* effectively are those who make it clear to students what is required of them and why it is being required, that is, how it fits into the total scheme of the class.

In summary, effective teachers are those who remember that the student is the most important part of the teaching-learning process. The success of second language teachers is ultimately measured by how well students have learned to communicate in the second language. I believe that success can best be attained by teachers who possess a sound knowledge of their subject matter and express warmth, sensitivity, and tolerance in imparting this knowledge.[5]

---

[5] Since finishing this paper, I came upon a report of a very recent study of what characterizes outstanding foreign language teachers (Moskowitz, 1976). Many of the findings in the study bear out what has been said here. The following are a few examples of the behavior identified in classrooms belonging to outstanding teachers: "the climate is warm and accepting"; "the teachers are expressive and animated"; "students exhibit more outward signs of enthusiasm to participate"; "there is a greater number of different activities per lesson"; "patience is exhibited by the teacher."

References

Hook, Sidney. 1976. Morris Cohen—fifty years later. *The American Scholar*, 426–436.

Lakoff, Robin. 1975. Linguistic theory and the real world. *Language Learning*, 25:309–338.

Moskowitz, Gertrude. 1976. The classroom interaction of outstanding foreign language teachers. *Foreign Language Annals* 9:135–157.

Robinett, Betty Wallace. 1969. Teacher training for English as a second dialect and English as a second language: the same or different? Georgetown University: Monograph Series in Languages and Linguistics 22:121–132.

Stevick, Earl W. 1971. *Adapting and writing language lessons.* Washington, D.C.: U.S. Government Printing Office.

——. 1976. *Memory, meaning, and method: some psychological perspectives on language learning.* Rowley, Mass.: Newbury House.

Wallace, Betty Jane. 1949. The importance of classroom atmosphere. *Language Learning*, 2:73–75.

Yorio, Carlos. 1976. Discussion of 'explaining sequence and variation in second language acquisition.' *Language Learning*, Special Issue 4:59 –63.

Face Validity in TESOL: Teaching the Spoken Language

J. Donald Bowen

The notion that any native speaker can teach his language to persons from other speech communities has been with us for a very long time. Actually the assumption seems reasonable; one should be able to teach something he does himself so easily and so well. Furthermore, would any of us be satisfied with a piano teacher who can't play the piano, or a ski instructor who can't ski? If these are inadequate, why should we settle for a language teacher who has not mastered the language well enough to sound authentic?

In many instances, however, the native speaker doesn't seek the job—the job seeks the native speaker. Notice boards in countries around the world carry messages that solicit English teachers, and with great frequency these include a specification that the teacher "must be a native speaker." How strange! One could expect "Must be trained," or "Must be experienced," or "Must be competent," but why will a prospective student be more concerned with a prospective teacher's speech habits than with his teaching skills? The answer seems to be that the native has "face validity"; he sounds right and therefore inspires confidence.

It is not that mastery of the language is considered of secondary importance for teachers; indeed it is usually acknowledged as a component in teacher training programs, with competence in the basic skills either assumed as a prerequisite to enrollment or the subject of specific instruction. But even when other skills are satisfactory, fluency in the pronunciation of the spoken language is often shaky, and rationalizations—"my students just need to read," or "they'll never talk to a native speaker anyway"—are not uncommon. I suggest that a high degree of competence in spoken English, in pronunciation and fluency, should be a goal of all teachers, regardless of whatever professional limitations their job assignment seems to suggest. Better communication skills are not only useful per se, they will enhance the teacher's self-respect and will encourage him to address his students with confidence and assurance.

Furthermore, I suggest that most non-native teachers are capable of greater competence than they have achieved, that with more accurate information and guidance and with focussed practice they can substantially improve the quality of their spoken English. The conviction that native-like English is extremely difficult has too often spawned the rationalization that minimally comprehensible English is sufficient for the typical teacher's needs, an assumption that will almost inevitably diminish the desire to improve. The *sine qua non* of better oral production is the conviction seriously held that it is both possible and desirable to perfect one's pronunciation and fluency. Then set out with sufficient orientation to do so.

If native English-speaking teachers were widely available, they could serve as a leavening, and the oral skills of non-native teachers might be less of an issue. But the demand for English instruction far outruns the available supply of teachers from English-speaking countries. For this reason and for others, English classes around the world are almost exclusively taught by local teachers. Even in the United States and Canada, where natives are abundant, a surprising number of classes offered to speakers of other languages are taught by non-native speakers of English. These teachers, in fact, have an important psychological advantage over the natives, because their situation says to the students: I learned English as a second language, and you can too.

Teachers need and can put to good use a generous amount of linguistic versatility. They especially need phonology in context. Such phonology courses as are typically available emphasize units and features of pronunciation: the phonemes and major allophones, usually in monosyllabic contrasting pairs of words such as *ship* and *sheep*, with drills stressing consistent aural discrimination and identifiable oral production. This is not a harmful component of pronunciation training, provided it comprises no more than ten to fifteen percent of the instruction. Too often it makes up ninety-five to one hundred percent.

So, what is missing? What needs to be added? Two aspects of spoken English need greater attention, one idiosyncratic, the other probably universal but with specific applications. The idiosyncratic feature is stress (or emphasis, or relative prominence of syllables compared to each other). This is an area of considerable complexity in English and one that affects naturalness and intelligibility in a major way, particularly since there are correlated patterns of occurrence for an equally complex vowel system or, more accurately, vowel systems. This gives rise to the complicated alternations of vowels in related English words, alternations that are disguised by the morphophonemic system of spelling which English employs. The disguise is so effective that many students—and, indeed teachers—are unaware that these alternations exist.

The second characteristic aspect or feature of spoken English is very probably a linguistic universal, though the exact consequences in English pronunciation depend on the phonetic inventory, the prevailing syllable structure, and the specific combinatory rules of the English phonological system. It is what might be called the flow of speech, characterized by the assimilations, contractions, and reductions that affect speech segments in a discourse.

These two areas of phonological realization are in fact the broad organizing principles of oral English production—and of course, therefore, of aural comprehension: the stress-vowel correlation fabric, and the patterns of influence that sounds in sequence exercise on one another. Let's look at some of the implications for each of these.

English words show three levels of stress: strong, medial, and weak, all shown in a word like /démənstrèyt/ (demonstrate), where the order is strong-weak-medial, observing an English preference for separating two higher stresses in sequence when possible. The strong and medial stresses are occupied by what we might call "full vowels," while the weak-stressed syllables are made up of "reduced" or "weak vowels." The two systems are shown on a traditional grid as follows:

47

Full   **Reduced**

iy ɪ		uw ʊ		iy ɪ	ə	uw
ey ɛ	ə	ow oy				ow
æ	ay aw a	ɔ				

If we are aware of the contrasts of these two systems and can keep in mind their distribution, a giant stride toward native-like English will be taken.

The word *demonstrate* cited above has three syllables, and therefore three vowels: /ɛ ə ey/. Writing the sequence of stress marks with the vowels produces the series /ɛ́ ə èy/. Note that the word *demonstrate* is related in form and meaning to another word: *demonstrative,* normally pronounced /dəmánstrətəv/. In both words the vowels marked with strong or medial stress are full vowels; syllables that are weak-stressed have the reduced vowel schwa, written /ə/:

demonstrate   /dɛ́mənstrèyt/
demonstrative   /dəmánstrətəv/

If we know the stress patterns, we can determine from the spelling what the pronunciation of the vowels will be. Basically *e o a* will be /ɛ a ey/, but only when stressed. Those left unstressed are subject to a special rule of English pronunciation—they change to schwa. Thus:

e o a —   /ɛ́ ə èy/   in /dɛ́mənstrèyt/
e o a —   /ə á ə/   in /dəmánstrətəv/
e o a —   /ɛ̀ ə éy/   in /dɛ̀mənstréyshən/

In this way English spelling represents what can be called the phonological deep structure of the language.

Native speakers often use English spelling rules to help them remember how to spell syllables that are pronounced with a schwa. For instance /mǽtər/ and /léybər/ both have /ər/ in their second syllable; but how should they be spelled? (Any English vowel letter *can* represent schwa, as in *collar, order, fakir, color, femur, satyr.*) Finding a related word with the /ər/ syllable stressed often reveals the spelling. So *material* and *laborious* supply the letters *e* and *o* respectively for the second syllables of *matter* and *labor*.

The interaction between stress and vowel quality is actually much more complex than the foregoing description indicates. Though the schwa is crucially important, there are four other exemplars in the reduced vowel system, all clustering in the high central region of the vowel square, and therefore in the mouth cavity of the English speaker. For the purposes of this short article, we merely note their presence, but all interact with their counterparts in the full vowel system and with schwa in the reduced system.

But the combined complexity of a three-level stress system and a correlated pattern of reduced vowels is still only part of the problem a learner of English faces. He must also cope with stress shifts seemingly catering to the English preference for avoiding juxtaposed high stresses. Hence we say /sèvəntíyn/ in 'She's seventeen', but /sévəntìyn/ in 'I've known her for seventeen years.' Additionally there is the ever-present pattern of contrastive stress, whereby *seventeen* shifts its stress to the first syllable when pronounced in counting sequence to show which syllable carries new information: /fíftiyn, síkstiyn, sévəntiyn/, etc.

By marking new information with contrastive stress, the speaker offers a redundant assist to his listener. Thus if a listener hears a garbled sentence like: "I wasn't (garble), but I also wasn't díscouraged," the contrastive stress on *díscouraged* identifies the lost word as "éncouraged." Likewise "Every plane has its (garble) and its dísadvantages," the stress on the syllable *dís*- tells us the lost word was "advantages." If the sentence had *disadvántages* with the normal syllable stressed, the garbled word would not be obvious, but the listener does know it isn't *advantages*, but maybe *problems* or *troubles* or something with a similar meaning.

Obviously the totality of problems associated with stress and stress-vowel correlations cannot be fully described in a single brief paper. Stress involves, besides intensity, correlated patterns of pitch, length, pitch shift, rhythm, the secondary or phrasal stress, etc., each in itself reasonably simple, but adding up to considerable overall complexity. But if individual points are taken up one at a time by a serious student, visible improvement will surely come. And even small gains will be magnified. Imagine, for example, how much improvement will result from a student merely being able to add schwa to his inventory. The gain in intelligibility—orally and aurally—would be impressive.

The other broad organizing principle is the flow of speech, by which we refer to the continuity of the speech signal and the effect adjacent sounds and forms have on each other.

Virtually all of our experience with language suggests discreteness. We think of words as units separated by space when we print a text, and indeed of letters as separate configurations of lines, curves, etc. They, too, are individually separate when we print, and only joined in strings in handwriting as a convenience so we don't have to lift the pen too often. We still clearly know when one letter stops and another starts.

Speech has been compared to a string of beads, with the beads in a fixed order representing sounds and words. Perhaps it would be more suggestive to think of it as a rope—continuous like strung beads, but with interwoven strands as the elements, and no clear signs to indicate when one strand ends and another begins.

The phenomena of speech flow touch the stress-reduced syllable pattern where weak-stressed vowels occur at word boundaries adjacent to another vowel. In a sentence like "Is Rosa over the flu?" compared with "Is Rose over the flu?", the weak-stressed second syllable of *Rosa* in the first example is influenced by the following vowel. Yet it is not completely swallowed up. In fact, it's a good illustration and practice exercise that shows just how brief a weak-stressed syllable can get without disappearing. In contrast, note how the schwa in *Rosa* is protected when it appears between consonants in a sentence like "Is Rose/ Rosa going?"

Words that may occur unstressed regularly have forms with reduced vowels. Notice the following three sentences:

Whattaya want with that cat?
Whattaya doin' with that cat?
Whattaya done with that cat?

50

The reduced 'word' /ə/ between *what* and *ya* is *do* in the first sentence, *are* in the second, and *have* in the third. Anyone who wants to handle real English in a communication situation must be aware of such reductions and must be able to quickly and accurately interpret the consequent phonological overlaps.

Most of the so-called particles (simple, one-syllable function words) of English have weak-stressed or reduced forms in which the full vowel of the form as stressed in citation alternates with a schwa. A very useful exercise can be built on the contrasts of full and reduced vowels correlated with a higher stress and a weak stress. Note the following:

Where's he at?	He's at home.	/ǽt/	ət/
Who's he for?	He's for Scranton.	/fɔ́r/	/fər/
What's it made of?	It's made of honey.	/àv/	/əv/
Where's she from?	She's from Luxor.	/frám/	/frəm/
Is Mr. Jones in?	He's in his office.	/ín/	/ən/
Who should I speak to?	Speak to the manager.	/tùw/	/tə/
He's the minister?	I think he is.	/híy/	/iy/
Where *are* they?	Where're they staying?	/ár/	/ər/

Another very general pattern of influence between contiguous sounds can be seen when an alveolar stop or sibilant is immediately followed by a /y/. The normal result, referred to as palatal assimilation, is a pattern of reciprocal influence that produces such pronunciations as 'Whatcher name, Whadja see there, Wherezher car, Is thisher pen.'

Notice the trouble we have spelling these pronunciations. The fact there are no acceptable spellings correctly implies that such assimilations are not acknowledged in polite society, in such places as schoolrooms. Yet they exist in the natural expression of native speakers of English, and to ignore them is to condemn still more students to a difficult transition from classroom to real life, a transition some students never succeed at.

The pattern of assimilation shows that the sounds in sequence affect each other, to produce a new or different sound. Though a great many second-language speakers of English are probably unaware of this pattern, it can be listed and illustrated very briefly:

/s/	/sh/	I miss your cooking.
/z/	/zh/	Who's your teacher?

51

/t/		/ch/	Has he finished yet?
/d/	+ /y/ →	/j/	Did you see him?
/ts/		/ch/	What's your name?
/dz/		/j/	He needs your help.

These assimilations are perfectly natural in English. In fact, native speakers who studiously avoid them may sound a bit strange, perhaps affected. Yet they are often avoided in English classes, for both first and second language learners. No harm is done native speakers studying their own language—they'll already have learned these patterns. But second language learners may miss needed exposure to the pattern, especially if they are studying in a non-English-speaking environment, and will be less well-prepared when they are left to make their way among native speakers.

Most students of English are made aware of a phenomenon called contraction, where parts of two words are put together in a new and usually shortened form. Though there are some teachers and some textbooks which try to avoid using any contractions—presumably in the interest of promoting the best possible style and usage—they are presented and used in most classes. A spelling convention applies to their written form: an apostrophe marks the point where sounds are omitted. So there are what could be called traditional contractions: *he's, we're, they're, isn't,* etc. An extension of this spelling pattern to other forms produces some marginal forms, usual in speech but criticized as unacceptable in writing: *there're, Jack'll, Ray'd, when'd, must've,* etc.

But other patterns of contraction characterize spoken English, such as *lemme, gimme, dunno, les, amana* for "let me, give me, don't know, let's, I'm going to." The form *whattaya* cited earlier is an example of this level of contraction. These are mostly individual forms, but among them there is a pattern that deserves special mention, the unorthodox contractions made up of a verb form plus the particle *to*: *gonna, gotta, usta, hasta, wanna, supposta,* etc. These must be acknowledged since they signal contrasts in meaning:

What do you have to eat?	(What food is available?)
What do you hafta eat?	(What diet is prescribed?)
So you got to go.	(You managed to take the trip.)
So you gotta go.	(You will have to take the trip.)

52

There are spellings for these forms, but they are seen only in the most informal of written texts, such as in the balloons of comic strip dialog. Many teachers would not admit them in serious pedagogical materials. Yet they exist and as indicated above they can be used to disambiguate meanings that otherwise may not be clear.

Finally some mention should be made of the reductions that occur in consonant clusters and sequences. Otherwise, we will go on expecting performances from our second-language students that even our natives can't and don't handle. For example, *textbook* is cut down to /téksbʊk/, with the medial /t/ deleted; we don't even *try* to say /tékstbʊk/. Only on rather formal occasions would we speak of /bə́rsts/ in a sentence like "There were many spontaneous bursts of applause." More likely we'd say /bə́rs/. And so on with many other examples, as /fífs/ not /fífəs/ in "three-fifths of a second," etc.

Curiously there are times when the simplification of a consonant cluster in English is best accomplished by adding a consonant. Thus when a past tense suffix *t* is added to the verb *dream*, the sequence *mt* is produced. But these two sounds are quite different from each other—one a voiced bilabial nasal and the other a voiceless alveolar stop. The cluster is made easier to pronounce by inserting between the two consonants a /p/, which is bilabial like the /m/ and voiceless like the /t/, producing the three-consonant cluster /mpt/ in /drémpt/. Similarly a /t/ is inserted between the final /n/ of *ten* and the ordinal suffix /ə/, producing /téntə/. But then we may wish to make *tenth* plural by adding an /s/; /téntəs/. The cluster /ntəs/ is just too much for the average English speaker, so he drops one sound—not the /t/ he inserted but the /ə/ which follows it, producing a form pronounced /ténts/ in 'two-tenths of an inch.'

The point to draw from this rather complicated description of intrusive consonant and subsequent simplification is that we should not expect our second-language students to maintain complex clusters which native speakers regularly simplify. Relevant examples with reductions are: *months* /mə́nts/, *acts* /æks/, *tempts* /témps/, *sixths* /síks/, *asked* /æst/, etc.

The main problem seems to be that a real world of English communication, the living phonology of English, has been systematically excluded from the classroom. English teachers have condemned such pronunciations and have even tried to pretend they don't exist. It is true they do not occur in the hot-house climate of formality that is traditionally maintained in our schools, where only prestige forms have been admitted. And the prestige form of English has tended to be formal and written. Perhaps now it's time to acknowledge informal and oral.

I don't suggest that formal, written English should be dropped from the curriculum; only that informal, spoken forms should be added. In first language instruction we can ignore informal forms—the students learn them in context and come to schools for training in the formal language. But second-language learners have no background experience to rely on; they learn only what is presented to them in their regular instruction. These students should be exposed to both kinds of English, each in an appropriate context. Otherwise their instruction will be out of balance. An effective drill procedure would be to use formal and informal forms as cue and response in a comparison drill.

The combination of unappreciated complexity (effectively disguised by the English spelling system) and a linguistic prudery that has ignored reality has placed a substantial burden on anyone interested in native-like pronunciation. Yet by analyzing and describing the details, by a systematic presentation, and by focussed practice on these details, it will be possible to substantially improve the quality of pronunciation for a motivated student. And motivating students to a higher standard of performance should be an easier task as more successful learners emerge from our training programs. The student should achieve an understanding of the patterns of pronunciation in English and the contrastive pressures which must be overcome. This should make possible effective self-monitoring, so the student can carry on after leaving the classroom and the teacher.

With perceptible improvement will come greater confidence and ease in handling the language, and the non-native teacher will be strengthened. Another substantial benefit is much more face validity and with it the ability to convince others that here is a teacher of demonstrable competence. Perhaps the fastidious customer in search of a qualified and superior teacher would even prefer him to an unwashed native speaker.

Polychronometry in Lesson Analysis

William F. Mackey

INTRODUCTION

The history of science is largely the history of measurement. Most developments in measurement have in the past been associated with the physical sciences. Since the turn of the century, however, advances in the social sciences have been associated with statistical methods. Most of these have been applied to the behavior of populations rather than to detailed observations of individuals or small groups and their behavior during observable events in their lives. It is the purpose of this article to present a method and an instrument for the analysis and measurement of such observable events, including language lessons.

Although there are established ways of measuring changes in environment, there are as yet few standard measures for variables of events that take place in the environment. Environmental changes in such things as temperature, humidity, radiation, and the purity of air and water are measured daily, and these measurements are used to solve a host of practical problems. We no longer rely on our feelings to find out whether a place is warmer or damper than another; we rely on such instruments as thermometers, hydrometers, barometers, and the like. The use of such instruments permits us to record measurements of things that are continually changing, enabling us to come to a number of general and practical conclusions.

On the other hand, in talking about events we have very few possibilities of measurement. A notable exception is the stock market where the selling and buying activity of individuals is recorded with precision and rapidity. In less than a few hours we can know how many shares have changed hands in such cities as London, New York, Toronto, and Tokyo, the value of these shares, and whether their price has gone up or down. But when talking about such fields as radio and television, sports, theater, ballet, and other forms of activitiy, we have nothing more than individual impressions and opinions, which may vary from individual to individual, when analyzing the same event. Opinions may vary as to how much action there was in one event as opposed to another, whether someone's performance was better than someone else's, and the like, because we have no objective way of analyzing and measuring the variables. The same symphony, opera or play presented a number of times, each time with changes in the tempo of its components can give a series of entirely different impressions.

Before any sort of evaluative conclusion is possible, however, the event must first be accurately observed, the variables isolated and measured, the results interpreted and the functional categories established. There are therefore four related problems the solution of which depends on the field, the situation, and the objectives. They are: the problem of observation, the problem of computation, the problem of interpretation, and the problem of categorization.

The Problem of Observation

Whether the event is observed directly as it is taking place, or indirectly as a recording or verbatim report, may depend on the possibility of obtaining information that is accurate or abundant enough to be worthwhile.

Direct observation—known or unknown to the subjects being observed—was all that was possible at the period when time-and-motion studies were first launched in industry. As recording facilities became more generally available, indirect observation through recorded material gained in popularity. These facilities permit a choice between verbal recording, vocal recording, cinematography, and videotaping.

Verbal records, especially the verbatim stenographic transcripts of the court clerk, have been of limited use in the study of duration and frequency of events, since they have recorded only what can be written according to the usual conventions (Flanders, 1970). Vocal recording, however, by means of disk and tape recorders, registers not only what is said but also how it is said, including the hesitations and silences, in real time. These have been used for the analysis of psychiatric interviews (Kasl and Mahl, 1965). If, however, one is interested more in the actions than in the speech of the subjects, simple cinematographic records may be what is required. This type of recording may also be used in the analysis of interview material (Sainsbury, 1954). The most complete record, of course, includes both the sound and the image. Both sound motion pictures and especially videotape have become widely accessible to record for later analysis events in many different fields (Mackey, 1968a). The superiority of videotape is that it gives the choice of either erasing the record once it has been analyzed, or of conserving it as a document or a model for purposes of training and research (Mackey, 1968b).

The means of observing the event—directly or indirectly—is only the beginning of the problem of description and analysis. Once we have the record, we must arrive at a means of compiling and computing the relevant data which it contains.

The Problem of Computation

What are the objectively measurable components of an event? The chief ones are time, sound, movement, and contact. Since both sound and movement must take place in time, they can be described and measured in temporal terms as continua of frequency of occurrence and duration. All phenomena distributed in time can be described in terms of frequency distribution and relative duration; these can be correlated with related phenomena as being significant, causal, or diagnostic.

In analyzing configurations of movement and sound as they unroll in time, one must know what units to look for and how to count them. The units themselves will depend on the type of event, the field of knowledge, and the purposes of the analysis. If one is studying interview transactions, one may be interested only in what a person says (content analysis). Or one may be

57

interested in how he or she says it (behavioral analysis), and this could include the person's rate of speech, the amount of talking, and the length and number of silences and interruptions.

A complete count of the time-units includes a record of their duration and frequency. The duration can be computed in arbitrary units of time—in minutes or seconds. Some researchers have used units of one minute (Melbin, 1954); others have been able to limit themselves to 30 seconds (Verzeano and Finesinger, 1949), five seconds (Sainsbury, 1954), and even to three seconds (Moskowitz, 1970). Both methods can be used with or without special recorders of elapsed time.

Frequency can be counted with the aid of special mechanical or electromagnetic counters (Matarazzo, Saslow, and Matarazzo, 1956), or by hand tallying with the aid of a stopwatch (Melbin, 1954). Hand tallying obliges one to use arbitrary time units, even though these may be of short duration; units as short as three seconds have been used along with hand tallying (Moskowitz, 1970).

Once the distribution of the frequency and duration of the event has been recorded and computed, it is often necessary to re-group and interpret the results in terms of certain indices.

The Problem of Interpretation

Interpretive indices may be independent of the time record. They may depend on practical and theoretical considerations in the analysis of the subject matter analyzed.

According to his interaction theory of personality, for example, Chapple interprets total durations of interruption minus the silences as an index of adjustment (Matarazzo, Saslow, and Matarazzo, 1956). Flanders (1970), on the other hand, interprets his data in terms of interaction matrices.

Such indices, matrices, and other numerical interpretations permit one to classify events and their participants into functional categories.

The Problem of Categorization

Categories often depend on correlation with other phenomena outside the event in question. For example, it may have been discovered through experience or experimentation that people with dominant personalities make poor servants but good masters, or that teachers whose lesson matrices show a lot of student initiative are successful at teaching certain subjects to certain age-groups. The activity of such teachers could be put into the category of 'indirect teaching' (Flanders, 1970).

The technology of visual and sound recording has become advanced and widespread enough to make the recording of all sorts of events practicable. Later analysis, interpretation, and categorization of the components of such events depends on the purpose, function, and state of knowledge and experimentation of the field observed. Computation of time variables, however, depends on advances in instrumentation. This is the aspect of the problem to which we shall now give our attention.

INSTRUMENTATION

One might say that the history of instrumentation in this field begins with the invention of the stopwatch, which was what many people interested in chronometric variables, including the writer, started using, until it became evident that such a simple instrument could not meet the complex requirements in the analysis of multiple time variables in behavior.

In the early 1940s, Chapple perfected a machine which would do most of the computing automatically. It was the first in a series of what became known as "Interaction Chronographs." On these, interviews were recorded by an observer using two keys; a computer, sometimes in a separate room, aided in producing a series of graphs at the end of the interview. After several years of use, however, more variables were needed in research than the first Chronograph could measure. A perfected model was therefore developed by the inventor in the late 1940s. In this model, the observer's box was equipped with push buttons, two of which turned the recording machine on or off, two were allotted to the participants (one for the interviewer and the other for the interviewee), and another button activated a counter. A computer was designed to supply the different measures by combining the frequency and duration of the stretches of speech and silences of the two persons.

Each of these measures was given a certain interpretation. For example, duration of a person's speech (or action) became

59

his activity index. The number of times he came out talking after an interruption became his dominance index (Chapple, 1949).

Although used widely for the analysis of interviews, it must be pointed out that the Interaction Chronograph, in the final analysis, dealt with only two first-order variables—activity and non-activity. Only two people were dealt with at a time—the interviewer and the interviewee. The process was too complicated even for some simpler purposes; the recording was not automatic; and the observer's reaction time and fatigue were sources of error.

In 1949 an attempt was made to eliminate the human observer of the interview—and at the same time reduce human error—by designing an automatic interaction analyzer to record and compute the speech activity of an individual. The speech was first recorded by individual microphones—one for each person. Each microphone fed a separate tape recorder and computer. Duration and frequency were computed in intervals of 30 seconds; a counter and totalizer of duration gave the frequency distribution in these 30-second units; and finally there was a counter and classifier of interruptions. The apparatus consisted of electromagnetic counters, time delay relays, a stepping switch, and a pulse timer (Verzeano and Finesinger, 1949). Although the machine was used in the field of psychiatry, for studies of free association, it was not universally applicable. The 30-second unit was arbitrary and too long for some studies, and a separate machine was needed for each person involved in an event.

In the 1950s a number of automatic devices came out for specific and limited operations in speech analysis. Some were designed only for the study of verbal activity during an interview (Kasl and Mahl, 1965). Others were invented for measuring rates of speech (Irwin and Becklund, 1953) and variables in verbal conditioning (Krasner, 1958).

In 1960 Starkweather conceived a speech-rate meter for verbal behavioral analysis. It produced a graphic cumulative record of pulses of speech, which showed a high correlation with the results of word-frequency counts obtained through typescripts (Starkweather, 1960).

These counters of speech units are to be distinguished from other automatic speech analyzers developed for phonetic research and language instruction, which go back to Homer Dudley's vocoder of the year 1928. The Bell Acoustic Spectograph was developed in the 1940s to make speech 'visible' (Potter, 1947); this later became the Kay Sonograph, a version of which was used in the study of voiceprinting, each person having his characteristic print, presumably as inalterable as his fingerprints. These, along with the Mingograph, and the Eric developed by Lucien LeBourhis at Laval, were all used for the purpose of breaking down sound into its acoustic components.

Also in another category are more than a dozen types of speech recognition devices, like the SAID (Buiten and Lane, 1965) developed under Harlan Lane in the mid-1960s to monitor practice in the learning of the intonation and rhythm of a foreign language. Here students record their speech on tape and look at a meter which displays the degree of acceptability of their utterance as far as the rhythm and intonation are concerned, after which the student reshapes his intonation to come closer to the model he is imitating. Another, more elaborate device also using a small computer analyzes and recomposes an intonation curve on a television screen; it was developed by Pierre Léon in the late 1960s at the University of Toronto to permit students to compare their tone curve with the model.

By the mid-1960s researchers were still working to improve on the Interaction Chronograph. In 1965 a description was published of a new device called the Interaction Recorder which consisted of a timer and a punch unit. The data recorded are the same as that of the Interaction Chronograph; but it permitted faster processing of these data. It recorded on punched paper tape the sequences of interview speech, and silence, keeping a record of when one or the other, both or neither of the persons was speaking. The tape was then fed into a Burroughs E101 computer which was programmed to produce a unit-by-unit analysis of the speech, silences, and interruptions of the interview (Weins, Matarazzo, and Saslow, 1965).

All these interaction recording devices have a great deal in common:

1. They deal with only three possibilities: activity, no activity, or no types.
2. The activity or nonactivity of only two persons is analyzed.

3. From these two first-order measures, other second- and third-order measures are derived.

4. They have narrow applicability, designed as they are mostly for interviews or for individual recording.

If other, more complex materials—lessons, games, television programs, and motion picture films—are to be analyzed, what is needed is a device that will record and compute variables in several types of activity and speech that can be used to analyze the simultaneous interaction of several people, a device that will give a greater number of first-order measures while being flexible and adaptable to different kinds of phenomena. This is what we attempted to do in developing the Polychronometer.

THE POLYCHRONOMETER

It was with a view to meeting the needs for wider ranging instrumentation in the analysis of time variables in behavior that the Polychronometer was developed. In the context of what has been done in this field, it will now be easier to understand the history and development of this instrument, its design, mechanism, uses, and special techniques.

History and Development

The development of the Polychronometer began in the mid-1960s when the present writer attempted to relate teacher performance to method analysis (Mackey, 1965). The analysis of the teaching materials having been quantified (Mackey, 1972), it was necessary to find a way of quantifying their use in teaching performance. After attempting to use chronometric techniques available at the time—all unsatisfactory—it was decided that the best long-term solution was to develop a machine for this and similar purposes. After a number of different designs and different types of instrumentation had been developed, a satisfactory working model was arrived at in late 1969, with the help of the chief technician of Laval University's Phonetics Research Laboratory, Lucien LeBourhis. After minor improvements and a few years of field testing, we are now ready to report on the features, design, mechanism, uses, and special techniques of this new device.

Main Features

The main features of the Polychronometer are as follows:

i) It is essentially a set of paired counter-timer units, each operated by a separate key.

ii) There are as many sets as there are fingers to operate them, that is, ten in number.

iii) This permits the analyst to make as many as twenty first-order measurements in a single run.

iv) Each key controls two types of measurement—duration and frequency.

v) Duration is measured in real time, since the electronic switches respond as quickly as an operator's reflexes.

vi) Each set is adaptable to automatic input (like speech recognition devices) or to computer output for first, second, and third order measurement.

vii) The machine is light in weight and easily portable.

viii) Since the keyboard is separate from the control box, the machine can be operated at a distance or by remote control.

Design

The ten sets of timer-counters are imbedded in a sloped control box containing the circuits and driving mechanism along with an on-off switch. The key board, with two sets of five concave keys, each designed for the varying length and shape of the fingers of each hand, is a separate unit which can be plugged into the control box at a distance. An optional remote control unit can operate videotape or magnetic tape playback machines for the analysis of recorded materials.

Mechanism

The mechanical problem in developing the machine was essentially one of circuitry and the coupling of appropriate relays to the activator keys (See Figure 1).

The electronic operation is briefly as follows:

1. When one of the keys is touched, an activator establishes a + HT on a corresponding relay.

a) The returning current passes through Q3 and R3, while Q3 remains active. (Base Q3 thru R3 and R4 to the HT, Q1 at rest.)
b) Contact S1 auto starts the relay.
c) Contact S2 discharges C2 on Base Q6 thru R1, which moves the corresponding key-touch counter ahead one unit, thru Q6.
d) Contact S3 starts the corresponding timer.
e) The tension developed by the Q3 emitter is not sufficient to start the monostable Q1-Q2, but sufficient to give to the base of Q5, thru R7, enough current to light the pilot light L1, indicating that one of the timers is active.

2. When another key is touched, its returning current, coupled with that of the previous one produces enough tension thru R3 at Point C (1 .volt) to start the monostable Q1-Q2, cutting the basic current Q3 (10 miliseconds). This unswitches the preceding relay while automatically putting a new relay into action behind the key which has just been touched. Anything over 10 milliseconds will thus be registered. The cycle is then repeated.

3. The stop button switches off all active relays. It must be pressed immediately after the end of the period of analysis. Otherwise, the timer set in motion by the last key will keep on counting.

64

THE POLYCHRONOMETER

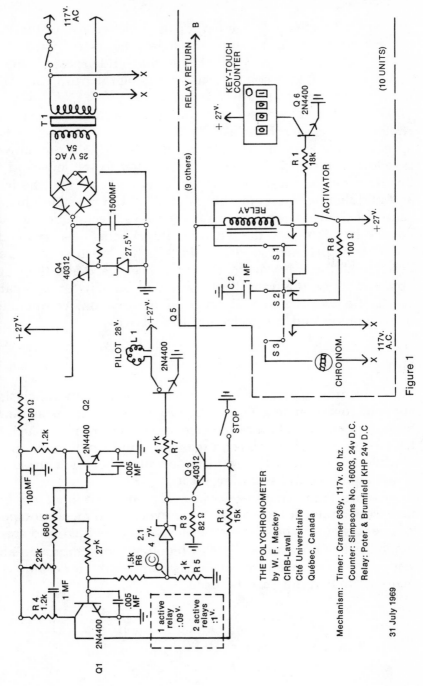

THE POLYCHRONOMETER
by W. F. Mackey
CIRB-Laval
Cité Universitaire
Québec, Canada

Mechanism: Timer: Cramer 636y, 117v. 60 hz.
Counter: Simpsons No. 16003, 24v D.C.
Relay: Poter & Brumfield KHP 24v D.C

31 July 1969

Figure 1

65

TECHNIQUES

Any special techniques needed for the efficient use of the Poly-chronometer can be mastered in a few hours of practice. Efficiency of use can be increased if the tendencies of the observer-operator and some basic psychological truths are taken into account. Here are a few suggestions:

Divide the categories, if possible, according to a basic dichotomy (e.g. teacher-class, interviewer-interviewee, action-speech, left side-right side, etc.). One side of the dichotomy can be allotted to the right-hand and the other to the left-hand key board. Allot the most frequent or likely categories to the index and middle finger (e.g. teacher talk). Avoid, if possible, the allocation of similar categories to adjacent keys. Techniques of usage have to be adapted to the type of material being observed and to the aims of the analysis. It would take too much space here to describe all the ways the machine has been used and the results obtained since the year 1969. This will be left for a separate article. So will the special types of observation, computation, interpretation and categorization (see above).

USES

The Polychronometer can be used for the quantitative analysis of any phenomenon that takes place in time. It can measure the frequency and duration of ten categories—according to such criteria as place, person, object, organism, sound, action, or speech —while the event is taking place, or after the event through a visual and/or sound recording of it.

If more than ten categories have to be accounted for, it is necessary to use a recording of the event on film, videotape or magnetic sound tape. The categories can be divided into sets of ten, and as many reruns made as required. For a thorough analysis of what can take place in a classroom lesson, for example, as many as four reruns can be used.

TABLE 1

POLYCHRONOMETRIC TECHNIQUE OF FOREIGN
LANGUAGE TEACHING ANALYSIS

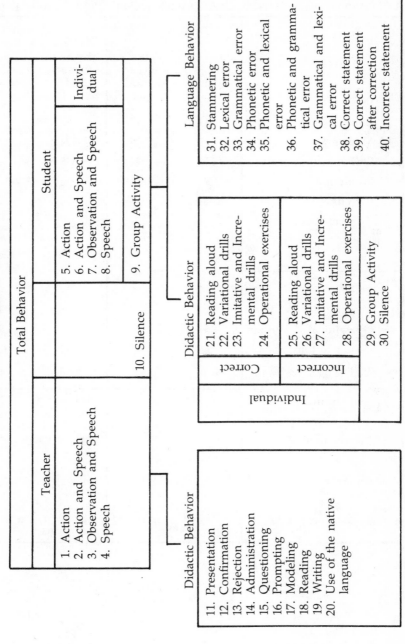

67

TABLE 2
TYPES AND DISTRIBUTION OF DIDACTIC BEHAVIOR IN TWO LESSONS

		Lesson A		*Lesson B*	
		duration (in seconds)	frequency (occurrences)	duration (in seconds)	frequency (occurrences)
T	Presentation	169	78	80	132
E	Confirmation	83	47	95	16
A	Modeling	41	19	124	19
C	Questioning	331	90	338	41
H	Prompting	32	18	12	9
E	Rejecting	16	8	0	0
R	Administration	4	1	7	3
C	Imitation	14	4	10	3
L	Variational Repetition	0	0	25	12
A	Operational Repetition	361	111	65	30
S	Group responses	266	64	311	132
S	TOTALS:	1317	440	1068	398
	Activity Index:	$\frac{1317}{440} = 2.9$		$\frac{1068}{398} = 2.7$	
	Variety Index:	$\frac{1317}{10} = 131.7$		$\frac{1068}{10} = 106.8$	
	Intensity Index:	$\frac{60 \times 178}{1317} = 8.1$		$\frac{60 \times 177}{1068} = 9.9$	
	Effectiveness Index:	$\frac{1317}{60} \times \frac{1}{78} \times 4 = 1.12$		$\frac{1068}{60} \times \frac{1}{68} \times 4 = 1.05$	

Lesson Analysis

In a language lesson there may be more than forty relevant variables which can be grouped for purposes of frequency-duration analysis. They can be divided into four groups of ten, requiring four runs through the video-playback. The first run analyzes the overall teacher-and-student classroom behavior; here the left hand can be allotted to the teacher and the right to the learners (silence recorded by the left thumb). The second run analyzes the teacher's didactic behavior; the third run, the learners' didactic behavior; whereas the fourth and final run is devoted to the analysis of language behavior (see Table 1).

For each of the forty types of behavior observed, the polychronometer will record both its duration and its frequency of occurrence. The figures can be analyzed in a variety of ways using a great range of available statistical techniques, depending on what one wishes to discover. For example, by dividing total class time in seconds by the sum of the frequencies of didactic behavior types (both teacher and learner activities), we obtain an activity index measuring the rate of interaction—an indicator of the interchange between learners and their teacher. Secondly, by computing the ratio between type of activity and total lesson time, in seconds, we obtain a variety index—a correlate of level of interest. Thirdly, by dividing the total number of individual and group responses in speech and action by total class time expressed in minutes, we can obtain an intensity index as an indicator of the average amount of participation. Fourthly, by token-counting acceptable phrases independently produced by individual learners, dividing this into total class time in seconds, and multiplying the result by the number of new teaching points presented, we may arrive at an index of effectiveness as an indicator of the newly acquired abilities of the learners to generate well-formed sentences from elements first encountered in the lesson. Several other indices can thus be calculated by grouping the variables in different ways, depending on what one wishes to find out about the lessons.

If a synthesis is required or if one wants an overall view of what the lesson looks like, the observed variables may be placed within a time-space framework by plotting frequency against duration (see below).

Comparing Language Lessons: an Illustration

Polychronometric techniques can thus be used to compare language lessons which supposedly 'teach' the same thing. By way of illustration let us take two lessons of elementary English of about twenty minutes duration (give or take a couple of minutes per lesson) in which the identical unit of the same method is taught. We first videotaped the two lessons (A and B) in two separate classes, each of thirty Grade-Five learners, taught by two different teachers. Each teacher taught Unit 23 of *Introducing English* according to the procedures explained in the teaching manual (Marquis and Saindon, 1962). From the videotape we made four separate analyses, as indicated above, transcribing from the polychronometer frequency and duration figures for all types of behavior observed. Such a polychronometric analysis of comparable lessons reveals how there can be differences in the teaching of the same lesson, which is purportedly uniform even though it is taught by different teachers. Such analyses can also illustrate how differences in teaching behavior condition different types of language behavior in the learners.

If, for example, we examine only the didactic behavior of teacher and class in the above lessons A and B, we note a difference in the use of such procedures as questioning, prompting, rejection, and the variation of elements in a pattern (variational repetition). On the basis of the cumulated totals we can also arrive at overall indices for purposes of comparison (see Table 2). In addition to this the characteristics of the two lessons can be plotted within a duration-frequency space continuum showing different profiles for each of the lessons(see Figures 2 and 3).

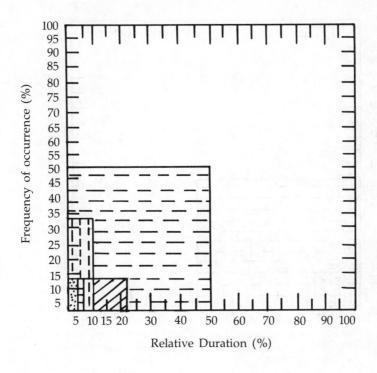

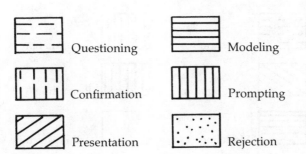

Figure 2: Frequency and Relative Duration of Teaching Behavior in Lesson A

71

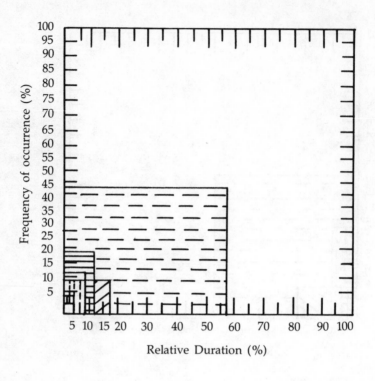

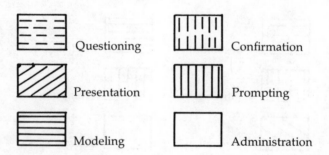

Figure 3: Frequency and Relative Duration of
Teaching Behavior in Lesson B.

The above analyses are simply meant as an illustration of what can be done. The forty variables suggested may be increased, decreased, modified, or replaced, depending on what features one wishes to quantify. Or an entirely new set of variables may be chosen such as the system of foreign language interaction analysis (FLINT) which stresses such features as dealing with feelings, encouraging and praising, using humor, using the ideas of the students, repeating verbatim the responses of the students, asking questions, giving information, correcting, giving directions, directing drills, criticizing behavior and responses, and using individual and group responses (open-ended or student-initiated), laughter, confusion, nonverbal activity, and the native language (Louisy, forthcoming).

Some teachers have used the Polychronometer exclusively for the analysis of audio-taped lessons and have claimed that this is sufficient for their needs. Others have used the instrument simply to compare in a single run the language content of the lesson as taught with that of the lesson as it appears in the method and materials. It may also be used in the analysis of automated language teaching which, being subject to the same basic didactic principles as any other form of teaching, is not *per se* because of its automation necessarily any better (Mackey, 1969). Indeed, polychronometric analysis may be applied to most of the perennial attempts to measure classroom behavior which have intermittently appeared in the past half-century—ever since Horn, in 1914, experimented with his system for measuring the distribution of pupil participation in a lesson (Medley and Mitzel, 1967).

SUMMARY AND ABSTRACT

There is a growing need for instrumentation which can enable us to observe and compute phenomena that take place in time. Although problems of observation, computation, interpretation, and categorization vary from field to field and from problem to problem, it is possible to design an instrument for use in any situation where time-variables have to be measured as duration and frequency. The Polychronometer is suggested for such purposes. It is essentially composed of ten paired counter-timer sets, each operated by a separate key. The ten keys are set in a keyboard which is plugged into the control box, each key being designed for a different finger of the left or right hand. A few hours of practice is sufficient to give an observer proficiency in operating the keyboard, sufficient to adapt to the rapidity of moving events. Further work is being done to develop different polychronometric techniques for the analysis of behavior.

References

Buiten, R. and Lane, H. 1965. A self-instructional device for conditioning accurate prosody. *International Review of Applied Linguistics* 3:205 –219.

Chapple, E.D. 1949. The interaction chronograph. *Personnel* 25:295–307.

Flanders, N.A. 1970. *Analyzing teaching behavior.* Reading, Mass.: Addison-Wesley.

Irwin, J.V. and Becklund, O. 1953. Norms for maximum repetitive rates for certain sounds established with the sylrater. *Journal of Speech and Hearing Disorders* 18:149–160.

Kasl, S.V. and Mahl, G.F. 1965. A simple device for obtaining certain verbal activity measures during interviews. *Journal of Abnormal and Social Psychology* 53:425–433.

Krasner, L. 1958. Studies of the conditioning of verbal behavior. *Psychological Bulletin* 55:148–170.

Louisy, P.C. (forthcoming). *Polychronometry Compared with FLINT in Analyzing Foreign Language Teaching Behavior.* Quebec: CIRB (International Center for Research on Bilingualism), Publication B.

Mackey, W.F. 1965. Method analysis: a survey of its development, principles, and techniques. Georgetown: *Monograph Series on Languages and Linguistics* 18:149–162.

———. 1968a. The new technology of teacher training. *English Language Teaching* 23:10–14. 1968. La nuova technologia nella preparazione glottodidattica. *Homo Loquens* 1:71–75 (trans.).

———. 1968b. Practice teaching: models and modules. *Les langues modernes* 3:94–100. 1968. Titocinio didattico: modelli e moduli. *Homo Loquens* 3:24–34 (trans.).

———. 1969. *The Computer in Automated Language Teaching.* Quebec: CIRB, Publication B.

———. 1965, 1967. *Language teaching analysis.* London: Longman; Bloomington: Indiana University Press. 1972 (new version). *Principes de didactique analytique,* Paris: Didier.

74

————. (in press). Quantifying performance in language teaching and learning. *Die neuren sprachen.*

Marquis, Michel and Saindon, Rosaire. 1962. *Introducing English.* Montreal: Holt, Rinehart & Winston.

Matarazzo, J.D., Saslow, G., and Matarazzo, R.G. 1956. The interaction chronograph. *Journal of Psychology* 41:347–367.

Medley, D.M. and Mitzel, H.E. 1967. Measuring classroom behavior by systematic observation. In N.L. Gage (ed.) *Handbook of Research in Teaching.* Chicago: Rand McNally, 247–328.

Melbin, M. 1954. An interaction recording device for participant observers. *Human Organization* 13, 2:29–33.

Moskowitz, G. 1970. *The foreign language teacher interacts.* Minneapolis, Minn.: Association for Productive Teaching.

Potter, R.K., Kopp, G.A., and Green, H.C. 1947. *Visible speech.* New York: Van Nostrand.

Sainsbury, P. 1954. A method of recording spontaneous movements by time-sampling motion pictures. *Journal of Mental Science* 100:742–748.

Starkweather, J.A. 1960. A speech rate meter for vocal behavior analyses. *Journal of the Experimental Analysis of Behavior* 3:11–114.

Verzeano, M. and Finesinger, J.E. 1949. An automatic analyzer for the study of speech in interaction and in free association. *Science* 110:45–46.

Wiens, A.N., Matarazzo, J.D., and Saslow, G. 1965. The interaction recorder: an electronic punch paper tape unit for recording speech behavior during interviews. *Journal of Clinical Psychology* 21:142–145.

Interaction in the Foreign Language Classroom

Reinhold Freudenstein

One area of language teaching which has increasingly attracted the attention of researchers and educators is the interaction process that takes place between teacher and students from the moment they enter the classroom to the end of a lesson. Until recently, observation and evaluation of teacher-student interaction were based on personal judgment and individual interpretation guided by the training and experience of the observers. These reactions were generally pertinent; in many cases the observers were able to identify the factors that could be considered responsible for the success or failure of a lesson. On-the-spot observations, however, are not systematic and do not cover all the activities which take place during a lesson. The resultant lack of objectivity may be the most serious drawback in the more traditional ways of observing teacher-student interaction.

Recent research in the field has resulted in observation methods which eliminate subjective factors as far as possible; but at the same time they have become very complicated and often too theoretical to be of practical value. Flanders (1970) offers an interaction analysis system which seems to be particularly appropriate for the foreign language field because it is concerned primarily with verbal behavior. Observable verbal behavior is broken down into ten categories, seven devoted to teacher talk and two to student talk; one category concentrates on "silence or confusion." The talk by the teacher is subdivided into "response" and "initiation," the first containing the categories: "accepts feeling," "praises or encourages," and "accepts or uses ideas of pupils"; the latter: "lecturing," "giving directions," and "criticizing or justifying authority." One category of teacher talk, "asks questions," falls into both subdivisions. The talk by the pupil can only be listed as "response" or "initiation."

In the Flanders system the observer has to assign a category to every three seconds of elapsed classroom time. Thus one ends up with hundreds of numbers which are only of quantitative value. They do not tell anything about the content of a lesson, the arrangement of instructional phases, or the problems which are specific to foreign language instruction. The system offered by Flanders is a research instrument; it cannot serve as a guide for the teacher who is interested in analyzing and evaluating his own behavior. A detailed look at Flanders' interaction system is offered by Bailey (1975), who points out its deficiencies in accuracy, reliability, and practicality. Bailey is also critical of an interaction system developed by Moskowitz (1970), who had expanded the Flanders system to twenty-two categories, thus making it even more complex and increasing its weaknesses. Another system is offered by Fanselow (1976) which can only be handled by trained specialists. Although it is not supposed to be an instrument to be used by the classroom teacher, it does provide a new and promising approach to research methods.

Another adaptation of the Flanders system was developed by Nearhoof (published in Grittner, 1969). He concentrates more specifically on the foreign language classroom, and his scheme has many advantages over the Flanders system: verbal behavior is observed on the basis of whether the talk involves the native or the target language; the categories are more equally divided between teacher and student talk; and classroom interaction is analyzed with special consideration to types and forms of exercises which normally occur in language-learning situations. This approach, however, suffers from some of the more serious limitations already discussed: observers have to assign a number every three seconds (thus interrupting the listening-observing process in the middle of a sentence or an expression), and the categories cover too many different verbal activities under the same heading. This can be illustrated by Category 1:

1. Teacher uses foreign language for communication
   a) to give directions which then elicit desired pupil action;
   b) to discuss ideas relating to cultural contrasts, geography, history, literature, etc.;

77

    c) to explain problems of structure, of sound system, of writ-
       ten system, or other pertinent concepts;

    d) to answer pupil questions.

As far as classroom interaction is concerned, these are activities which differ in many respects and should be listed under separate subcategories.

In response to these weaknesses, a system was developed at Marburg University which attempts to be more specific without becoming too complicated. This system employs research methods for the practical needs of the classroom teacher. The following listing of the Nearhoof categories (indicated by the numbers in brackets which refer to the Marburg form) shows that each Nearhoof category is covered by at least two, often three, and sometimes four categories on the Marburg form. Three Marburg categories (1, 2, and 10) are not included in the Nearhoof system. This indicates that our form offers a more detailed and differentiated analysis of a foreign language lesson. We do not concentrate on verbal behavior alone, but we have tried to study further aspects of the teaching-learning process as well. As can be seen below, Nearhoof focuses on the use of the foreign language vs. the mother tongue almost exclusively:

1. Teacher uses foreign language for communication (3, 4).
2. Teacher uses foreign language for reinforcement (3, 4, 7).
3. Teacher uses mother tongue to clarify meaning or provide a cue (3, 4).
4. Teacher uses mother tongue as the functional classroom language (3, 4).
5. Student uses foreign language for rote response (1, 3, 5, 8).
6. Student uses foreign language to recombine prelearned material (1, 3).
7. Student uses foreign language to ask a question which he himself has originated (1, 3).
8. Student uses foreign language spontaneously (1, 3).
9. Student uses mother tongue for classroom communication (1, 3, 5).
10. Noninteraction activities, e.g. silence, confusion, organization, other language activities such as language laboratory, singing, silent reading, etc. (6, 8, 9).

The Marburg form was not designed for research purposes. It was developed as a practical aid for teachers and student teachers with no other objective in mind than the wish to provide a scheme for a systematic observation of activities during a foreign language lesson. Analysis is the basis for evaluation. It is to be hoped, therefore, that the statistical information collected on our form may serve as a starting point for further interpretation.

Each Marburg form is supplemented by a listing of general data. These provide information on the situational aspects of the lesson which has been observed: the date; the time; the sex and age of the teacher; the type of school; the size of the class; the year of foreign language learning; the target language. The data also includes information on the objectives of the lesson; the linguistic and cultural content of the lesson; and the material or textbook used.

We ask our observers to summarize their findings in time units of three minutes each. This enables them to concentrate on classroom activities in a more natural manner than shorter time periods permit. We arrived at time units of three minutes after experimentation with systematic observation of live and videotaped lessons. Time units of three minutes each guarantee the summing up of enough data to give a systematic and overall view of classroom activities as they develop during a lesson of 40 or 45 minutes. They also give the observers the freedom to make professional and intelligent judgments on their own within a limited observation period. They can mark their entry at any time within the limits of the given time unit. (Normally they start marking after half of the time or during the second and third minute.) The decision to be made is: which activity and type of interaction is most typical for the period of foreign language instruction under observation during the given time unit? They then mark the relevant categories which normally involve three to five entries and which, through their particular arrangement, indicate typical patterns of language teaching.

The Marburg form offers ten categories as shown in the chart on page 82. They are:

1. *Phases of instruction.* Listed are the most common phases during the period of language teaching and learning. Should other or unforeseen events take place, they can be marked and specified under "Other." Other remarks can be made throughout the period in the space provided at the bottom of the observation form.

79

2. *Homework.* This category is not covered by any other system although it refers to an activity which generally occurs in every language lesson.

3. *Interaction.* Here again the most common forms of interaction are listed but there is also room for other processes that might be observed. "Open" interaction refers to free language use, e.g. during discussions (the observer marks "o" in the column); "controlled" interaction refers to questions to which there is only one correct answer, e.g. in a pattern drill.

4. *Teacher language.* We assume that in a foreign language lesson the teacher will generally use the foreign language, because we feel that the objective of teaching a foreign or second language automatically leads to the use of that language during most of the time of instruction. "Faulty" means that the teacher is able to communicate in the foreign language freely but that he or she does make mistakes which do not, however, prevent him from getting his or her message across. The subdivision under "Mother Tongue" covers most areas in which it is likely to occur.

5. *Student language.* Here again we assume that during a foreign language lesson students normally speak in the language they are learning. Our interest focuses on the question: How often, when (during a lesson), and why do they use their mother tongue?

6. *Skills drilled.* This category is used only in connection with the subcategory "Exercises" (learning the new material) of Category 1 (phases of instruction). It gives information on which skill is being practiced.

7. *Correction.* This category is also typically used in connection with Category 1, subcategory "exercises." It can give answers to the questions: How often does the teacher actually allow classroom time for the correction of student responses? Is there any observable result of his effort? Does he delegate this task to (brighter) students?

8. *Media use.*

9. *General atmosphere.* This seems to be the weakest category of the Marburg form; however, we feel that we should not neglect this very important aspect of interaction. We know that entries in this category are very subjective but we also

have discovered that entries by different observers bring about results that are markedly alike. Nevertheless, we hope to develop this category further, possibly using the data collected by Moskowitz (1976).

10. *Student participation.* This can be judged by observing how many students raise their hands when responses are required, etc.

By studying a completed observation form it is easy to discover the sequence of activities during a given lesson and to interpret the data. We often find that an increasingly large number of entries under "students bored" corresponds to the lack of change in Categories 1, 3, or 8. We also discovered that the most critical moments in a foreign language lesson in terms of student boredom are minutes 18 to 21. Only a change in the type of interaction, media use, or a change of instructional phases (Category 1) can help to motivate students during this part of a lesson.

Observation entries can be made by a person sitting in during the lesson. They can also be made by watching a videotaped lesson. If a teacher has no assistance, a lesson can be recorded on a tape recorder and the form filled in after the lesson (while listening to the tape).

The form discussed above has proven to be practical although it must be considered to be a compromise solution: it allows for a restricted personal evaluation but forces the observer to concentrate on specific aspects in a systematic way. Undoubtedly, more experimentation with the form will contribute towards its further development.

When looking at the Marburg form one can easily see that it has been developed to serve the needs of the classroom teacher. It is less sophisticated than other analysis systems although these are not free of shortcomings either (Bailey 1975). We feel that the role of the teacher in the evaluation of classroom activities is not only to be the object of outside observation. Teachers should also have the opportunity to analyze and judge the interaction in which they have been involved. If this can be done with the help of the Marburg form in a less subjective way than in the past, the new system will have served its purpose.

FOREIGN LANGUAGE CLASSROOM OBSERVATION FORM

V-Center, Marburg University, FR of Germany

Time in minutes

Category	Item	3	6	9	12	15	18	21	24	27	30	33	36	39	42	45
PHASES OF INSTRUCTION	Repetition—Warming Up															
	Presentation (of new material)															
	Learning (the new material)—Exercises															
	Using (the new material in other situations)															
	Other:															
HOMEWORK	C=Control A=Assignment															
INTERACTION o = open c = controlled	Lecture T=Teacher S=Student															
	Teacher Question—Student Answer															
	Student Question—Teacher Reaction															
	Student—Student															
	Other:															
TEACHER LANGUAGE	Foreign Language c=correct f=faulty w=wrong															
	Mother Tongue — Instructions															
	Mother Tongue — Grammar Work															
	Mother Tongue — Explanations (D= Discussion)															
	Mother Tongue — Other:															
STUDENT LANGUAGE—	Asking for Explanations															
	Answer to Teacher Questions															
	Discussion															
Mother Tongue	Among themselves															
	Other:															
SKILLS DRILLED	L=Listening S=Speaking R=Reading W=Writing TF=Translation into Foreign Language TM=Translation into Mother Tongue															
CORRECTION	T=Teacher S=Student += successful -= unsuccessful															
MEDIA USE T=Teacher S=Student	B=Textbook V=Blackboard W=Workbook O=Overhead Projector S=Worksheet T=Tape Recorder Other:															
GENERAL ATMOSPHERE	Teacher — More authoritarian / More democratic															
	Students — Motivated / Bored															
	S=Silence C=Confusion															
STUDENT PARTICIPATION	A=All M=Many F=A Few N=None															

( ) = Short occurrence only

Other Remarks:

References

Bailey, L.G. 1975. An observational method in the foreign language classroom: a closer look at interaction analysis. *Foreign Language Annals*, 8, 4:335–344.

Fanselow, J.F. 1976. Beyond Rashomon. Paper read at the 1976 TESOL Convention, New York City.

Flanders, N.A. 1970. *Analyzing teacher behavior*. London: Addison-Wesley.

Grittner, F.M. 1969. *Teaching foreign languages*. New York: Harper & Row.

Krumm, H.J. 1973. *Analyse and training fremdsprachlichen lehrverhaltens*. Weinheim, Beltz.

Moskowitz, G. 1970. *The foreign language teacher interacts*. Minneapolis: Association for Productive Teaching.

————. 1976. The Classroom Behavior of Outstanding Foreign Language Teachers. Paper read at the 1976 TESOL Convention, New York City, *Foreign Language Annals*, (in press).

Some Differences between Teaching English as a Second Dialect and English as a Second Language

Kenneth R. Johnson

Although second language teaching techniques have been used to teach standard English to speakers of Black dialect, the use of these techniques presents some serious problems in the teaching of a second dialect. The pedagogical applications are not identical for teaching standard English as a second language and as a second dialect. The problems inherent in the teaching of standard English as a second dialect are unique to Black dialect speakers.

The difference between the two situations was identified as long ago as 1968, at the convention of the National Council of Teachers of English in Milwaukee, Wisconsin during a meeting of educators and linguists interested in investigating Black dialect and/or developing programs based on second language techniques for teaching standard English to disadvantaged Black children. Since then, the controversy of whether or not to use second language teaching techniques has continued. Specifically, the question is: what special pedagogical problems occur when second language techniques are used to teach standard English to Black children who speak Black dialect?

The most important consideration is the attitude of teachers toward Black dialect. Teachers—especially English teachers—have often labeled the speech of disadvantaged Black children as "bad, sloppy, and ungrammatical." The literature of education is full of examples of this kind of negative attitude towards the speech of disadvantaged Black children. Language is a label which identifies the speaker with all those who speak the same variety of English (the speaker's primary cultural group). When teachers label Black children's speech as "bad, sloppy, and ungrammatical," they are rejecting these children and their culture. This attitude and others like it only alienate Black children from the instructional program. They are unlikely to accept the standard English that teachers attempt to teach them. If teachers reject the students' language, then the students cannot easily accept the teachers' language. The speakers of foreign languages do not experience this same kind of attitude; teachers working with foreign speakers do not usually make the negative value-judgments about the speakers of foreign languages—foreign languages are generally accepted and recognized as legitimate and viable communication systems, and imply no derogatory qualities about the speakers.

The first problem then in teaching standard English to disadvantaged Black children involves teachers' attitudes toward Black dialect. Teachers must try to accept it. They must refrain—by implication or direct statements—from extending any negative attitudes they may have about Black dialect.

Teachers' negative attitudes towards Black dialect also reflect their ignorance of this dialect. Teachers have not recognized it as a variety of English that consists of unique phonological and grammatical systems. Instead, the deviations from standard English in the speech of disadvantaged Black children have been viewed as "errors" or "careless disregard" of the rules of standard English. (This assumes that these children have a knowledge of standard English, and that they are too careless or too unconcerned to adhere to these rules.) On the other hand, teachers working with speakers of foreign languages recognize that their students' errors are a natural part of the language learning process, and they are sympathetic towards these speakers. Disadvantaged Black children are not given this sympathy, because teachers are ignorant of the systematic organization of Black dialect.

Teachers' negative attitudes towards Black dialect have inevitably created the same attitude in the children who speak it. The children are often ashamed of their language . . . and ashamed of themselves. Perhaps this is one of the reasons they are reluctant to express themselves in the classroom; and consequently, they have often been labeled as "nonverbal." They do not, however, seem to be "nonverbal" once they leave the classroom. Their shame towards their language is evidently related to location and audience.

The need for teachers to accept Black dialect is apparent. As soon as teachers attempt to display this acceptance and build it in the children, however, they encounter another problem that teachers of foreign language speakers do not encounter. The children don't trust the teachers; they fear that the teachers who suddenly advocate acceptance of Black dialect are just pulling one more trick to force them to learn standard English. In the language of their ghetto, the teachers are "running a game" on them.

If the teachers do get Black children to accept their own Black dialect, or even if the children already accept their own dialect, there is another problem that is not encountered by teachers of foreign language speakers. William Labov has labeled this problem "functional interference," which here is the refusal to learn standard English because it is "white folks' talk." This phenomenon is the result of Black pride. Black people are proud of their history, their music, their physical appearance, their customs . . . and their language. As a result, many Black children will not want to learn standard English because it is identified with white culture.

Functional interference does not usually occur with speakers of foreign languages. Usually, these speakers have a definite reason for learning standard English, and they do not identify the learning of standard English with an "enemy" group or a denial of their own cultural identity.

Another problem faced by teachers utilizing second language techniques in teaching standard English to Black children is that standard English is not reinforced in the children's social environment. Segregated living patterns help to insulate many Black children. All they may hear is Black dialect. The only time they encounter standard English in a structured instructional setting is the comparatively brief period they are in school. Of course, they hear standard English on television and on the radio or in the movies, but these are not structured instructional situations; nor is their attention focused on standard English patterns. There is also a strong tendency in Black environment which forces children to use the Black dialect. Anyone who speaks differently—specifically, anyone who speaks standard English— is likely to be ostracized, because he or she is different and may be considered "uppity." Again, the teacher of foreign language speakers does not have to consider this problem in the same way. Foreign language speakers learning English in the United States are living in a social environment where English, regardless of the variety, is the primary communication system. Even if foreign language speakers spend a great deal of their time in an environment where their native languages are spoken, they will encounter many situations in which some variety of English is spoken, and the contrast between their language and English is so great that it is immediately recognized, and reinforcement can take place. This is not true for Black children who speak Black dialect. The contrasts between their dialect and standard English are so subtle that they often go undetected and no reinforcement occurs. As long as Black children continue to live in a segregated environment where only Black dialect is spoken, reinforcement outside the school will not take place.

One question that must be answered by teachers of Black children who speak Black dialect is: "Why should these children learn standard English?" In other words, they have to answer a question of motivation. For the teachers of foreign language speakers learning standard English, the answer is obvious and motivation is easy to achieve. Black children, however, are not as obviously and easily motivated to learn standard English. The real question is: "Will these children be able to use standard English even if they learn it?" Stated another way, the question is: "Will society offer the opportunities to them in which standard English is operable?" The segregated nature of our society and the lack of opportunity for Black people make it difficult to give a positive answer to this question. Society must "open up" for Black people, and afford them opportunities for full participation in society before they are motivated to learn standard English.

It is especially difficult to motivate younger Black children to learn standard English. Teachers can't point out to young children the vocational, social, and academic advantages of learning standard English. Young children are unaware of the advantages of learning standard English. As long as they remain in their segregated social environment, they will not learn standard English. Black children must be able to see that they will have opportunities to use standard English—and this requires society to admit more Black people into positions where standard English is the communication system used. The more Black people in these positions the more there will be positive and concrete motivating forces.

Some second language techniques require that instruction be focused on points of interference between standard English and Black dialect. These interference points are often so subtle, however, that Black children can't determine the differences. They often think they are reproducing standard pronunciation and grammatical features when they are not. Yet their nonstandard features are apparent to standard speakers and these nonstandard features serve as social markers on which negative value judgments are made. For example, many nonstandard speakers, or speakers of Black dialect, do not recognize the difference between the /d/ they substitute for the initial voiced /th/ in: *the, this, them,* and so on. Or they do not recognize the difference between the final voiceless /th/ and the /f/ they substitute for it, in *south, with, both, mouth, path,* and so on. While these differences are unrecognizable to them, standard English speakers do hear the difference. The contrasts between foreign languages and standard English are easily recognized. The subtlety of difference between standard English and Black dialect makes contrastive analysis exceedingly difficult.

The kinds of drills and exercises used in second language techniques present another problem when working with Black children. Pattern practice, slot drills, answering drills, memorization of short paragraphs, audio-discrimination drills, and so on, are simple exercises for speakers *who already speak English.* Black children understand standard English, even if they do not speak it; and the drills and exercises used in second language teaching techniques do not present much of a challenge for these children. To maintain their attention, interest, and motivation, drills and exercises must contain sentences that are interesting, humorous, or provocative. It is difficult, however, to write these kinds of exercises and at the same time focus on those structures where nonstandard and standard English differ. It is far less difficult to compose drills for foreign speakers.

The time allotted for stimulus and response must be reduced sharply when using second language drills and exercises with Black children. That is, when the stimulus is presented, the children must answer immediately. Drills and exercises must progress much faster for Black children than for foreign language speakers. This sustains interest. However, the faster the pace, the more inclined these children are to slip into Black dialect when they respond. Thus, they must constantly be reminded to respond in standard English. Also, the longer the drill or exercise, the more likely they will slip into Black dialect. Drills and exercises, therefore, should be brief and move at a fast pace.

Role playing is a popular technique in second language teaching and enjoyed by Black children as well. It is difficult, however, for them to sustain standard English while they are in the role. They often become so engrossed that they forget about the standard English appropriate to the role. On the other hand, the foreign language speaker speaks English throughout the duration of the role, and receives all of the intended practice.

Finally, one more unique problem exists in using second language techniques with Black children who speak Black dialect. These children already speak English, even if it is a nonstandard variety. Thus, teachers cannot tell them they are learning another language. They know they are speaking English, and it would be confusing to tell them that they are going to "speak English." Instead, they must be told that they are learning another dialect of English. They must be given information about the nature of dialects, the causes of their development, and various American dialects and their social implications.

The areas that should be emphasized in teacher-training programs are obvious. The *amount* of emphasis that should be given to each area, however, is debatable. Yet careful consideration of the instructional problem of teaching standard English to dialect or foreign language speakers implies that there is a kind of priority of emphasis for the areas that must be included in a training program for teachers.

The area that should receive the greatest emphasis in teacher-training programs is cultural anthropology. In order to teach any student effectively, the teacher must understand the student. Since students are really products of their cultures, teachers must understand the cultures of their students. An understanding of the culture of the students also indicates to the teacher what to emphasize in terms of concepts, ideas, situations, and all that language envelops. In other words, an understanding of culture enables the teacher to know what motivates students to learn a second dialect.

Linguistics is the area that should receive the next greatest emphasis in a program for training teachers of standard English as a second dialect. That is, teachers must have an understanding of the structures of the native and target dialects of the students. Because culture and language are so closely related, it is difficult to separate the culture of the students and their native language or dialect. The emphasis in the area of linguistics, however, should be on the way the language system of the students differs from standard English. This will help teachers to identify the specific sound and grammatical features in the target language that students must learn. An understanding of linguistics helps teachers develop a language program that is sequential, proceeding from the easy to the difficult features. Finally, an understanding of linguistics suggests ways that the target language can be taught. Specifically, linguistics suggests ways to devise drills, to present features to be learned, and to explain the target language in terms the students can understand.

Educational psychology is the third area of emphasis. Teachers should understand the psychology of language learning.

They must understand the ways in which individuals learn language and the ways another language or dialect can be taught efficiently and effectively to students who speak a different language or dialect.

Methodology and techniques and a knowledge of materials and instructional media are other areas to emphasize in a teacher training program. These areas are ranked last in the order of emphasis because the effectiveness of teachers in these areas is inversely proportional to the teachers' understanding in the other areas mentioned. That is, the more teachers understand the culture of the students, the structure of the language of the students and the target language, and the psychology of teaching and learning language, the less methodology, materials, and media need to be emphasized. Greater understanding in these other areas will help teachers develop effective methodology on their own, and suggest ways to use materials and instructional media. There is an undesirable effect of over-emphasizing methodology, materials, and instructional media. These areas are often emphasized at the expense of other areas. The implication here is that teachers who understand only the other areas can be effective language teachers, and teachers who understand only methodology, materials, and media cannot be effective language teachers. An understanding of cultural anthropology, linguistics, and educational psychology in addition to knowledge of methodology, materials, and media creates a total preparatory program for teachers.

In addition, teachers should have the personal and professional characteristics intrinsic to successful teaching. First, teachers should really like to teach. An enthusiasm for the teaching-learning process can very often compensate for the lack of understanding in other areas. Second, teachers must be individuals who are sensitive to others. Sensitivity in this context means an awareness of the cues that students give to indicate if they are learning, if they are interested. In short, teachers must be empathetic to their students. Next teachers must be good speech models. That is, they must be good models of the target language so that students learn the target language, not a distorted version. Finally, teachers should be individuals who enjoy the learning process. This is an important characteristic, because of

91

the rapid increase in the discovery of effective ways to teach language, the frequent introduction of new materials and instructional media, and the many discoveries about the nature of language and the ways to teach language revealed through greater research in linguistics and related areas. All these require that teachers be individuals interested in professional growth.

Even if good programs for training teachers are developed, and individuals who have the personal and professional characteristics intrinsic to successful teaching complete their training, many current problems of teaching standard English as a second dialect remain. Language is best learned in situations that permit maximum face-to-face interaction and much individual attention. Students do not have these opportunities in crowded classrooms. Furthermore, there is a shortage of *good* instructional materials that are appropriate to the various maturity levels of the students and their levels of standard English. This problem, however, can be overcome somewhat if quality teachers are involved. A good teacher constructs materials that are appropriate for the students' maturity level and the teachers' own "teaching styles."

The greatest problem in teaching standard English as a second dialect is the economic deprivation of the students. Economic poverty prevents students from acquiring the experiences on which the curriculum is based. Specifically, economic poverty causes such problems as poor nutrition, family breakdown, restricted experiential backgrounds, severe emotional problems, and so on. Even if all other conditions for a good program were met (quality teachers, small classes, adequate materials, and so on), the deprivation of many students would retard success. Eliminating the effects of economic deprivation is the basis for academic success in language learning and all other subjects. As long as students are disadvantaged, their chances for success are slight. Eliminating deprivation or, at least, finding ways to overcome the debilitating effects of economic deprivation is the main problem today in teaching standard English.

References

Dillard, J.L. 1972. *Black English*. New York: Random House.

Feigenbaum, Irwin. Spring/Summer 1969. Using foreign language methodology to teach standard English: evaluation and adaptation. In: Aarons, Gordon, and Stewart, (eds.), *Linguistic-Cultural Differences and American Education. The Florida FL Reporter.* 116–122.

Stewart, William A. (ed.). 1964. Nonstandard speech and the teaching methods in quasi-foreign language situations. In: W.A. Stewart (ed.) *Nonstandard Speech and the Teaching of English.* Washington: Center of Applied Linguistics, 1–15.

Wolfram, Walt and Fasold, Ralph. 1974. *The study of social dialects in American English.* Englewood Cliffs, N.J.: Prentice-Hall, Inc.

PSYCHOLINGUISTIC
INSIGHTS

Remarks on Creativity in Language Acquisition

Heidi Dulay
Marina Burt

It may seem superfluous to devote a paper to general remarks on creativity since it appears that virtually no one today would deny the creative participation of the learner in the language acquisition process. The combined effects of Chomsky's revival of the "creative aspects of language use" as a major focus of theoretical linguistics, along with the complementary efforts of Piaget in developmental psychology, have given creativity a central place in contemporary psycholinguistics.

Thus far in psycholinguistic research, however, we have not been able to specify with much clarity or precision the ways in which the learner is creative. While analyses of developing learner speech generally support the view of the learner as an active and creative participant in the acquisition process, the absence of specific principles to explain all the facts that have been accumulating in journals and anthologies is perhaps the greatest difficulty apparent in the "creative" approach to language acquisition. It seems important, therefore, to attempt to operationalize at least some of the aspects of creativity that seem basic to an explanation of language learning behavior.

We briefly review two widely used and different notions of creativity and present a partial model of certain creative aspects of second language (L2) acquisition. A variety of facts collected from the existing empirical literature are then gathered together to demonstrate 1) the mediating (creative) role of affective and cognitive structures on input during the acquisition process and 2) the role of input factors in a creative construction framework. Special emphasis is given to frequency of occurrence of grammatical structures in the learner's input. In light of the apparent interaction between learner and environment, we suggest how

95

frequency might be viewed within a creative construction framework.

DEFINITION OF CREATIVITY

The term "creativity" has been used in several disciplines—education, psychology, linguistics, and language acquisition—in two distinct and, in some respects, contradictory ways. Although in both senses of the term some notion of independence is implied, the notion of creativity often used in education and psychology is substantially different from that used in linguistics and language acquisition.

In education, "creative thinking" and "creative writing" often connote an ability to produce ideas, solutions to problems, or twists of words and phrases that do not conform to what is most frequently produced by most people. For example, using cooked rice as glue would be considered a creative use of rice. And the phrase "as cold as a polar bear's whiskers" would be considered more creative than "as cold as ice" (cf. Renzulli, 1973). Creativity in this sense refers to the independence of some individuals from some tendency or norm set by the majority.

This use of the term derives much of its theoretical basis from the thinking and empirical research on creativity in psychology, largely inspired by the work of J.P. Guilford and his associates on a structure-of-the-intellect model (cf. Wallach, 1970). Guilford introduced the notion of creativity as "divergent thinking"—a cognitive process that involves coming up with many different possible alternatives in response to a problem or to the task of processing information—as opposed to "convergent thinking," which refers to zeroing in on the one correct answer (cf. Guilford, 1967).[1] For example, to answer the question "Which state borders California on the north?" one would employ convergent

---

[1] Torrance (1966a) extends Guilford's concept of creativity to include any problem-solving or hypothesis-generating activity whether it be convergent or divergent in nature. He defines creative thinking as "a process of becoming sensitive to problems, deficiencies, gaps in knowledge, missing elements, disharmonies, and so on; identifying the difficulty; searching for solutions, making guesses, or formulating hypotheses about the deficiencies; testing and retesting these hypotheses and possibly modifying and retesting them; and finally communicating the results" (Torrance, 1966: 6). This construct is operationalized in a battery of instruments he designed to measure individual creativity (Torrance, 1966b).

thinking skills in order to arrive at the one correct answer (Oregon). However, the instruction "Name as many uses of a shovel as you can." taps divergent thinking skills. Someone who offered twenty uses of a shovel would be considered more creative than one who offered only five, and the less conventional the use, the more creative. An artist's use of a shovel as a "found object" to display in an art gallery might be considered highly creative. In this sense of creativity not everyone is creative, and those who are exhibit a certain independence from conventional thinking and behavior.

In linguistics on the other hand, the essence of creativity is the use of rules and conventions of a language. Speakers can express an indefinite and infinite number of thoughts using sentences never heard before because they have internalized a system of rules that governs ordinary language use (cf. Chomsky, 1965:6). Because speakers regularly produce and understand sentences never heard before, they are said to use the language creatively. For example, "Grandmother had a hair transplant yesterday" or "Ed is overjoyed that his paper is finally done" are ordinary sentences. They are creative in the linguistic sense, however, because the speaker generated such sentences from an internalized rule system rather than as a result of having heard, imitated, and memorized them. Linguistic creativity then is not the privilege of a select few who might be poets. It is characteristic of all normal speakers of any language.

Creativity in language acquisition derives from the linguistic notion; it is also attributed to all normal learners. It too refers to *a degree of learner independence from external input factors* such as the exact form of modeled utterances, frequency of occurrence, or rewards for correctness. While for mature speakers creativity stems from a control of the rules of the language they speak, for language *learners,* creativity stems from the structure of those mental mechanisms responsible for learning the rules of a new language. Thus, as has been suggested elsewhere, "creative construction" in language acquisition refers to the process by which learners gradually reconstruct rules for speech they hear, guided by innate mechanisms which cause them to formulate certain types of hypotheses about the language system being acquired, until the mismatch between what they are exposed to and what they produce is resolved.

97

Examples of this creativity abound. Valdman (1974), for example, studied American college students in a beginning French class who had little opportunity to hear French outside the classroom. He states that the "most striking feature of the data . . . is the relatively high incidence of the *wh*-fronting type of question, e.g., *Où Jean va?*, [in spite of the fact that] the subjects were exposed only to the inversion and *est-ce que* types of question," (e.g., *Où va Jean?* and *Qu'est-ce que vous étudiez ici?*, respectively). He concludes that "it can be asserted with confidence that the *wh*-fronting type questions they produced were generated by some sort of reconstructing process rather than direct imitation" (p. 14).[2] Examples of this sort from children learning a first or second language have been presented in numerous papers, as we shall see later. In sum then, creativity in language learning refers to the human learner's predisposition to organize input in ways that exhibit a certain independence from external environmental characteristics. This aspect of language acquisition is believed to be rooted in innate and universal structural properties of the mind.

The last discussed notion of creativity is the sense in which we use the term in this paper. It has inspired both first and second language acquisition researchers to undertake extensive investigations of learners' developing speech in order to determine whether learners were in fact creative—whether their verbal behavior could be considered reflections of universal cognitive structure. Much of the research supports the position that creativity is an essential factor in explaining language acquisition behavior, though some of the recent research indicates a discomfort with attributing much of the learner's progress to internal processing mechanisms, to the neglect of input factors. It seems timely, therefore, to place into perspective the role of internal

---

[2] He also points out that the "corresponding structure in L1 can be rapidly eliminated as a potential source," as "the EST-CE QUE construction provides the best one-to-one matching of the surface structure features of the English construction" (Valdman, 1974: 15). He compares:

Où	est-ce que	Jean	travaille?
↓	↓	↓	↓
Where	does	John	work?

pointing out that both languages have semantically empty elements occurring in the same linear order. The same observation holds for "semantically full" auxiliaries.

"creative" mechanisms vis-à-vis input in language acquisition. One might simply ask: When does input—its form, its frequency, and its intensity—*not* affect learning, and when does it exert its influence? We begin with the first half of the question: In what specific ways does the human mind mediate input? In other words, in what ways is language acquisition creative?

Given the myriad conscious and unconscious internal factors interacting with input to produce the speech products we study, it may not be possible to isolate certain of these entirely. Nonetheless, given the data available at the present time, it appears we may attribute certain discrepancies between input and learner output to at least two very general but distinct sources: *affective delimitors* and *cognitive organizers*. "Affective delimitors" refer to conscious or unconscious motives or needs of the learner which contribute, among other things, to: 1) individual preferences for certain input models over others, 2) prioritizing aspects of language to be learned, and 3) determining when language acquisition efforts should cease. For example, depending on various criteria, a learner will "tune in" more to certain speakers of the language rather than to others, or learners will learn certain types of verbal routines or vocabulary items rather than others, or learners will apparently stop acquiring the target language at a point before they reach native-like proficiency. These behaviors may be attributed to affective factors which delimit to a significant extent the input data which is made accessible to the cognitive organizers.

"Cognitive organizers" refer to the internal data processing mechanisms responsible for the construction of the grammar we attribute to the learner. They contribute, among other things, to: 1) the error types that occur systematically in developing speech, 2) the progression of rules that learners use before a structure is mastered, and 3) the order in which structures are acquired.

A third source of creative activity is the "monitor" (Krashen, in this volume, 1976, and in press), which may be defined as the conscious editing of one's own speech. The degree to which speech is edited depends on both individual criteria and the nature and focus of the task being performed. For example, extent of concern over grammatical correctness is an individual criterion operating in many individuals which often results in a great deal of editing, as seen in numerous hesitations or constant self-correction. In addition, tasks which cause speakers to focus on communication tend to bring on less self-editing, while tasks whose focus is linguistic analysis (such as fill-in-the-blank or translation) seem to invite more editing. The construct of the monitor has been suggested by Krashen to explain a number of previously puzzling aspects of adult second language behavior.

It seems useful to think of internal processing as the successive operation of affective delimitors, cognitive organizers, and the monitor, in that order.

FIGURE 1
Working Model for Some Aspects of Creative Construction in Language Acquisition.

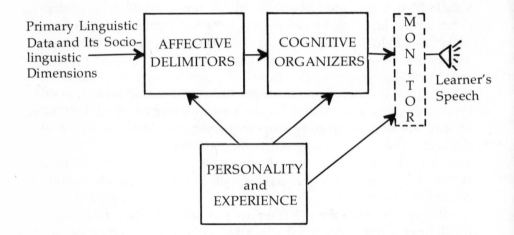

Figure 1 illustrates the partial model proposed: primary linguistic data (including its sociolinguistic dimensions) undergo the successive operation of affective delimitors and cognitive organizers. This ordering reflects research data which suggest that internal affective factors delimit to a significant extent the external linguistic input which the learner takes into account to reconstruct the target language system.

The monitor operates under certain circumstances on the output of the cognitive organizers. A detailed discussion of the operation of the monitor and of other internal factors such as personality and experience (including the role of first language acquisition experience and knowledge on second language acquisition)[3] is beyond the scope of this paper. We simply wish here to indicate their suggested place in this scheme. We will discuss in greater detail, however, research data that points to affective delimitation and cognitive organization of input.

EVIDENCE FOR AFFECTIVE DELIMITATION OF INPUT

Upon reviewing the second language research literature, the clearest examples of affective delimitation of input involve an apparent preference for certain speaker models over others under certain circumstances, e.g., preference for peers over teachers, peers over parents, and own ethnic group members over non-members.

Preference for certain models is clearly demonstrated by learners acquiring one of two dialects to which they are exposed in daily communication. Milon (1975) reports that a seven-year-old Japanese-speaking child who had immigrated to Hawaii learned the Hawaiian Creole English of his agemates rather than the Standard English of his teachers during his first school year. When he moved to a middle class neighborhood the following year, however, he quickly picked up the Standard English that his new friends spoke. In explaining this phenomenon, Milon states that "there is no question that the first dialect of English these young immigrant children learn is the dialect of their peers and that they learn it from their peers. If they learn productive control of the dialect of their teachers, it is not until later . . ." (Milon, 1975: 159).[4]

---

[3] For a detailed discussion of issues on this topic, see Dulay and Burt, 1972, 1974a, and 1975a, and Hernández-Chávez in this volume.

[4] It is interesting to note that one cannot explain the early acquisition of Hawaiian Creole here by appealing to the idea that its syntactic structures are somehow a "simplification" of Standard English. Compare several Hawaiian Creole structures produced by Milon's subject to their Standard English equivalents:

HCE: Over here got one.
SE: There's one over here.

HCE: How come no more any of those?
SE: Why are those all gone?

The differences in the forms of the corresponding utterances cannot be described by any notion of "simplicity" advanced to date in the L2 literature.

A similar example—in this case showing L1 learners' preference for peers' speech over parents'—is provided by Stewart (1964, in Dale, 1976: 281) who reports that the Black children he studied in Washington, D.C. learn the dialect used by their peers (a dialect of Black English that is most different from Standard English), rather than the dialect used by their parents (a dialect of Black English closest to Washington, D.C. Standard English). Likewise, Labov (1972) finds that both Black and White children in a middle class area of northeastern New Jersey learn to pronounce the r's before consonants as their New Jersey friends do, rather than drop the r's as their New York-raised parents do. These data, too, show "that children learn more language behavior from members of their own peer group than from their parents . . ." (Stewart, 1964 in Dale, 1976: 281).

Finally, Benton (1964) reports that Maori children learn the English dialect of their own ethnic group rather than standard New Zealand English. In some cases this model preference is consciously articulated:

> One teacher reported that a Maori child had told her: "Maoris say *Who's your name*, so that's what I say." Maori English is often an important sign of group membership and a source of security for these children (Benton, 1964:93 in Richards, 1974: 169).

The examples we have presented here demonstrating the individual's affective delimitation of input through model preference represent only one of many types of end-products whose source lies in the basic psychological need to identify with and belong to a social group (peers over non-peers, etc.). Since language is an important identification marker of social groups, it is to be expected that language learners and users should show the kinds of preferences we have seen for speaker models representing their preferred group.[5]

More in depth investigations of affective delimitation of input would probably be closely tied to the study of sociolinguistic features of primary linguistic data. A full treatment of these im-

---

[5] There are many examples, of course, of proficient speakers who interact at a variety of levels and with more than one social group. These speakers typically control the languages, dialects, or styles appropriate for interaction with the particular group at the appropriate time.

portant issues is unfortunately beyond the scope of this paper. Here we simply suggest that affective factors cause learners to delimit their linguistic input in particular ways, resulting in various observed differences between learner speech and that of the total input. We are suggesting that such differences cannot be explained by appealing to a description of linguistic input alone; rather, such descriptions must be accompanied by a specification of the various kinds of internal forces which operate on linguistic input and the conditions under which they operate. These are just beginning to receive serious attention.

EVIDENCE FOR COGNITIVE CREATIVITY

As was mentioned earlier, the notion of creativity in language acquisition entails the assumption that internal processors make a contribution to learning progress that is independent of the contribution made by input. Part of the evidence for cognitive creativity, therefore, involves demonstrating discrepancies between the actual characteristics of the learner's output and what might be predicted if input factors alone were responsible for the learner's progress (taking into consideration, of course, possible effects of affective delimitation of input). The research findings summarized here are grouped according to the input factors which have been shown to be mediated in systematic ways. They include the form, perceptual salience, and frequency of input structures; corrective feedback; and reinforcement.

Form of Input Structures: Contiguity of Elements in Speech Patterns

The systematic deviations from the structure of the sentences learners hear in their environment comprised the initial glimpses of creativity in language acquisition. Researchers noticed that language learners systematically produced constructions they could not have heard before, and which could thus be explained only by an appeal to human cognitive organization. Utterances such as *Adam hit ball* (Brown, 1973b), *No wipe finger* (Klima and Bellugi, 1966), and *Mommy sock* (Bloom, 1970) have become part of the standard repertoire of first language acquisition researchers, as have "overgeneralizations" such as *digged, goed*, and *childs,* which have even found their way into papers on adult foreign language learning, as well as child second language acquisition. The observed deviations from well-formed sentences are not haphazard lapses of memory nor poor attempts at imitation. Rather, the occurrence of systematic errors comprises ". . . the best evidence we have that the child possesses construction rules" (Brown, 1973a).

Countless first language (L1) acquisition studies have made this point, including L1 research on some thirty-three languages other than English (cf. Brown, 1973a: Ch. 1). See, for example, Klima and Bellugi (1966), Cazden (1972), Brown (1973a), among others, and Dale (1976) for a comprehensive review of that literature.

Second language acquisition research, following closely on the heels of the advances made in first language studies, provides similar evidence. Since this research has been summarized elsewhere (cf. Dulay and Burt, 1975a and b), suffice it to mention here that error types that can best be explained by positing some creative restructuring process on the part of the learner have been observed in child second language speech (Dulay and Burt, 1972 and 1974; Hernández-Chávez, 1972; Venable, 1974; and Ervin-Tripp, 1974, among others), as well as in adult second and foreign language performance (Richards, 1971 and 1974; Valdman, 1974; and Taylor, 1975). Additionally, L2 learners, like L1 learners pass through certain steps in the acquisition of negatives and interrogatives. (For negation see Hernández-Chávez, 1972; Milon, 1974; and Gillis and Weber, 1976. For *wh*-questions, see Ravem, 1974.)

Learners' systematic use of novel construction rules during the process of acquiring syntactic structures comprises the bulk of the research evidence for the role of cognitive organizers in language acquisition.

Perceptual Salience

Perceptual salience is an input factor that has not as yet been precisely defined, though general descriptions such as "amount of phonetic substance, stress level, usual serial position in a sentence, and so on" (Brown, 1973a: 409) have been used to give it a general meaning in the research literature. Salience may be defined solely in terms of input characteristics (in which case it would be analogous to the notion of "stimulus intensity" in behaviorist learning theory); or its definition may include internal processing factors which cause certain features in the learner's input to *become* salient. This discussion refers only to the former sense of the term which is implied in most of the relevant literature.

Perceptual salience is commonly mentioned by some L2 researchers as a potential predictor of order of acquisition; that is, the more perceptually salient an item is, the sooner it should be learned if its effects remain unmitigated. There is evidence, however, that learners do indeed regulate potential effects of perceptual salience: they do not acquire grammatical morphemes that are equally salient at the same time, nor are the potential effects of the different degrees of salience of certain structures realized.

Consider, for example, some of the s-morphemes whose order of acquisition in oral production has been studied extensively for both first and second language learners. In L2 research, it has been found repeatedly that the contracted form of the singular copula (as in "He's fat") and the short plural morpheme (as in "windows") are learned early. The short possessive (as in "the king's") and the third person indicative (as in "sees") are learned much later, however. (See for example, Dulay and Burt, 1974b and 1975a; Burt, Dulay, and Hernández-Chávez, 1976; and Fathman, 1975 for children; and Krashen, Madden, and Bailey, 1975; and Larsen-Freeman, 1976 for adults.) It is clear that perceptual salience, generally defined, cannot underlie this acquisition order, since the phonetic substance and stress levels of these s-morphemes is virtually the same. The early acquisition of the contractible singular copula is especially interesting, since its sentence medial position presumably makes it less salient than it would be in, say, final position. (The differential acquisition of these morphemes was also found by Brown for his L1 learners, although some of the specific items were ordered differently.)

The last example we will mention in this context (though there are many more) is the late acquisition of the long plural morpheme, -es relative to the short plural -s. Even though the long plural is syllabic and the short plural is not, the long plural is acquired much later than the short plural (Burt, Dulay and Hernández-Chávez, 1976; or Dulay and Burt, 1974b or 1975b). The opposite order would be predicted by perceptual salience.

Frequency of Occurrence

When frequency is discussed as an input variable in language acquisition research, it refers to the number of times a given structure has presumably occurred in a learner's immediate linguistic environment. For example, one might count how many times *wh*-questions occurred in the speech of a mother to her child during some discourse situations that might be representative of the child's total input. The count would be considered the frequency of *wh*-questions in the child's input. The relation of this input variable to learner speech has received considerable attention in language acquisition research.

Perhaps the most systematic and extensive evidence of the unpredictable relationship between external frequency and language learning comes from first language acquisition research. It is now well known that the order of acquisition of morphemes found by Brown for his three children learning English barely correlated with the frequencies with which those morphemes occurred in the speech of the children's parents in parent-child discourse. The Spearman rank order correlation (rho) between the rank order of acquisition (averaged across the children) with the rank order of frequency (averaged across the pairs of parents) was very low, +.26, leading to Brown's conclusion that "no relation has been demonstrated to exist between parental frequencies and child's order of acquisition" (Brown, 1973a: 362).

A second example of the mitigation of external frequency pressures—this time in second language acquisition—may be extracted from the data presented in Wagner-Gough and Hatch (1975). In their observations of a child learning English as a second language, they report that although two types of questions occurred with equal frequency in their subject's linguistic input, only one type of question was produced correctly and not the other. The *wh*-questions *What's X?* and *Where's X?* were produced correctly, whereas the question which required copula inversion *(Is this X?)* was not. Thus, we observe the selective

106

leaning of one question type, in spite of the equal frequency of occurrence of two types in the input data.

Of course, all of the novel constructions and systematic errors found in learner speech (see above) remain the most pervasive phenomenon that cannot possibly be attributed to input frequency. Recall, for example, Valdman's finding, described earlier, that a significant number of American college students learning French in his class in the U.S. produced an intermediate question form which did not occur in their input at all.

Finally, consider the well-known fact that specific grammatical morphemes in English occur more frequently than specific major content words; and yet, "the early absence and long delayed acquisition of those more frequent forms has always thrown up a challenge to the notion that frequency is a major variable in language learning . . ." (Brown, 1973a: 362). The relatively late acquisition of grammatical morphemes compared to content words has also become an established fact for second language learners. Here again it seems as though factors other than frequency are operating to determine learning priorities.

Corrective Feedback

Experienced language teachers have long known that providing students with the correct forms of their imperfect utterances can be immensely frustrating. Although students say they want corrective feedback (Cathcart and Olson, 1976) and teachers try to provide as much as they can, it is all too obvious, and painful for both teachers and students, that many errors are impervious to correction. In fact, Cohen and Robbins (1976) found that the effects of correction in the written work of university ESL students in the U.S. did not actually influence the production of errors. Although the authors believe this lack of influence was caused by factors relating to the quality and systematicity of the corrections, we see no justifiable reason to expect significantly different results with better or more systematic correction techniques.

In first language acquisition, Cazden's experiment (Cazden, 1965) on the effect of "expansions" is the classic study along these lines. It was hypothesized that systematic modeling of the grammatically correct versions of children's utterances (expansions) might be a major force in acquisition progress. To most everyone's surprise, Cazden found that expansions had no effect whatsoever on the speech of the children she studied.

These findings suggest that more "systematic" feedback may not be the answer. More *selective* feedback, tailored to the learner's internal level of linguistic development, may be more effective.[6] We return to this later.

Reinforcement

Another input factor that has received some attention, albeit only in the first language literature so far, is reinforcement. Although Chomsky (1959) has shown that an examination of the notion of reinforcement in the psychological literature reveals no consistent definition of "reinforcing behavior," the appeal of intuitive notions of reinforcement is so widespread that some pertinent research results may be worth mentioning here.

Using Skinner's notion that any sign of approval constitutes reinforcing behavior (Skinner, 1953: 78), Brown and Hanlon (1970) studied the effects of positive and negative reinforcement on children's developing speech. They used parental approval (determined by responses such as *That's right, Correct, Very good*, and *Yes*), and disapproval (as indicated by *That's wrong, That's not right,* or *No*) as indicators of positive and negative reinforcement. Brown and Hanlon report that there was not even "a shred of evidence that approval and disapproval are contingent on syntactic correctness" (p. 47); but rather that these are linked to the truth value of the proposition contained in the child's utterance.

Brown and Hanlon found a similar result when they studied a different form of reinforcement, namely "relevant and comprehending reactions" to the child's utterances, as opposed to irrelevant reactions, or no reaction at all. Here again, they found that reinforcing input does not affect the child's progress in acquiring grammatical forms.

---

[6] A criterion for selective correction, based on ease of comprehension, has been suggested and worked out by Burt and Kiparsky (1972). See also Burt (1975).

Summary

So far, we have summarized available empirical data that indicate the influence of human cognition and affect on the course of language acquisition. Specifically, we have presented cases where certain input factors alone cannot possibly account for the speech produced. As we have seen, frequency, perceptual salience or intensity, corrective feedback, reinforcement, and contiguity of elements in a structure cannot, by themselves, account for specific learning outcomes.

These observations must not be taken to imply that input factors are unimportant or negligible; rather that any theory or account of language acquisition, whether first or second, must take into account the independent and central contribution of internal mental mechanisms to the construction of the new language system.

Within this framework, and given the data presented so far, one might well ask with due concern, "What then is the role of input factors in the acquisition of productive syntactic rules?"

ROLE OF INPUT FACTORS

An increasing number of studies have attempted to describe the external environment of the language learner and have suggested input variables that affect the learning of syntax and morphology. What is usually presented are cases where certain learner outcomes mirror input factors, such as the observation that the relative frequency of *What's this?* and *Where's that?* matches their early use. The interpretation of such observations is typically that the given input factor is an "important determinant" of progress in language acquisition. However, as discussed earlier, high frequency or highly salient items, etc., are not always learned first. This dilemma leads one to suggest that the formulation of accurate and predictive principles concerning the effects of input factors on progress in acquisition might best be accomplished *by specifying conditions under which external factors will have an effect.* Such conditions may have to do with relationships among several input factors operating at the same time, and between input variables and internal processing factors.

A clear and important example of such an effort is the recent series of investigations conducted by Piagetian psychologists B. Inhelder, H. Sinclair, and M. Bovet (1974), who studied the effects of certain training procedures on children's progress in cognitive development. Although the study does not investigate language development per se, its assumptions, procedures, and findings should be extremely useful to language acquisition researchers interested in the effects of input factors.

Inhelder et al. conducted a series of learning experiments on the acquisition of the process of conservation and class inclusion. They selected thirty-four children aged 5:1 to 7:0 from the Genevan State nursery and primary schools. The children were selected on the basis of cognitive developmental levels; they ranged from those who never made a conservation judgment (Level I) to those who made such judgments most of the time (Level IV). The experimentors then provided various types of training sessions to see what their effect on the children's learning would be.

The training sessions "resembled the kind of situation in which [cognitive developmental] progress takes place outside an experimental set-up," that is, where children interact naturally with features of the environment provided by the experimentors, observing characteristics of objects and making judgments about them. "Experimental situations that might almost automatically elicit the correct answers were avoided" (Inhelder et al., 1974: 24).

The training sessions, which were the same for all the children, had virtually no effect on the fifteen children at the nonconservation level. Only two of those children improved substantially, while most of the intermediate level children (nineteen) progressed substantially. In other words, the more advanced children made real progress in cognitive development, while the less advanced children did not, despite the fact that the input provided in the experimental conditions was the same (pp. 51–52). The authors take pains to point out that *all* the children noticed *all* the relevant observable features presented to them; however, only the more advanced children were able to use the information for solving the problem at hand. The beginners simply did not know how to use the observations they had made (p. 53). Apparently, then, the effects of the "observable

110

features" of the input help children develop their reasoning insofar as these features can be integrated into their developing cognitive system. The provision of appropriate input, therefore, accelerates cognitive development when the learner has reached a certain cognitive level that permits the formulation of certain kinds of judgments.

Although the findings of Inhelder et al. do not deal specifically with second language acquisition, they illustrate the importance of specifying principles of interaction between input factors and mental factors (rather than suggesting a conflicting relationship between internal mental mechanisms and external input or environment) in the explanation of learning. This approach makes it possible to predict when a certain type of input, in this case a type of training procedure, will significantly affect learning and when it will not.

Another treatment of input along these lines is included in E. Hernández-Chávez's seventeen-month longitudinal study of a Spanish-speaking child's acquisition of English grammatical structures and semantic relations (Hernández-Chávez, 1977 and in this volume). Hernández-Chávez made biweekly tape-recordings of his subject Güero's verbal interactions with his nursery school classmates and the adults at the school. He found that a large portion of Güero's utterances during the first eight months seemed to be comprised, at least in part, of imitated elements of modeled utterances, e.g.,

> Adult: You don't want it?
> Güero: No want-it. I no want-it.

(where *want-it* is the reproduced portion of the modeled utterance). These he called "quasi-spontaneous utterances," since part of the utterance was freely produced and part was imitated from the model.

Upon closer examination and analysis of the discourse transcripts, Hernández-Chávez noticed that there was much speech addressed to the child that was not integrated in quasi-spontaneous utterances until much later in the study, if at all. For example, although the imperative subject "you" (in the context of an imperative sentence such as *You look at me, OK?*) occurred regularly in the speech addressed to the child in every succes-

111

sive taping from month 2 on,[7] Güero did not make any attempt to use it until month 5.5, when it finally appeared in a quasi-spontaneous utterance:

> Model: You read it.
> Güero: You read that.

The structure was produced totally spontaneously shortly thereafter (in month 6). Many other examples of this sort are discussed at length in Hernández-Chávez (1977), where he demonstrates that for the ten grammatical functions analyzed, a similar order of emergence in spontaneous and quasi-spontaneous utterances was evident.

From such observations, Hernández-Chávez argues that the child was imitating input *selectively* based, at least in part, on the state of his developing grammar.[8] The only exceptions seemed to be a few "stretches of speech that were memorized and associated with very specific nonlinguistic contexts, such as games." He suggests that the child's apparent memorization and imitation of input must be placed into a wider creative context if these phenomena are to be fully understood.[9] Here again, as with the Inhelder et al. studies, the specification of an interaction between internal states and external input serves to increase the predictive power of a statement on the effects of input.

From these kinds of findings, it is clear that the investigation of the explanatory power of input in a theory of language acquisition is an important undertaking for both basic psycholinguistic research and for pedagogical advancement. Others share this view. For example, Hatch and Wagner-Gough (1976), Larsen-Freeman (1976a), and Wagner-Gough and Hatch (1975) attempt to link various input factors with the order in which syntactic and

---

[7] Hernández-Chávez, personal communication. As frequency information was not reported in his paper, Hernández-Chávez provided us with this information.

[8] The state of the child's construction of the new grammar also influences the structures used in code switches. For example, Güero produced *Este es yours* at the time he was "trying out" English possessives.

[9] Other researchers have also described the incorporation of apparently imitated portions of input by language learners (Clark, 1974-L1; Hakuta, 1974-L2; Wagner-Gough and Hatch, 1975-L2, among others). Hernández-Chávez is unique, however, in going beyond the description of the phenomenon to an attempt to relate the child's level of grammatical development to what is likely to be imitated.

morphological structures are learned. It is unfortunate, however, that these efforts have not resulted in a clear description of the role, weight, or precise functioning of the factors proposed. Characteristics of the input language, such as semantic value, communicative function, salience, frequency, number of forms, etc., are proposed to "account" for the early or late production of specific structures. For example, high frequency is suggested to account for early acquisition of *What's X?* and *Where's X?*, while the later acquisition of *be*-inversion questions, e.g., *Is this a book?*, (which occur with the same frequency as the *What's X* and *Where's X* questions) is attributed to the low "semantic value" of *be* and its number of variant forms (Wagner-Gough and Hatch, 1975: 299). Is it not the case, however, that the semantic value and potential number of forms of the copula in the first acquired structures is the same as that in the later to be acquired structures? Moreover, if the *'s* in the *wh*-questions cited is not a productive part of the child's grammar, but rather, part of an unanalyzed fragment, the *wh*-questions cannot be said to have been productively acquired yet. Even without these difficulties, one would expect a discussion of why these factors operate only some of the time.

It has been pointed out by others who have attempted to explain language learning behavior that input is the "other side" of the learning process. The unresolved question is the exact nature of the contribution of input. Brown and Hanlon ask, for example, "Why do data have an impact at some times and at other times no effect at all?" (1970: 50). Brown (1973a), Chomsky (1959 and 1975: Ch 4), Piaget (1970: Ch 4), and others discuss various aspects of the possible role of input at some length. It seems, however, that these discussions have gone largely unnoticed in the papers mentioned above. For example, consider the following suggestion concerning how we might prioritize explanations of language learning data:

> Everyone of us has our biases and could assign priority to our favorites. For example, I happen to think that low semantic value, number of forms, number of functions, and perceptual salience account for late acquisition of the English definite article much more clearly than language universals or contrastive analysis. Most people who have taught students from Japan, Korea, and China would disagree. . . . Perhaps an interesting

113

experiment might be set up where we ask everyone who is working on second language learning . . . to look at sets of data and give explanations for each. Finally, they could rank or weight their explanations as they like (Hatch and Wagner-Gough, 1976: 54–55).

Surely such an approach does not represent the kind of methodology required to advance our understanding of language acquisition. It seems more likely that attempts to deal with input factors in relation to learner factors within a cohesive theoretical framework and a well-developed methodology (such as Inhelder et al. and Hernández-Chávez have done) may prove more productive.

Correlations and Causality

Another potential weakness in the study of input effects on learning is the erroneous treatment of statistical correlations as *causal* relationships between factors studied. For example, Larsen-Freeman (1976a and b) found that the frequency order of nine morphemes based on the speech of 1) the parents of Brown's three young children learning English as a first language and 2) university ESL teachers, correlated significantly with the morpheme acquisition order found for child and adult L2 learners. These correlations led her to conclude that "morpheme frequency of occurrence in native-speaker speech is the principal determinant for the oral production morpheme order of second language learners" (1976a: 132). It is erroneously assumed, however, that because two things go together (e.g., Brown's parents' morpheme frequency and L2 learners' acquisition order), that one causes or determines the other. This type of assumption is a well-known source of erroneous beliefs (see, for example, Huff, 1954 and Hays, 1963). The error lies in assuming that if B goes together with A, then A has caused B. Clearly, it could easily be the other way around; or perhaps neither caused the other; they may both be the result of some third factor, etc. Brown (1973a), in reporting "no relationship" between parental frequency and child order of L1 acquisition was of course aware of this basic distinction when he added that even "if a relation had been demonstrated to exist, it would still have been necessary to make a case for causality or determination" (p. 362). In the study under consideration, no such case has been made.

114

The tenuous value of the use of correlations in the investigation of cause and effect is clearly illustrated in Larsen-Freeman's own findings: While the frequency of morphemes in the speech of Brown's parents to their two to four-year-old children correlates significantly with the acquisition order of *university level* ESL students (the 3 rho's computed = +.79, +.80, +.93), the parents' morpheme frequency hardly correlates with the acquisition order of their own children (rho = +.26)! Additionally, the morpheme frequency in the speech of teachers of *university* ESL students correlates more highly with acquisition orders of public school *children* learning English as a second language (6 rho's range from +.70 to +.78) than with university ESL students (6 rho's range from +.43 to +.73, the two lowest not reaching acceptable significance levels). Since it is well known that adults' speech addressed to children differs from that addressed to other adults[10] (e.g., correlations between Brown's parents' morpheme frequency and that of the ESL teachers studied were relatively low: 6 rho's ranged from .42 to .63, with two not reaching .05 significance levels), the meaning of such correlations is far from clear.

The confusion of a statistical correlation with a cause-and-effect relationship is not uncommon. It seems important therefore to remind the untrained reader that even though a given relationship "has been shown to be [statistically] real, the cause and effect nature of it is only a matter of speculation" (Huff, 1954: 98).[11]

The preceding discussion is not intended to imply that input frequency has no effect on language acquisition, only that its effects remain largely unspecified in the L2 research literature to date.

---

[10] See for example Wagner-Gough (1975) and Landes (1975) for a review of the relevant studies.

[11] As one of the more amusing examples of this difficulty, Huff cites the close relationship found between the salaries of Presbyterian ministers in Massachusetts and the price of rum in Havana. "Which is the cause and which the effect? . . . are the ministers benefiting from the rum trade or supporting it?" Of course, it is much more likely that both figures are growing because of "the influence of a third factor: the historic and world-wide rise in the price level of practically everything" (p. 90).

Some Effects of Very High Frequency

There are items, phrases, and utterances whose frequency is extremely high in general discourse, or which are primarily associated with specific and frequent functions, such as certain types of social interaction. These appear to have a variety of effects on learner speech.

Although Brown (1973a) found no general correlation between frequency and acquisition order, he did find a relationship between very frequently used items and certain speech behavior (also reported in Cazden, 1972). When the parents of his three children produced certain *wh*-questions (e.g., *What's that?*) at a very high rate during a period when the children did not yet know the structure of *wh*-questions, the children learned to produce the two most frequently repeated ones on "roughly appropriate occasions" (*What's that?* and *What are you doing?*). When, much later, "the children began to produce all manner of *wh*-questions in the preposed form (such as *What he wants?*), it was interesting to note that *What's that?* and *What are you doing?* were not at first reconstructed in terms of the new analysis . . . In terms of [the children's] new rules, they ought to have said *What that is?* and *What you are doing?* but instead, they at first, persisted with the old forms" (Brown and Hanlon, p. 51).

Thus, one effect of very frequently occurring forms is that at least some of them somehow will be represented in the child's performance "even if its structure is far beyond him." The child will render a version of it and will form a notion of the circumstances in which it is used. Such constructions will, in Brown and Hanlon's words, "become lodged in his speech as an unassimilated fragment"[12] (p. 51). Furthermore, they suggest that extensive use of such unanalyzed or mistakenly analyzed fragments probably protects it, for a time, from reanalysis. Here then, especially high frequency seems to interfere with the learners' productive integration of certain structures into their grammatical system.

---

[12] These should not be confused with the quasi-spontaneous utterances discussed earlier, whose occurrence does not depend on high frequency but probably on the state of the child's developing grammar together with the availability of the structure in the child's input.

We found a similar type of phenomenon in a recent study we conducted on the acquisition of English by Keres-speaking Indian children and Spanish-speaking Mexican American children. Using the ordering·theoretic method described in our earlier studies (Burt, Dulay, and Hernández-Chávez, 1976; Dulay and Burt, 1975b), we analyzed the natural speech protocols of elementary school children collected by speech clinicians in New Mexico,[13] and speech collected with a structured conversation technique similar to the *Bilingual Syntax Measure* (Burt, Dulay, and Hernández-Chávez, 1976). The following progression was obtained for a subset of related *wh*-questions structures:

What's that?[14]

↓

What are those?

↓

I don't know what those are.

↓

I don't know what that is.

where "↓" indicates that the acquisition of the structure at the top of the arrow precedes the acquisition of the one at the bottom.

Focusing on the order of the copula and demonstrative pronoun in the *wh*-constructions alone, we see that *What's that?* was acquired first. Its correct use preceded the correct production of *What are those?*, which differs only in number. (Its intermediate form, *What those are?*, however, appeared together with *What's that?*) Both correctly formed simple *wh*-questions preceded the acquisition of the two types of embedded *wh*-questions (plural and singular). Finally, and of special interest here, we observe that the correct form of the embedded plural *wh*-question precedes the acquisition of the embedded singular *wh*-question, i.e., *I don't know what's this* persisted even while *I don't know what*

---

[13] Under the direction of Professor Dolores Butt of the Department of Communicative Disorders at the University of New Mexico, Albuquerque, New Mexico.

[14] *This* and *that* appeared interchangeably in the singular context and *those* and *these* in the plural context for these constructions.

those are had been acquired. This evidence, too, suggests a "protected" status for the *What's X?* sequence.

It appears then, that Brown's suggestions concerning the effects of high frequency on first language learning are applicable to second language learning as well.

Frequency in Creative Construction

The effects of frequency on the acquisition of syntactic and morphological structures seem to be far from clear or simple. We have seen some cases where certain structures are produced and not others, despite equal input frequency; other cases where structures are produced that did not even occur in the input; and still others where some very high frequency phrases are memorized before the child knows their internal structure, apparently to the temporary detriment of their productive integration into the child's developing target language system.

These findings are not entirely mysterious if one assumes that the developmental state of the learner's cognitive organizers is of major importance in determining how linguistic input data will affect it; and further, that a defining characteristic of the developmental state is the organizational level of the learner's internal grammar of the target language.[15] Given these assumptions, we might expect that the potential effects of input frequency on learning are directly related to the state of the learner's internal target language grammar. In this view, one might suggest that *frequency serves primarily to increase the probability that those structures which the learner is ready to process will occur, thus increasing the chances that the learner will be able to attend to and process them.*[16]

If this is the case, one might expect that the rate at which acquisition takes place may be increased if maximal exposure of

---

[15] See Pylyshyn (1973) for a careful and exhaustive treatment of the role of competence theories in cognitive psychology.

[16] It is important to distinguish at least three different ways in which a language learner might use a structure in speech: 1) as a productive rule that has been integrated into the learner's target language grammar, 2) as a quasi-spontaneous utterance where the learner is "getting ready" to use the structure productively, and 3) as an unanalyzed fragment. The effects (or non-effects) of frequency on the first two may be similar, but effects on the third may differ from the first two.

a precise sort at specific times over an appropriate period of time is provided. This assumes of course that the affective delimitors will "let the input through," and that the critical characteristics of the "right sort" of exposure have been determined.

These kinds of suggestions, which receive some support from experiments such as those conducted by Inhelder et al., assume some knowledge of the developmental steps in the learning process. That is, to the extent that the right kind of exposure depends on the level of grammatical development of the learner, to that extent we must know what the developmental steps are. Although a great deal of research and experimentation has been devoted to this end in cognitive psychology, similar investigations intended to uncover steps in the development of a second language have just begun. The kind of results obtained by Inhelder et al., however, are cause for optimism. They suggest the correctness of recent attempts to learn about the acquisition process by careful observation of those who are in the process of acquiring a second language.

Summary and Conclusions

The ultimate source of creativity in language acquisition is the structure of the human mind. Because the mind in action is not directly observable (recent advances in neuropsychology notwithstanding), creativity will remain, at least for the foreseeable future, an inference from observable fact. This paper has attempted to gather the empirical evidence available in the current literature that points to the necessity of positing the independent contribution of the mind to the language acquisition process, in particular, L2 acquisition.

We reviewed evidence that learners do not necessarily acquire a variety of speech they are exposed to regularly—not because they are somehow lacking in language learning ability, general intelligence, or social class—but because they tune in to certain models over others. Internal affective forces, such as the need to identify with a social group, delimit the input to the learner in important respects; i.e., affective delimitors narrow down what will be admitted for cognitive processing.

Evidence for the independent effects of cognitive organizing mechanisms on the learning process consists of empirical findings that demonstrate discrepancies between the characteristics of the learner's output and what might be predicted if input factors alone were responsible for the learner's progress. Examples of the mitigation of the potential effects of the form, the frequency, and the perceptual salience of linguistic structures in a learner's environment and of the potential effects of corrective feedback and reinforcement, all point to the force of creative mental factors on learning outcomes. If one assumes a creative construction framework to account for language acquisition, input factors take on a specific role. They provide the raw material which the mind digests and alters in accordance with its structure. In this view, (external) frequency serves to increase the probability that the learner will encounter in the environment what he or she is "ready" for or "needs" to be exposed to in order to continue development.

To know what the learner is "ready for," or "needs to be exposed to" requires a description of the developmental levels that reflect the process of language acquisition (where certain characteristics may differ for L1 and L2 or for child and adult L2 learners).

So far we have information on the acquisition orders for certain structures of English.[17] The linguistic structures themselves do not comprise the defining characteristics of the levels; they are so to speak symptomatic of the levels—instances of more general characteristics. For example, in the development of cognition, a child's perception that there is the same amount of water in a tall, slender glass as there is in a short, wide glass is but an instance of the general operation of conservation in the child. Other instances of conservation of quantity abound.

The task of specifying the defining characteristics of levels or steps in the L2 acquisition process still remains before us. In L1

---

[17] Despite differences in age, language, and formal instructional background, there are strikingly similar acquisition orders in oral production for groups of grammatical morphemes across child second language learners when their focus is communication. (Dulay and Burt, 1975a and b; Burt, Dulay, and Hernández-Chávez, 1976; and Fathman, 1975.) Orders of acquisition similar to those found for children learning L2 have been observed for adults' oral production (Krashen, 1975 and Larsen-Freeman, 1975a). Finally, d'Anglejan and Tucker (1975) have found a developmental order for the comprehension of linguistically complex English structures by French-speaking adults. The order was similar to that found by C. Chomsky (1970) for English first language acquisition by children five to ten years old.

acquisition research, one of the few serious hypotheses advanced to attempt to explain acquisition order was Brown's derivational complexity hypothesis. It relied on the early (1965) model of transformational grammar that grew out of the basic framework of mental creativity that Chomsky had outlined. The actual derivational history proposed by transformational grammarians, coupled with a metric of semantic complexity, was used to try to explain order of acquisition. (Cf. Brown, 1973a; Dulay and Burt, 1975b for a critical review of such attempts.) From the vantage point of hindsight, one might think that the ultimate fate of the derivational complexity hypothesis was predictable, given the still evolving status of transformational grammar and Chomsky's own cautionary remarks concerning its function (cf. Chomsky, 1965:9). At the time, however, the lack of even a hint of a working model of speech perception, production, or acquisition that seriously acknowledged the learner's independent contributions left few serious alternatives. Generative grammar was such a long overdue departure from both the linguistic and verbal learning theories available in the 1950s that the instant canonization by psycholinguists of even its narrowest aspects was almost inevitable.

It is now clear, however, that the initial hope on the part of psycholinguists that aspects of a model of generative grammar might predict language acquisition behavior has dissipated (see Fodor and Garrett, 1966; Fodor, Bever, and Garrett, 1974; and Dulay and Burt, 1975b for discussion). Not only has research along these lines been relatively unproductive, but the 1965 "Aspects model" used in most of the psycholinguistic research has undergone significant change (see Chomsky, 1975, Ch. 2; and Bresnan, 1976). It is also becoming more and more apparent that although theories or models appropriate for generative grammar, speech perception-production, first-language acquisition, and second-language acquisition might all fall within a framework of human creativity, the specific models for each will probably be quite different.

It is to be hoped, however, that the immensity of the task before us will not stifle but rather inspire continued and creative (in the educational-psychological sense) research into these important areas of inquiry.

References

d'Anglejan, Alison and Tucker, G. Richard. 1975. The acquisition of complex English structures by adult learners. *Language Learning* 25, 281–296.

Benton, Richard. 1964. *Research into the English language difficulties of Maori school children, 1963–1964.* Wellington, New Zealand: Maori Education Foundation.

Bloom, Lois. 1970. *Language development: form and function in emerging grammars.* Cambridge, Mass.: M.I.T. Press.

Blumenthal, Arthur L. 1970. *Language and psychology.* New York: John Wiley and Sons, Inc.

Bresnan, Joan. 1976. Toward a realistic model of transformational grammar. Paper presented at the M.I.T.-A.T.&T. Convocation on Communications, M.I.T., Cambridge, Mass., March 1976.

Brown, Roger. 1973a. *A first language.* Cambridge, Mass.: Harvard University Press.

———. 1973b. Development of the first language in the human species. *American Psychologist.* February 97–102.

Brown, Roger and Hanlon, Camille. 1970. Derivational complexity and order of acquisition in child speech. In J.R. Hayes (ed.), 1970.

Burt, Marina. 1974. Error analysis in the adult EFL classroom. *TESOL Quarterly* 9, 53–63.

Burt, Marina and Dulay, Heidi (eds.). 1975. *New directions in second language learning, teaching, and bilingual education.* Washington, D.C.: TESOL.

Burt, Marina, Dulay, Heidi, and Hernández-Chávez, Eduardo. 1975. *Bilingual syntax measure (English, Spanish, and Pilipino editions).* New York: Psychological Corporation.

———. 1976. *Bilingual syntax measure: technical handbook.* New York: Psychological Corporation.

Burt, Marina and Kiparsky, Carol. 1972. *The gooficon: a repair manual for English.* Rowley, Mass.: Newbury House.

Cathcart, Ruth and Olson, Judy. 1976. Preferences for correction of classroom conversation errors. Paper presented at 1976 TESOL Convention, New York.

Cazden, Courtney B. 1972. *Child language and education.* New York: Holt, Rinehart and Winston.

———. 1965. Environmental Assistance to the Child's Acquisition of Grammar. Ph.D. dissertation, Harvard University, Cambridge, Mass.

Chomsky, Carol. 1970. *The acquisition of syntax in children age 5 to 10.* Cambridge, Mass.: M.I.T. Press.

Chomsky, Noam. 1959. A review of B.F. Skinner's *Verbal Behavior. Language* 35, 26–58. Reprinted in J. Fodor and J. Katz (eds.), 1964.

———. 1965. *Aspects of the theory of syntax.* Cambridge, Mass.: M.I.T. Press.

———. 1975. *Reflections on language.* New York: Random House.

Cohen, Andrew D. and Robbins, Margaret. 1976. Toward assessing interlanguage performance: the relationship between selected errors, learner's characteristics, and learner's explanations. *Language Learning* 26, 45–66.

Clark, Eve. 1974. Performing without competence. *Journal of Child Language* 1, 1–10.

Dale, Philip S. 1976. *Language development: structure and function.* New York: Holt, Rinehart & Winston.

Dato, Daniel (ed.). 1975. *Developmental psycholinguistics: theory and applications (Georgetown University Round Table on Languages and Linguistics, 1975).* Washington, D.C.: Georgetown University Press.

Dulay, Heidi and Burt, Marina. 1972. Goofing: an indicator of children's second language learning strategies. *Language Learning* 22, 235–252. A more complete version of this paper appears in J. Richards (ed.), 1974.

———. 1974a. Errors and strategies in child second language acquisition. *TESOL Quarterly* 8, 129–136.

———. 1974b. A new perspective on the creative construction process in child second language acquisition. *Language Learning* 24, 253–278. Note: Error in Figure 4 (Hierarchy for *s*-morphemes) corrected in Volume 25, No. 1.

———. 1975a. Creative construction in second language learning and teaching. In M. Burt and H. Dulay (eds.), 1975. 21–32.

———. 1975b. A new approach to discovering universals of child second language acquisition. In Dato, Daniel (ed.), 1975. 209–233. This paper is an expanded version of H. Dulay, and M. Burt, 1974.

Ervin-Tripp, Susan. 1974. Is second language learning like the first? *TESOL Quarterly* 8, 111–127.

Fathman, Ann. 1975. Language background, age and the order of acquisition of English structures. In M. Burt and H. Dulay (eds.), 1975. 33–43.

Fodor, Jerry A., Bever, Thomas G., and Garrett, Merrill F. 1974. *The psychology of language.* New York: McGraw-Hill Book Company.

Fodor, Jerry A. and Garrett, Merrill. 1966. Some reflections on competence and performance. In J. Lyons and R. Wales (eds.), 1966. 135–162.

Fodor, Jerry A. and Katz, Jerrold J. (eds.). 1964. *The structure of language.* Englewood Cliffs, New Jersey: Prentice-Hall, Inc.

Gillis, Mary and Weber, Rose-Marie. 1976. The emergence of sentence modalities in the English of Japanese-speaking children. *Language Learning* 26, 77–94.

Guilford, J.P. 1967. *The nature of human intelligence.* New York: McGraw-Hill.

Hakuta, Kenji. 1974. Prefabricated patterns and the emergence of structure in second language acquisition. *Language Learning* 24, 287–298.

Halle, Morris. 1975. Confessio grammatici. *Language* 51, 525–535.

———. 1976. New approaches to a realistic model of language. Paper presented M.I.T.–A.T.&T. Convocation on Communications, M.I.T., Cambridge, Mass., March 1976.

Hatch, Evelyn and Wagner-Gough, Judy. 1976. Explaining sequence and variation in second language acquisition. *Language Learning,* Special Issue No. 4, H. D. Brown (ed.). 39–57.

Hayes, John R. (ed.). 1970. *Cognition and the development of language.* New York: John Wiley and Sons, Inc.

Hays, William L. 1963. *Statistics.* New York: Holt, Rinehart and Winston.

Hernández-Chávez, Eduardo. 1972. Early code separation in the second language speech of Spanish-speaking children. Paper presented at the Stanford Child Language Research Forum, Stanford University, Stanford, Calif.

———. 1977. *The Acquisition of Grammatical Structures by a Mexican American Child Learning English.* Ph.D. dissertation, University of California, Berkeley, California.

Huff, Darrell. 1954. *How to lie with statistics.* New York: W.W. Norton & Co.

Inhelder, Barbel, Sinclair, Hermine, and Bovet, Magali. *Learning and the development of cognition.* Cambridge, Mass.: Harvard University Press.

Klima, Edward S. and Bellugi, Ursula. 1966. Syntactic regularities in the speech of children. In J.R. Lyons and R.J. Wales, (eds.), 1966.

Krashen, Stephen D. 1976. Formal and informal linguistic environments in language acquisition and language learning. *TESOL Quarterly* 10, 157–168.

———. (in press). Individual variation in the use of the monitor. In W. Ritchie, (ed.).

Krashen, Stephen D., Madden, Carolyn, and Bailey, Nathalie. 1975. Theoretical aspects of grammatical sequencing. In M. Burt and H. Dulay (eds.), 1975. 44–54.

Labov, William. 1972. *Language in the inner city: studies in the black English vernacular.* Philadelphia: University of Pennsylvania Press.

124

Landes, James E. 1975. Speech addressed to children: issues and characteristics of parental input. *Language Learning* 25, 355–380.

Larsen-Freeman, Diane. 1976a. An explanation for the morpheme acquisition order of second language learners. *Language Learning* 26, 125–134.

———. 1976b. ESL teacher speech as input to the ESL learner. *Workpapers in TESL.* UCLA, 1976.

Lyons, John and Wales, R.J. (eds.). 1966. *Psycholinguistic Papers.* Edinburgh: Edinburgh University Press.

Milon, John P. 1974. The development of negation in English by a second language learner. *TESOL Quarterly* 8, 137–143.

———. 1975. Dialect in the TESOL program: If you never you better. In M. Burt and H. Dulay (eds.), 1975.

Mussen, Paul H. (ed.). 1970. *Carmichael's manual of child psychology (Volume I).* New York: John Wiley and Sons.

Piaget, Jean. 1970. *Structuralism.* New York: Basic Books.

Pylyshyn, Zenon W. 1973. The role of competence theories in cognitive psychology. *Journal of Psycholinguistic Research* 2, 21–50.

Ravem, Roar. 1974. The development of *wh*-questions in first and second language learners. In J. Richards (ed.), 1974.

Renzulli, Joseph. 1973. *New directions in creativity.* New York: Harper & Row.

Richards, Jack C. 1971a. Error analysis and second language strategies. *Language Sciences* 17, 12–22.

———. 1971b. A non-contrastive approach to error analysis. *English Language Teaching* 25, 204–219. Reprinted in J. Richards (ed.), 1974.

———. 1974. *Error analysis: perspectives on second language learning.* London: Longman.

Ritchie, William (ed.) in press. *Second language acquisition research: issues and implications.* New York: Academic Press.

Skinner, B. F. 1953. *Science and human behavior.* New York: Macmillan.

Taylor, Barry. 1975. The use of overgeneralization and transfer learning strategies by elementary and intermediate university students learning ESL. In M. Burt and H. Dulay (eds.), 1975. 55–69.

Torrance, E.P. 1966a. *Torrance tests of creative thinking: norms—technical manual.* Princeton, New Jersey: Personnel Press.

———. 1966b. *Torrance tests of creative thinking: directions manual and scoring guide; verbal test and figural test (Research Edition).* Princeton, New Jersey: Personnel Press.

Valdman, Albert. 1974. Error analysis and pedagogical ordering. Reproduced by Linguistic Agency University at Trier, D-55 Trier, West Germany.

Venable, Gail P. 1974. *A Study of Second-Language Learning in Children.* 641 M. Sc. (Appl) II Project, McGill University. Author now at Scottish Rite Institute for Childhood Aphasia, Dept. of Special Education, San Francisco State University, 1600 Holloway, San Franciso, Calif. 94132.

Wagner-Gough, Judy. 1975. *Comparative Studies in Second Language Learning.* M.A. thesis, University of California, Los Angeles, California.

Wagner-Gough, Judy and Hatch, Evelyn. 1975. The importance of input data in second language acquisition studies. *Language Learning* 25, 297–308.

Wallach, Michael A. 1970. Creativity. In P.H. Mussen (ed.), 1970, 1211–1272.

The Development of Semantic Relations in Child Second Language Acquisition

Eduardo Hernández-Chávez

Introduction

In the two decades since the beginning of the Chomskian revolution in grammar, the central occupation of theoretical linguists has been the attempt to understand the human capacity for language. Linguists are interested in learning what the precise nature of the knowledge is that speakers must have in order to use their language, what the kinds of internalized structures are that permit the creation of and the ability to comprehend instantly entirely novel sentences, and what the relationships of those structures are to other cognitive abilities. Questions such as these have stimulated intense research in generative syntax, semantics and phonology, the design of mathematical models of language, and the search for universals in linguistics.

Since the early 1900s an extremely important area of research that has been given impetus by the Chomskian movement is the investigation of child language acquisition. The study of child language constitutes not only a testing ground for the theoretical constructs that are the result of work in other branches of linguistics but also an important, and even indispensable, key for unlocking some of the answers to the major questions that linguists ask. For if we can gain some insight into how young children discover that abstract and very complex object that is language, how they take a highly variable and incomplete input and, in the course of three or four years, construct a generative grammar that is effectively identical to that of colinguals who receive a different input in vastly different circumstances, then we can begin to understand the nature of the human capacity for language.

One of the important issues in linguistic theory, and one which is of crucial interest to developmental psycholinguistics, revolves around the question of an innate *faculté du langage*. Few scholars today will doubt the existence in the human neonate of a predisposition to learn language, but the character and extent of any such genetically determined ability is still very much an open question. How much of grammatical structure, if any, are infants preprogrammed to learn and how much is the sole result of experience and generally high intellectual capacity? Are there universal processes or strategies that learners employ to arrive eventually at mature control of linguistic structure, and if so, what is their nature? Studies of the acquisition of language by children are uniquely suited to investigate these questions. One of the important conclusions of such research has been that reinforcement of children's responses is not one of the core mechanisms by which language is learned (Miller and Ervin, 1964; Brown and Hanlon, 1971). Another is that children's developing language does not consist of imperfectly imitated adult speech, but rather is the result of a creative construction process upon which the child brings to bear his own cognitive faculties (Dulay and Burt, 1975a). Substantively, we have learned that the order in which the grammatical structures of a language are acquired is highly systematic and in many respects predictable (Brown, Cazden, and Bellugi, 1968). Cross-linguistic comparison demonstrates a surprising degree of agreement in the kinds of structures that children acquire and the developmental stages in which they acquire them.[1]

These findings are important evidence in support of theories of universal grammar. But in recent years, the increasing interest in semantic and functional analysis has raised other increasingly complex questions concerning the relationship of the language learning capacity of children to their other cognitive abilities. Thus, we may ask whether the cross-subject and especially cross-linguistic uniformity that has been found is due more to

---

[1] See Slobin, 1973, for a discussion of the burgeoning cross-linguistic research.

the common properties of human conceptual development than to any inborn and specifically linguistic mental processes. For example, we should not expect to find, nor do we find, linguistic forms such as tense or temporal adverbs before the child is capable of conceptualizing the nonlinguistic notion of time. Similarly, the acquisition of adjectives is dependent upon the knowledge that qualities may be attributed to things.

Considerations such as these make much more problematical the question of universals of language acquisition. Learning sequences and acquisition strategies may reflect the maturation of children's nonlinguistic conceptual systems and thus may not be strictly linguistic at all, or they may reveal an intimate relationship between distinct but closely tied cognitive functions. Studies of the acquisition of a first language will continue to provide data that will increase our understanding not only of these problems but also of such important questions as what kinds of formal devices are easier to learn and by what processes various aspects of grammatical structure are acquired.

Within the last decade, growing attention has been given to the description of language acquisition in bilingual environments. These efforts were spurred by the same intellectual excitement that generally pervaded work in generative linguistics.[2] Most of these studies have tended to focus on the relationship between the incipient bilingual's two languages.[3]

One of the important theoretical issues that the study of childhood bilingualism is particularly able to address concerns the relationship of the semantic component of a developing grammar and the learner's other cognitive abilities. One way to view this relationship is that since the sequential second language learner has an already well-developed cognitive apparatus by the age of three, for example, when he begins to acquire the

---

[2] Earlier work in child bilingualism outside the generative tradition has also had an important impact on more recent studies. In the U.S., Leopold's work remains unsurpassed as a diary account of the acquisition of two languages (Leopold, 1939–1949).

[3] There is a growing literature in this field that is concerned with linguistic, psychological, and educational aspects of the acquisition of bilingualism. Studies are especially numerous in sequential second language acquisition. For some of the pace-setting studies in the area, see in particular Imedadze (1960), Mikes (1967), Ravem (1968), Richards (1971), Hernández-Ch. (1972), Selinker (1972), Dulay and Burt (1974 *inter alia*), and Milon (1974).

second language, the order of acquisition and the strategies that the child employs will surely reflect purely formal linguistic processes.[4] A strong implication of this view is that the bilingual individual possesses a single conceptual system for which he acquires separate linguistic means of expression. A different view, which suggests certain Whorfian ideas, considers the semantic component of a grammar to be on a different plane from the conceptualization of experience. This view holds that the structure and semantic content of a language develop independently from, though in close coordination with, experimental concepts, and, in a strong version of this view, would mold the learner's cognition of experience to the shape of the particular language. The resolution of this issue will provide us with deep and interesting insights into the nature of language, its relationship to cognition, the role of culture in the formation of both, and similar questions that have long intrigued language scholars.

This paper reports on some recent research that, it is hoped, will help to elucidate some of the problems concerned with the underlying processes involved in language acquisition. We will address two related questions in particular. First, we will attempt to show that the semantic structure of children's language develops, at least to some extent, along different lines from their other cognitive functions, and that the language learning faculty includes processes which enable the learner to construct both the formal and the semantic systems of his language.

The semantic system that we are concerned with is a specifically *linguistic* system. It is distinct from other systems of concepts that may include beliefs or numerical systems or such things as shape, distance, and configurations, etc. More crucially, we will claim that the linguistic semantics are distinct from such concepts as things, qualities, and time and from such relations as actors, actions, and things acted upon. These have their analogues in grammatical functions like noun and tense or

---

[4] Language learning of course involves other, noncognitive factors, especially the sociolinguistic conditions in which the child is inevitably immersed. We omit any such considerations from this discussion, though we recognize their great importance.

subject and verb. Roger Brown has demonstrated that there is an intimate relationship between actions and verbs and between things and nouns (Brown, 1957), but we will try to show that they are not identical.

Secondly, we will be concerned with the question of the relationship between the semantic system of the bilingual learner's first language and the acquisition of the semantic relations of the second. Recent work in syntax strongly suggests that a bilingual's second language follows patterns of development that are essentially autonomous. For example, this writer recently presented evidence that the developing structures of Spanish-speaking children learning English were extremely similar to those reported for children learning English as a first language (Hernández Ch., 1972). Moreover, the English utterances of these children showed no clear examples of the transfer of Spanish structures. Dulay and Burt have analyzed the speech of 179 bilingual children and have found that in less than five percent of the utterances could interference from English reasonably be interpreted as the source (Dulay and Burt, 1974). Their research also shows that the order in which grammatical structures are learned is systematically patterned for both first and second language learners although the particular orders for these two classes of learners may be different (Dulay and Burt, 1975a, 1975b).

While the question of syntactic interference is by no means settled, there is growing agreement that children who are learning a second syntax maintain it essentially separate from that of the first language. However, there is a general assumption that, because of the advanced cognitive development of the sequential second language learner, the *semantics* of the first language are automatically and completely available to the child as he learns a second language. This paper will attempt to show that this is an unwarranted assumption and that, in the part of the semantic system that pertains to the grammatical functions, transfer from the native language to a second language is not a major principle of acquisition.

Several related kinds of evidence will be presented in support of these positions. We will discuss the orderly emergence of semantic relations and syntactic structures[5] in the developing speech of a bilingual child, and we will show that their order of development does not depend upon the existence of those functions in the first language. In addition, we will demonstrate the existence of a number of learning strategies by which the child organizes new linguistic functions and incorporates them into the structures he is learning.

Development of the Early Syntax

The findings presented here are from the study of Güero, a three-year-old Mexican-American boy whose first introduction to English was in a day-care center in Oakland, California.[6] The child's progress was followed for a period of slightly more than sixteen months by means of biweekly tape recordings of his spontaneous speech in interaction with other children and Center personnel. Among the children and staff were monolingual English speakers, bilinguals, and dominant Spanish-speaking persons. The total English output collected over the sixteen-month recording period included well over 4,000 utterances. The great bulk of these occurred in the final eight months of study. However, in this paper we will concentrate on the first eight months of the recording period which, though it yielded a relatively small amount of production, demonstrated a fairly rapid development of the basic structures which are of greatest interest for our purposes.

---

[5] These are not to be confused. *Semantic relations* include the major sentential functions —subject, object, predicate, benefactive, etc. These may in turn be composed of other semantic relations such as person or plurality, as well as inherent features of lexical and grammatical categories, such as ostentive or inanimate. The *syntactic structures* refer to the temporal orderings, configurations, and forms that realize the underlying grammatical functions and meanings. For example, categories such as *VP*, concatenations such as *Det. + N*, or formatives such as *Modal* and the rules that organize them are elements of syntax. Thus, we adhere essentially to the Hjelmslevian opposition between content and expression. The boundary between semantics and syntax is not a sharp one, and this important distinction is blurred further by the use of the same term to refer now to semantic, now to syntactic phenomena. For example, *possessive, definite, plural, past,* etc. are both semantic notions and labels for syntactic categories.

Another possible source of confusion in this paper is the fact that syntactic phenomena, as the only directly observable aspects of the child's language, will be used heavily to infer his semantic intentions and his control or lack of control of a semantic relation. We believe this is a methodologically sound procedure, but we wish to caution our readers.

[6] For details of the learning conditions, see Hernández-Chávez (1977).

During this time, represented by 14 taping sessions, Güero produced a total of 740 English utterances[7] of which 342 were reproductions, i.e., either exact repetitions of a model or responses which incorporated some portion of the model. The majority of the reproductions were forms which we call quasi-spontaneous utterances. These are said spontaneously or in response to another's utterance, but they differ from fully spontaneous forms in that at least some of the material in the utterance has been heard by the child at an earlier time in the same transcript, usually with a small amount of intervening material and most frequently with a time lapse of between four or five seconds to a minute or more. These are not counted as spontaneous utterances because of the possibility that the child can hold the model or a part of it in short-term memory, and, if he practices it covertly, may recall portions of the model even after a considerable lapse of time. Of 402 fully spontaneous utterances, 55 involved some use of Spanish with the utterance, leaving 347 utterances which formed the central corpus for this analysis.

During the first eight months after his introduction to English, Güero's grammatical acquisition concentrated on the development of the basic phrase structure of the language. The earliest syntactic construction to appear,[8] at month 2 (M-2), was an equational sentence with a subject and a predicate-possessive.

---

[7] For the purpose of a simple count of utterances, no rigid criteria were followed. Phonetic material between pauses was most frequently interpreted as a single utterance, though this procedure was not always completely reliable. In practice, decisions about what constitutes an utterance were in most cases easy to make. In some instances, however, decisions required the use of a number of interrelated criteria which we will not discuss here. For the purpose of this paragraph, repetitions of words or phrases such as "Hey, lookit; hey, lookit" were counted as two utterances. On the other hand, certain fairly long sequences were counted as a single utterance, as for example, when the child chants "Jingle bells, jingle bells" over and over or when he mimics an utterance, obviously engaging in vocal play. In one such sequence, Güero repeated "What" 46 times.

[8] Since the data are entirely the result of the collection of naturalistic speech, it was impossible to rely on a large number of occurrences in order to attribute a grammatical structure to the child. Various kinds of evidence were productive. Indispensable among these was that the form in question must have been produced completely spontaneously and entirely in English. Recurrence of the form in succeeding transcripts was also considered crucial, since a few, obviously memorized utterances appeared that contained grammatical elements far in advance of the child's development. Additionally, there was a strong reliance in the early period upon supporting facts from nonspontaneous utterances and from sentences with a combined Spanish and English structure.

133

The only subject permitted in this construction was the demonstrative pronoun *this* (alternatively, *this-one* or *that*); the predicate-possessive was restricted to the pronoun *for-me* (e.g. *This-one for-me*). The element *for-me* soon gave way to *my* and did not recur until months later with a benefactive function. For the first several transcripts, this subject-predicate construction was the only productive syntactic nucleus to occur.

Six weeks later at M-3.5 we find the sudden appearance of sentences such as those in Example (1) which are the first constructions with verbs. It is important to note that all of these sentences are subjectless and

(1) Lookit that
Lookit Lisa
Gimme pa-pow (=gun)
Gimme one
Gimme more
Hey, stop-it

have an imperative meaning, and that the object position is filled by a number of different types of words including indefinite pronouns, a demonstrative, and a proper noun. In this same transcript, a single example of a nonimperative verb occurs: *I make-it* [ai̯mɛ́kɪ]. Within the next two weeks a number of similar structures appear, all of them without direct objects, and all with either *I* or *you* as subjects. It seems clear that the single example at M-3.5 was indeed the first recorded productive use of the subject-finite verb construction.

Several observations are important at this point. One is that analogous functions in these various kinds of sentences govern different privileges of occurrence. That is, subjects, objects, modifiers, etc. develop differently depending upon whether they are in equational, imperative, or nonimperative structures. For example, the subject of an equational sentence may only be a demonstrative which does not occur as subject of a verbal nucleus; verbs of imperative sentences do not appear in nonimperatives and vice versa.

134

TABLE 1
Emergence of Three Major Sentence Types

TIME OF APPEARANCE	SENTENCE TYPE	EXAMPLE
Month 2.0	Equational	This for-me
Month 3.5	Imperative	Gimme one
Month 4.0	Indicative	I wannit

A second observation is that each of the major sentence types enters the child's active production at clearly separate times. As Table 1 illustrates, we first find equational sentences of the type *This for-me*. The next kind of sentence six weeks later is the imperative such as *Gimme one,* and finally, two weeks later, nonimperative or indicative sentences such as *I wannit* become productive. We may further observe that nonimperative verbal nuclei first develop without an object function while imperatives, which may have direct objects, do not take a subject. Because of considerations of this sort, we find it reasonable to posit three distinct sentence types which develop their major nuclear functions independently of each other. This independent development of the major sentence types continues to be an important feature of Güero's development throughout the recording period and suggests a fundamental and far-reaching division in the child's grammar.

TABLE 2
Differential Development of Syntactic Categories According to Semantic Function

SYNTACTIC CATEGORY	SEMANTIC FUNCTION					
	Equational Sentence		Imperative Sentence		Indicative Sentence	
	Subject	Predicate	Subject	Object	Subject	Object
Demonstrative Pronoun	2.0 mos.	— mos.	* mos.	3.5 mos.	8.25 mos.	3.75 mos.
Possessive Pronoun	9.25	2.0	*	4.5	—	7.5
1st Person Pronoun	9.5	—	*	12.0	3.5	7.0
2nd Person Pronoun	7.5	—	6.0	—	3.75	11.0
Noun	8.0	5.0	*	3.5	9.5	5.5

* Category does not normally occur with this function.
—Category does not occur in the corpus with this function.

135

The separate development of syntactic categories within analogous sentence relations continues for most of the early period, and for some categories, well into the later period. Table 2 illustrates this principle for a number of the more important components of noun phrases. Each syntactic category, e.g. demonstrative pronoun, emerges at distinct times for each of the major semantic relations. We notice in the table, for example, that possessive pronouns first function only as predicates; two and a half months later they may function as objects of imperative sentences, and not until three months later are they found as objects of indicatives. We can observe clearly analogous developmental patterns with the noun and the other pronoun categories. The blank cells in the table either represent later developing forms such as the 2nd person reflexive pronoun in imperative objects (and possibly the personal pronouns as predicates), or else they are due to the rarity of the communicative conditions that call for the form in question.

Complex noun phrases, too, develop differentially according to the semantic relations they express. The first noun phrases to appear at M-5.5 combine nouns with possessive pronouns or indefinite articles; these may function only as predicates. Other functions are learned gradually. Table 3 shows the permissible noun phrase configurations at the end of four different time periods for each of several major semantic relations. At M-6 we note that all NP configurations are represented, but each is severely restricted as to the sentence relations it may express. Thus, while the category NP may express various semantic relations, there are systematic constraints on the co-occurrence of its components. The result is that we cannot yet represent these different configurations as a unified syntactic category.

In M-7.5, there is a dramatic increase in the number of sentences containing NP's and a sudden relaxation of many of these constraints. By M-8, the constraints on NP are effectively lifted, and an NP, once it expresses a particular relation, occurs freely in any of the configurations that it manifests. A clear illustration of this comes with the subject relation in indicative sentences. No NP's are permitted until M-9.5. By M-10, every configuration is found except *Indefinite-Pronoun + Noun* which we consider to be a gap in the communicative probabilities rather than a seman-

TABLE 3
Semantic Constraints on Occurrences of Four NP Categories

Time	Equational Subject	Equational Predicate	Imperative Object	Indicative Subject	Indicative Object
M-6.0	—	Poss. + N	—	—	—
	—	—	Demons. + N	—	—
	—	Indef. + N	—	—	—
	—	—	Def. + N	—	Def. + N
M-7.5	—	Poss. + N	Poss. + N	—	—
	Demons. + N	—	Demons. + N	—	Demons. + N
	—	Indef. + N	—	—	Indef. + N
	Def. + N	Def. + N	Def. + N	—	Def. + N
M-8.0	Poss. + N	Poss. + N	Poss. + N	—	Poss. + N
	Demons. + N	—	Demons. + N	—	Demons. + N
	Indef. + N	Indef. + N	—	—	Indef. + N
	Def. + N	Def. + N	Def. + N	—	Def. + N
M-10	Poss. + N	Poss. + N	Poss. + N	Poss. + N	Poss. + N
	Demons. + N	—	Demons. + N	Demons + N	Demons + N
	Indef. + N	Indef. + N	Indef. + N	—	Indef. + N
	Def. + N	Def. + N	Def. + N	Def. + N	Def. + N

tic constraint. These tables show clearly how, although a syntactic category may be fully productive, the *semantic relations that it expresses are still in a stage of development.*

In this brief description of the development of a portion of English phrase structure, one fact stands out in bold relief. Not only is the concatenation of forms into various configurations of English syntax learned in a systematic fashion—a finding that is not unexpected—the child also follows a definite and orderly sequence of development in the acquisition of the semantic relations of English grammar. That is to say, the underlying semantic relations of English sentences are learned in a step-by-step fashion which is not identical with the development of the syntax. We shall see that this has important consequences for our view of the relationship between the linguistic and nonlinguistic conceptual systems.

Relationship of the Spanish and English Semantic Systems

The orderly development in Güero's speech of English semantic relations raises important questions about the relationship between the semantic system of the learner's two languages. Among most researchers who have written on the subject, there is an underlying assumption that in sequential second language acquisition, learners approach the task with a relatively well-developed conceptual structure upon which they map the new mode of expression. Stated another way, the prevailing wisdom holds that a semantic system, once learned for a single language, becomes the base for the subsequent learning of a second language. Only the syntax or expression requires explicit learning; the semantics or content is given as previously learned. Underlying this belief is the theory of a universal base: the deep structure of a grammar defines the fundamental semantic relations which are shared by every natural language; the syntax of particular languages then specifies the temporal orderings and other manifestations of the linguistic elements. We should thus expect that the semantic structure acquired in first language learning will be fully available to the child as he or she approaches the learning of a second.

But the facts of Güero's acquisition of English are not consistent with such a view. We have seen that the syntactic categories develop differentially according to the grammatical function that they serve. That is, the systematic exclusion of a learned category from an existing semantic relationship demonstrates that the child must learn the meaning of the category; in still other words, that meaning is not a given. More critically for our argument, the orderly emergence of the semantic relations is unexplainable by a theory that attributes to the learner a single, undifferentiated semantic system. If the semantic relational system that a child has acquired in learning the first language is also the same one that the child has available in the acquisition of a second language, we should expect to find all of the grammatical functions developing equally for both languages, and in the earlier stages of syntactic acquisition of the second language, no discernible autonomous development of semantic relations.

It is central to our argument that not only does Güero not express in English the notions we attribute to him in Spanish, he does not intend to express them. In order to demonstrate this, we will present evidence that particular semantic relations exist in the child's Spanish. We will show that he does not attempt to express these in English by demonstrating that certain forms which appear to express particular notions in fact do not, and that careful observation can reveal a given intention even in the absence of an overt form.

The semantic relations that Güero knows in Spanish are, already by the early English learning period, quite sophisticated.[9] We may first observe that of the grammatical functions that gradually emerge during the first eight months, all of them are present in Spanish at the time of the child's first introduction to English. At M-1, the following forms, among others, are recorded:

(2) a. Es el camión. 'It's the truck'
   b. Acá está mi casa. 'Here is my house'
   c. Mira un carro. 'Look at a car'
   d. No quiero desto. 'I don't want (any of) this'
   e. Voy a hacer una casa, mira. 'I'm going to make a house, look'

Examples (2a) and (2b) are instances of the subject and predicate relations in equational sentences. In addition, (2b) includes a locative. An imperative with a verb object is seen in (2c), while (2d) reveals a negative indicative verb with 1st person subject as well as a demonstrative object. And in (2e) appears the auxiliary that corresponds to English *gonna*. In addition to the presence of these relational notions, we can also note any number of purely formal processes such as appropriate word order, verb morphology, and subject deletion, but these are not material to our discussion.

The existing knowledge of these notions in Spanish, in contrast to their gradual acquisition in English, is extremely problematical for a theory that assumes a single unified semantic sys-

---

[9] The Spanish data for Güero are not nearly so extensive as those available for English. He very early defined the day-care center as a principally English-speaking setting. We have been forced therefore to make inferences about his knowledge of Spanish from forms that recur but rarely. All of his Spanish use is with persons that the child knows are Spanish-speakers, and virtually all of his production is spontaneous. In spite of the paucity of data, we are confident that the structures we cite are indeed productive forms.

tem. But in addition we find in the child's Spanish a number of more complex grammatical functions, some of which do not appear in English until much later in the recording period, and others which do not appear at all.

Example (3) provides instances of semantic relations that occur in Güero's Spanish but which are not expressed in English during the early syntatic period.

(3) a. ¿Se acabó?   'Is it finished?'
    b. Se me cayó.   'I dropped it.'
    c. Con ventanas.   'With windows.'
    d. Porque tenía.   'Because it had some.'
    e. Por favor, póngamelo. 'Please put it on me.'
    f. ¿Le das ese a Chiqui? 'Will you give that to Chiqui?'
    g. Que lo meta.   '(I want him) to put it in.'

Examples (3a-b) reveal the existence of past tense in Spanish verbs. Yet there are no examples in English before M-7 in which the child unambiguously intends a past tense. The conversation given below illustrates the single instance in which one could conceivably attribute such an intention to the child. It occurred at M-3.75.

(4) a. Adult: You want to make a man?
    b. Güero: Man.
    c. Adult: (Pause) O.K. What did you make?
    d. Güero: I make man (softly).
    e. Adult: What did you make?
    f. Güero: I gonna make . . . I gonna man . . . I make man.

Man is not yet a completely productive form for Güero, and *make* occurred just once previously, in the preceding transcript. The exchange (4c)-(4d) contains the utterance at issue. The child was drawing on a piece of paper. After he had drawn a design, the adult asked him the question, clearly in the past. The response seems to indicate that the child understood and gave a semantically appropriate, though structurally not well-formed response. However, the fact that both *man* and *make* are partial reproductions of the adult model casts doubt on the child's full comprehension of the exchange and thus on the actual appropriateness of the response. The exchange that immediately follows in (4e)-(4f) tends to confirm our suspicion that (4d) does not contain a past tense intention. The child is talking about what he is doing and what he expects to do rather than what he has done.

All other utterances that contain a verb are either imperatives or have an obviously nonpast meaning. Not until M-7 do we find the child responding verbally to a situational context that requires a past tense meaning. In one of the first such instances, Güero is playing near a pool with another child. The second child splashes water on Güero who then pushes him. When the second protests, Güero says *You squirt me*. Under these conditions, we can safely attribute a past meaning to the child despite the lack of any formal marking.

Example (3c) provides a further illustration of the same point. This has a plural noun clearly intended as a plural. Plural forms in Güero's English do not clearly emerge until M-8. At that time, situational, morphological, and syntactic data provide evidence of a productive rule that generates a plural formative. However, the emergence of such a rule at M-8 does not preclude the possibility that the notion of plurality forms part of the child's English semantic system prior to that time. In fact, there is some evidence that it exists several weeks before M-8, though this evidence is not strong enough to warrant positing a rule of the phrase structure. Thus in M-5.5 we record this sentences:

(5) Lookit the elephants aquí. [lûkətəǽləfɔ̃səkí]

Because of elements of the nonlinguistic context, there seems to be no question that the child was indeed referring to an aggregation of elephants, and from the form of the word uttered we infer that he was intending to express a plural. However, not only is this the only plural form encountered prior to M-8, it is the sole example of an utterance in which the child can reasonably be said to attempt to express a plural. In our transcripts for M-2, we find the following dialogue:

(6)   Adult: What are those?
      Güero: ¿Y éste? What that?
      Adult: Do you know what those are?
      Güero: Those car.   [dõ̞ʊk'á·r]
      Adult: They're what?
      Güero: They're car.   [dêkʰá·r]

141

The adult was referring to a group of toy cars. The child had used the word *car* several times previously in spontaneous utterances and evidently knew the word and its pronunciation. The important facts to note are that 1) the 'plural' forms *those* and *they're* are direct imitations of a portion of the model; 2) they do not recur, either as imitations or as spontaneous forms until M-8; and 3) there are no other instances of an attempted plural until the example given in (5). All his other utterances in which a noun occurs either refer to a single object or express the notion of 'recurrence' with *another* or *more*.

It is not possible from our data—and it may be impossible in principle—to know without a doubt that a child does not possess a particular intention. We can only show that he does not *attempt* certain meanings or that he does attempt them but with an incorrect surface form. At the same time, surface forms such as those in (6) tell us virtually nothing about his intentions, and without further evidence, we conclude that the child does not possess the notion 'plural' for English before M-5.5 though Example (3) above demonstrates that he does have it for Spanish.

Let us return now to the remaining examples in (3) which are less problematic though equally instructive for the point we are making. The semantic functions expressed in these few examples include some which are relatively late in first language acquisition. For example, (3d) expresses an imperfective past, (3e) has a benefactive meaning, and (3f) an indirect object. Example (3g) is in response to the question *¿Qué quieres?* (What do you want?) and uses a subjunctive clause to express an optative function. None of these meanings is ever expressed in English by the child by the end of the recording period with the sole exception of the indirect object. We observe, then, a number of basic semantic functions that the child already possesses in one language which are not expressed in the other and which we claim there is no intention to express.

This finding appears to run counter to the general cognitive principle that Dan Slobin extends to linguistic development (Slobin, 1973, p. 184), namely that new forms first express old functions. If by "new forms" we can mean the syntax of a new language, then we ought to find that, as the child acquires the syntax of a second language, it is brought into play to express other semantic relations that the child already knows from the

142

first language. Our evidence suggests that this process is not followed by second language learners, but rather that they must learn which functions the second language expresses before they can learn *how* to express them.

The learning strategies that are used by the child can thus provide an important line of evidence for understanding the relationship between the child's two languages and the organization of his semantic system. In the remainder of this paper, then, we propose to examine three of Güero's learning strategies in the light of Slobin's principle in order to gain a better understanding of the semantic structure of the incipient bilingual. We will first examine the role of holophrases in the development of grammatical functions. Following that, we will discuss how the child employs quasi-spontaneous utterances and code-alternations as learning strategies.

The Role of Holophrases in the Development of Grammatical Functions

Güero's first English utterances contain no overt syntax. In the earliest transcripts, most of his production involved single-word utterances with a few multiple-word productions that are clearly unanalyzable syntactically. Phrases such as *open shut them* and *my name* are found in the first transcripts before the acquisition of any productive syntax. These phrases are obviously stretches of speech that are memorized and associated with very specific nonlinguistic contexts, especially games, and can be thought of as linguistic gestures with no generalized meanings.

In the very first transcripts we also find a small number of single-word forms that are used in more general contexts, which recur, and which very obviously have meaning for the child. Such one-word meaningful utterances have come to be known as *holophrases*. Most scholars have considered these to be unitary, grammatically unanalyzable complexes of meaning. Some recent work, however, has suggested that this is not a completely accurate view. For example, Paula Menyuk proposes that the holophrase has an internal structure based upon the use of intonations with different meanings (Menyuk, 1969, p. 25 ff). Lois Bloom recognizes that at least in the case of two or more

143

one-word utterances said in succession or in the case of an expansion from one-word to two-word utterances, a grammatical relationship between the words can be attributed to the child (Bloom, 1968, p. 57). Patricia Greenfield carries this notion further by attributing grammatical relations to holophrases themselves, without the condition of successive utterances or expansions (McNeill, 1970, pp 23–29).

The data for Güero also show that holophrases must be assigned as internal structure. Because of considerations of space, we will not present our full evidence here (see Hernández-Chávez, 1977, for a full discussion), but a few examples may be illuminating. The evidence that is used to infer the grammatical meaning intended by the child is of two principal kinds: the nonlinguistic situation and the linguistic context in which the utterance is spoken. The situation by itself will on occasion be sufficient to provide a good indication of the grammatical function of the utterance as when the child says *Look* while pointing at an object, or when he tugs at the clothing of an adult, saying *Come-on*. In these cases, we can be fairly confident that the child is intending an imperative meaning. Often the child will respond to an utterance in such a way that his response together with the situational context makes clear his meaning. So, for example, if the teacher is naming objects in a picture book then asks Güero *What's this?*, he may respond with an appropriate noun, e.g. *Car*. The child is not merely attributing a label to the object, but rather is making a predication about the immediate situation that he is experiencing, i.e. the pointing of the teacher, the question—however vaguely understood—and the object to which he is referring.

At other times Güero uses sentences that include elements from both languages that give us important information about his grammatical intentions. One example demonstrates that holophrases may have a direct object function as when the child says *Mira house. House.* The imperative *look* appears by itself many times in the same transcript but Güero does not yet combine English words. The mixed sentence appears to be an effort to resolve that restriction. The word *house* of *Mira house* is clearly the direct object. The most reasonable interpretation of the holophrase that follows is that it, too, has a direct object function.

Also in the first transcripts Güero uses the form *mine* [maɪ]. The situations in which this form is used are consistent with a possessive meaning, but they are also consistent with other meanings. Conceivably, in what we interpret as a possessive, the child could be intending a command, i.e. something equivalent to *gimme;* or he could be expressing a desire to obtain the object in question. Even if we accept its possessive meaning, its sentential function as a subject, an object, or a predicate is indeterminate in these utterances. Fortunately, we have also recorded the following exchange at another point in the same session:

(7)　Adult: What's this?
　　　Güero: This mine, That's mine, That mine.

The child is undoubtedly learning the subject function of *this* and *that* and is beginning to acquire the ability to concatenate forms. But the demonstrative does not appear spontaneously until the following month, so we do not yet consider it productive. The point of the example here is that the child demonstrates his grasp of the predicate function for the possessive pronoun. We can confidently label the earlier holophrastic occurrence as a possessive which may function at least as the predicate of an equational sentence.

The internal relational structure of holophrastic utterances becomes extremely important when we observe the emergence of syntactic constructions. The establishment of a semantic relation in holophrases in every case precedes the development of that relation in sentences with overt syntactic structure. (It does not follow, however, that every syntactically expressed relation is first found holophrastically.) We have seen that at M-1 the child learned the semantic relation of several grammatical categories including nouns as imperative objects, nouns and possessive pronouns as predicates, and verbs as imperatives. It is just these sentential functions that in the succeeding weeks the child first learns to concatenate into syntactic structures.

So for example, we have seen that the first syntactic construction to appear at M-2 has the structure [Demonstrative] subject + [Possessive] predicate. These relations occurred holophrastically at M-1. Similarly, when imperative sentences appear at M-3.5, they concatenate [V] verb and [Noun] object, relations that have already been learned holophrastically.

Moreover, as development progresses other holophrases arise which themselves anticipate the syntactic use of the semantic relations they express. In M-3, for instance, the first use of a locative occurs in holophrastic utterances with a predicate function. It is not until several weeks later, at M-4.5, that we begin to find the predicate-locative concatenated with other forms. The demonstrative pronoun occurs only as a subject of equational sentences until M-3, at which time there is evidence that it is used holophrastically as a direct object. In the following session two weeks later it is recorded in construction with an imperative verb functioning as its direct object (cf. Example 1, p. 134) and two weeks later it appears as the direct object of an indicative. Other examples of this process could be cited, but the general principle seems clear: holophrastic utterances in Güero's speech serve to establish the functional possibilities of particular categories of words. Once the grammatical function of the categories is learned, the child can then establish the temporal order and other syntactic characteristics that express the functions overtly.

Quasi-spontaneous Utterances and Code Alternation as Learning Strategies

Above we gave a few examples of "quasi-spontaneous" utterances and sentences involving code alternation in support of the claim that holophrases have internal grammatical structure. The term quasi-spontaneous refers to freely produced utterances, portions of which reproduce elements of a model. Example (8), below, gives several examples of these kinds of utterances. They differ from imitations in that they reproduce only portions of the model and have a communicative function. They are not fully spontaneous in that material from the model seems to provide a lexical and grammatical context into which the child's response is embedded.

Code alternation is the more appropriate term for what we have referred to above as "mixed sentences," i.e. those kinds of sentences that are produced with lexical and syntactic elements from more than one language. For example, *Este es yours* or *Un boot de la niña* incorporate English forms in Spanish constructions while *Gimme one, Gimme este* uses the English sentences as the context.

We will see that these kinds of sentences are used by Güero in the same way as the holophrases. That is, code-alternating or quasi-spontaneous sentences serve to introduce new grammatical functions into the child's grammar. In fact, as his syntactic capability grows, these devices become increasingly important while the holophrastic introduction of new structure takes on a reduced role. There are many examples of this process in our data, but we will cite only a few.

Indicative verbs do not appear spontaneously until M-3.5 and not until M-5.5 do they occur with a noun object. During the early period we record the following exchanges at various times:

(8) M-2   a.   Adult: You don't want it?
                        Güero: No want-it. I no want-it. I no want-it.

      M-3   b.   Adult: Let's see-it.
                        Güero: I (let's) see-it.   [aídɛsíɛ]

      M-3.5 c.   Child: I don't have no milk.
                        Güero: I drink milk.

Example (8a) is very similar to the kind of build-up that is often reported for children's speech with the exception that the constant portion is taken from a model. In that sense, (8a) and (8b) are the same. The model serves as a context for the subject pronoun. In (8c) the subject and object become the context in which the child tests the grammatical water for the verb, so to speak. At M-3.5, Güero uses *I make-it* spontaneously, and by M-4 several other verbs are used together with a demonstrative object. Exchanges such as those of (8) help the child to "try out" new grammatical functions and their syntactic privileges.

A very similar process can be observed with code alternation. We have already mentioned the direct object example in the sentence *Mira house.* The object function is embedded in a Spanish contect long before it is used freely in an English sentence. Another example concerns the possessive pronouns. The first person of the possessive participates in the very first syntactic construction. No other possessive constructions appear until M-5.5 at which time not only do the second and third person

147

pronouns appear, possessives may also combine with nouns into a complex NP. At M-4, however, we find:

(9) Este es yours. 'this is yours'

(10)   Adult: That's Mark's.
       Güero: That's my tortilla.

In (9), the second person of the possessive is seen to function as a predicate and in (10) the old first-person possessive has a new function as a determiner. Both of these uses are first introduced by the device of code alternation. Moreover, in (10) we notice that part of the child's response is, in addition, modeled by the adult.

Thus, it becomes evident that a variety of devices are employed by the child to do the work of ferreting out the functional potentials of grammatical categories. Holophrases, quasi-spontaneous utterances, and code alternations each serve the purpose of introducing and trying out structures that the child is preparing to develop in his productive syntax. We will cite a final example of this process. As has been noted, the locative does not appear spontaneously until M-4. But at M-3 we find these sentences:

(11)   a. Ves este in-here?   'Do you see this in here?'
       b. Van in-here.   'They go in here.'
       c. Ese es Chiqui here.   'That's Chiqui here.'

The only other examples of locatives prior to this time are three holophrastic utterances in the same transcript and a quasi-spontaneous use of the month before, given as Example (12).

(12)   a. Güero: Here. Right here.
       b. Adult: (to a third person) He's putting a piece of puzzle
                                     together.
          Güero: Put this in-there.

In these examples we observe three different processes all converging on the same function: locatives are produced first in holophrases, in code-alternating sentences, and in quasi-spontaneous utterances before they are freely used in fully spontaneous forms.

None of these cases provides a clear-cut demonstration of the principle enunciated by Slobin that new forms first express old functions except in the sense that when the child finally produces a fully spontaneous syntactic construction, he is expressing in a new way functions which he has learned by other means. But this leaves open the question of what those other means are. We have attempted to demonstrate three of those processes, and we may tentatively suggest a somewhat different principle from Slobin's, namely that familiar functions are used as a context for unfamiliar functions.

Conclusions

In this paper we have presented certain data from a Spanish-speaking child beginning to learn English. Our main interest has been to attempt to elucidate some of the problems that concern the relationships between the semantic systems employed by bilingual learners and between the linguistic and nonlinguistic conceptual systems. Among our principle findings are that the second language learner does not merely "syntactify" the semantic relations that he already has learned in his first language. Rather, he uses a number of different strategies to acquire the fundamental semantic relations of his second language in a step-by-step and systematic fashion. Only then does he begin to concatenate the forms into the syntactic patterns of the second language.

The interpretation of our evidence is by no means a straightforward matter. It would be possible to say that the child possesses but a single semantic system and, in testing the *syntactic* possibilities of his new language, discovers which of the existing semantic relations are also used in his second language. However, we would then have to explain why in the earlier stages of acquisition he does not "test the syntactic possibilities" of more complex semantic structures which he already possesses. Yet we have seen that he does not do this. The conclusion seems inescapable that the sequential bilingual learner acquires two distinct (though obviously very closely related) semantic systems, i.e. he proceeds under the basic assumption that the new language may express quite different semantic functions. In the event that the two systems are very similar, as they evidently are for Spanish and English, we may speculate that the similar functions come to be identical for the learner. It is this possibility which has made the study of semantic differences in adult bilinguals so problematical.

Güero does not transfer wholesale into English his prior knowledge of Spanish semantic functions. Furthermore, new semantic functions are learned in an orderly progression. These findings lead us to conclude that the semantics of the grammatical functions are distinct from (though, again, intimately related to) the nonlinguistic conceptual system. Güero's cognitive system at age 3.0 is obviously quite advanced. Yet in the early period of acquisition he did not attempt to express semantic relations beyond the most fundamental ones.

Moreover, if the linguistic and nonlinguistic conceptual systems were, in reality, identical, Güero's Spanish semantic system would constitute his total cognitive system which would obviously then be at the child's complete disposal in learning his second language. The basic grammatical relations, as semantic entities, would not need to be learned, and the gradual development that we have described in this paper would have no basis. Thus, not only must the semantic system of a language be considered separate from the conceptual system of experience, we must also consider that each language possesses a different set of semantic relations which makes up the set of grammatical functions that it can express.

References

Bloom, Lois M. 1968. Language Development: Form and Function in Emerging Grammars. Ph.D. dissertation, Columbia University.

Brown, Roger, 1957. Linguistic determinatism and the part of speech. *Journal of Abnormal and Social Psychology* 55, 1–4.

Brown, Roger, Cazden, Courtney, and Bellugi-Klima, Ursula. 1968. The child's grammar from I to III. In J. P. Hill (ed.) *Minnesota Symposia on Child Psychology*, vol. 2. Minneapolis: University of Minnesota Press, 28–73.

Brown, Roger and Hanlon, C. 1970. Derivational complexity and order of acquisition in child speech. In J. R. Hayes (ed.) *Cognition and the Development of Language*. New York: Wiley, 11–53.

Dulay, Heidi C. and Burt, Marina K. 1975a. Creative construction in second language learning and teaching. In M. K. Burt and H. C. Dulay (eds.) *New Directions in Second Language Learning, Teaching and Bilingual Education*. Washington, D.C.: TESOL, 21–32.

————. 1975b. A new approach to discovering universals in child second language acquisition. In Daniel Dato (ed.) *26th Annual Roundtable: Developmental Psycholinguistics* (Monograph Series on Languages and Linguistics), Washington, D.C.: Georgetown University Press, 209–233.

————. 1974. Errors and strategies in child second language acquisition. *TESOL Quarterly* 8.2:129–136.

Greenfield, Patricia. 1968. Development of the Holophrase. Unpublished paper, Harvard University, Center for Cognitive Studies. Cited by McNeill (1970), 23–29.

Hernández-Chávez, Eduardo. 1972. Early Code Separation in the Second Language Speech of Spanish-speaking Children. Paper presented at the Stanford Child Language Research Forum, Stanford University, Stanford, California.

————. 1977. The Acquisition of Grammatical Structures by a Mexican-American Child Learning English. Ph.D. dissertation, University of California, Berkeley, California.

Imedadze, N. V. 1960. K psikhologicheskoy prirode rannego dvuyazychiya. *Vopr. Psikhol.* 6:1. 60–68. Translated by Dan I. Slobin in Translation Abstracts #5, Psychology Department, University of California, Berkeley, California.

Leopold, Werner. 1939–1949. *Speech Development of a Bilingual Child: a Linguist's Record*. 4 vols. Evanston, Illinois: Northwestern University Press.

Menyuk, Paula. 1969. Sentences children use. Research Monograph #52. Cambridge: MIT Press.

Mikes, M. 1967. Acquisition des catégoires grammaticales dans le langage de l'enfant. *Enfance* 20:289–298.

Miller, Wick R. and Ervin, Susan M. 1964. The development of grammar in child language. In Ursula Bellugi and Roger Brown (eds.) *The Acquisition of Language*. Monograph of the Society for Research in Child Development 29, 1:9–35.

Milon, John. 1974. The development of negation in English by a second language learner. *TESOL Quarterly* 8:137–43.

McNeill, David. 1970. *The acquisition of language: the study of developmental psycholinguistics*. New York: Harper and Row.

Ravem, Roar. 1968. Language acquisition in second language environment. IRAL 6:175–185.

Richards, J. 1971. Error analysis and second language strategies. *Language Sciences* 17:12–22.

Selinker, Larry. 1972. Interlanguage. IRAL 10:209–231.

Slobin, Dan I. 1973. Cognitive prerequisites for the development of grammar. In Charles A. Ferguson and Dan I. Slobin, (eds.) *Studies of Child Language Development*. Holt, Rinehart, and Winston, Inc., 175–208.

151

The Monitor Model for Adult Second Language Performance

Stephen D. Krashen

This paper presents a model of adult second language performance that attempts to account for several perplexing phenomena, such as discrepancies in oral and written second language performance, differences between careful classroom speech and students' casual conversation, and the observation that certain students display a firm grasp of the structure of the target language yet seem unable to function in the language, while others do poorly on structure tests and appear to be able to communicate quite well.

It is proposed that adult second language learners concurrently develop two possibly independent systems for second language performers, one *acquired*, developed in ways similar to first language acquisition in children, and the other *learned*, developed consciously and most often in formal situations. The phenomena mentioned above, as well as certain experimental results, can be accounted for by positing a model in which adult linguistic production in second languages is made possible by the acquired system, with the learned system acting only as a monitor. The monitor, when conditions permit, inspects and sometimes alters the output of the acquired system.

Language Acquisition and Language Learning

The technical term language *acquisition* is used here to refer to the way linguistic abilities are internalized "naturally," that is, without conscious focusing on linguistic forms. It appears to

152

require, minimally, participation in natural communication situations, and is the way children gain knowledge of first and second languages. Research in language acquisition has indicated that the acquired system may develop, through a process of "creative construction," in a series of stages common to all acquirers of a given language, resulting from the application of universal strategies (Brown, 1973; Slobin, 1973; Ervin-Tripp, 1973; Dulay and Burt, 1974b and 1975a). Each successive stage approximates more closely the adult native speaker's set of rules (Brown, 1973; Klima and Bellugi, 1966; Dulay and Burt, 1974a).

Language acquisition is a subconscious process. Language *learning*, on the other hand, is a conscious process, and is the result of either a formal language learning situation or a self-study program. Formal learning situations are characterized by the presence of feedback or error correction, largely absent in acquisition environments, and "rule isolation," the presentation of artificial linguistic environments that introduce just one new aspect of grammar at a time (Krashen and Seliger, 1975).

The "switch" from acquisition to learning has been thought to occur at around puberty (Lenneberg, 1967). The model presented here, while maintaining the acquisition-learning distinction, modifies this view. While most language teaching systems presume that second language skills are best gained by adults via learning (Newmark, 1971, describes an interesting exception), there is some suggestive evidence that adults are able to acquire language to at least some extent.

First, several recent studies have found that errors made by adults in second language learning are, to a large extent, common to learners with different mother tongues, and are analyzable as incorrect hypotheses about the second language, as are errors made by first language acquirers (Buteau, 1970; Richards, 1971). These results are consistent with the hypothesis that adults have access to the creative construction process, or language acquisition. Other hints of adult acquisition can be found in studies by Braine (1971) and Wakefield, Doughtie, and Yom (1974) (see Krashen, 1975, for extended discussion).

The most spectacular evidence for adult acquisition, however, comes from research that shows that under certain conditions, adult second language learners show a difficulty order for aspects of second language grammar that is very similar to that seen in younger acquirers, indicating some similarity in language processing between children and adults. The details of these studies, to be discussed below, provide direct evidence for the Monitor Model of adult second language performance.

When "the Monitor" Operates

The Monitor Model for Adult Second Language Performance

learning (the Monitor)

acquisition ——————————————————————output
(a creative construction
    process)

The diagram illustrates the operation of the Monitor Model for syntax in adult second language speech production. Speech production is initiated in adult second language by an acquired system. When conditions allow, the consciously learned system can intrude and alter the syntactic shape of the utterance before it is spoken.

The existence of the Monitor in first language use was first suggested by Labov (1970), who noted that under conditions in which monitoring would be difficult, earlier acquired dialects became evidenced in speech production. Labov suggested that maintenance of prestige forms that are learned later in life is done via conscious audio-monitoring, and these forms may fall away when conditions make monitoring difficult ("when the speaker is tired, distracted, or unable to hear himself"—Labov, 1970, p. 35). We are suggesting here that similar principles apply to adult second language performance.

The model predicts that the nature of second language performance errors will depend on whether monitoring is in operation. Errors that result from performance based on the acquired system alone will be consistent across learners/acquirers, regardless of first language, as acquisition is guided by universal principles. Errors that result from situations in which monitoring is possible will be more idiosyncratic, as they will reflect each learner's conscious mental representation of linguistic regularities in the target language. These predictions are borne out by the experimental data in the literature: we find the "natural order"—the child's acquisition or difficulty order—just in those

154

situations where monitoring appears to be most difficult. Bailey, Madden, and Krashen (1974) evaluated adult ESL performance for eight grammatical morphemes, and reported a difficulty order that was very similar to that seen in children acquiring English as a second language (Dulay and Burt, 1973; see Krashen, Madden, and Bailey, 1975, for an extended discussion of much of the literature on grammatical morpheme sequences). The first languages of the subjects did not seem to affect the results; Spanish and non-Spanish speakers performed nearly identically. The Bailey et al. data was elicited using the field test version of the *Bilingual Syntax Measure* (BSM) (Burt, Dulay, and Hernández, 1973), which consists of a set of cartoons and an accompanying set of questions which the subject is asked. The BSM is designed to elicit a range of syntactic and morphological structures in natural conversation.

Larsen-Freeman (1975) also used the BSM for adult ESL learners and got similar results: the difficulty order she obtained was nearly identical to that found in Bailey et al. and was not significantly different from that found in children acquiring English as a second language. Larsen-Freeman, however, also administered four other tests that clearly focused on artificial problem-solving rather than on just natural communication: Listening (choosing which of three spoken sentences correctly describes a picture), Reading (choosing which of three spoken sentences or sentence fragments is correct in the context of a story), Writing (filling in blank spaces in a story context), and Imitation. From Larsen-Freeman's description and personal communication it seems that these extra tests, with the possible exception of Imitation, did not focus on natural communication, as did the BSM. Larsen-Freeman found that they gave less consistent and somewhat different rank orderings of the grammatical morphemes studied. There was less agreement among different first language groups, and the orderings produced by the different tasks were not identical. This could mean that these tasks were tapping a non-linguistic problem-solving ability that is not necessarily utilized in natural conversation or in the performance of tasks such as the BSM.[1]

---

[1] It is interesting to note that the Imitation test, which probably allowed the least monitoring time of all the supplementary tests, showed the most consistency in rank order across subjects, next to the BSM.

Similarly, Krashen, Sferlazza, Feldman, and Fathman (1976) found the "natural order" for adults on Fathman's SLOPE test, an oral production test involving 20 structures of English. Again, no difference among different first language groups was found; the adult rank order correlated significantly with the child second language order (Fathman, 1975; Dulay and Burt, 1974a); and again, the conditions were such that little monitoring was likely to have occurred. Also, no significant rank order difference was found between "formal" learners—those who had a great deal of ESL schooling and little informal exposure—and "informal" learners—those who had acquired nearly all their target language competence outside the classroom. This result is predicted by the Monitor Model: the formal learners did not have sufficient time for the intrusion of their consciously learned knowledge. A written version of the SLOPE revealed changes in the rank order. High accuracy prevented rank ordering, but there were obvious changes that were consistent with the model. For example, the third-person-singular ending for verbs, an item that is acquired relatively late but learned (or at least presented) very early, jumped in rank from 19/20 to 8/20.

Individual Differences

A virtue of the Monitor Model, as well as a demonstration of its validity, is its ability to predict variation in second language learning among adults. The model predicts that performers will vary with respect to the degree to which conscious monitoring is used. At one extreme, there are performers who seem to monitor whenever possible, and who therefore show variable performance. A good example is a subject studied by Krashen and Pon (1975), who analyzed the errors made in casual (unmonitored) speech by a very advanced speaker of English as a second language. This subject was a woman in her 40s who had spent many years in the United States and who began to learn English as an adult. This analysis showed that nearly all the subject's errors were correctable by the subject herself. When presented with an error that she had made in casual speech, the subject was able to recognize it as an error and give the correct form. Her gaps did not, therefore, represent only those areas of English syntax that were conceptually too difficult but were in easily describable domains. She was also capable of describing the relevant rules that were broken in the errors she made. Analysis of the subject's written (academic) English revealed virtually no errors.

What is hypothesized is that this subject's unguarded speech production is governed by her acquired system alone. This acquired system has evolved to a point close to, but not identical with, the native speaker's grammar, or has "fossilized" (Selinker, 1972).[2] She is able, however, to achieve the illusion of native-like speech in situations where she can utilize her monitor, such as in slow speech and writing.

Cohen and Robbins (1976) describe two similar cases in their in-depth study of learner characteristics. Ue-lin, like Krashen and Pon's subject, is able to self-correct her own errors and describes her errors as "careless." She reports that she likes to be corrected and has the practice of going over the teacher's corrections of her written work. Her background includes formal training in English in her own country. Eva, another Monitor user, makes some very revealing statements that indicate an awareness of the utilization of conscious rules to alter to pre-production written output:

> . . . sometimes I would write something the way I speak. We say a word more or less in a careless way. But if I take my time, sometimes go over it, that would be much easier . . . Whenever I go over something or take my time, then the rules come to my mind.

At the other extreme are adult second language performers who do not seem to use a Monitor at all, even when conditions would allow it. Such performers, like first language acquirers,

---

[2] Note that the use of the term "fossilized" to mean an acquired form that is not equivalent to the native speaker's rule and has ceased its evolution toward the native speaker's rule is quite similar to Selinker's use of the term. Selinker notes that "fossilized forms tend to remain as potential performance, re-emerging in the productive performance of an IL (interlanguage) even when seemingly eradicated. Many of these phenomena reappear in IL performance when the learner's attention is focused on new and difficult intellectual subject matter or when he is in a state of anxiety or other excitement, and strangely enough, sometimes when he is in a state of extreme relaxation." In terms of the model presented here, the imperfectly acquired grammar manifests itself when the speaker, for one reason or another, does not monitor his or her speech.

are not influenced by error correction (which speaks directly to the Monitor), and rarely utilize conscious linguistic knowledge in second language performance.

An example of such a performer is Hung, also described by Cohen and Robbins. Hung is, for the most part, unable to self-correct his own errors in written English and does not have a conscious knowledge of the rules he breaks. When he does attempt to self-correct, he reports that he does so by "feel." ("It just sounds right.") Hung reported that his English background was nearly entirely "submersion." He came to the United States at ten and did not receive formal training in ESL. Also, he reports that he does not like "grammar."

The Monitor Model predicts other possibilities. For example, one often sees performers who claim that rules are very important in second language performance, but who in reality admit that they hardly ever use them. On the other hand, one also sees performers whose overconcern with conscious rules prevents them from speaking with any fluency at all. For case histories of such performers, see Covitt and Stafford (1976).

Aptitude and Attitude

The Monitor Model also allows a parsimonious explanation for what had appeared to be a mysterious finding: both language aptitude (as measured by standard language aptitude tests) and language attitude (affective variables) are related to adult second language achievement, but are not related to each other.

Aptitude appears to relate directly to Monitor competence, and its effects appear when the tests involved encourage monitoring. The significant positive correlation found between test scores and high foreign language grades (Pimsleur, 1966) is consistent with this, as grades are generally a reflection of performance on such tests.

Attitude measures, such as integrative motivation, empathic capacity, and favorable attitudes toward the learning situation (summarized in Schumann, 1975), appear to relate directly to acquisition. Since the acquired system is necessary for all language production, this means that affective variables will show a relationship to second language proficiency for all tests of second language performance in adults.[3]

In Monitor-free measures of second language proficiency, we would expect to see a stronger relation to attitude and little if any relation to aptitude. Consistent with this are Lambert and Gardner's findings that integrative motivation and second language proficiency are consistently related "especially in the oral-aural features of proficiency" (Gardner and Lambert, 1972, p. 130).

Conclusion

It has been suggested here that while children inevitably *acquire* language, adults both *acquire* and *learn*. Given this, the ideal classroom might be one in which both acquisition and learning are possible. Experienced teachers know this already: the creative construction process is stimulated by contextualized exercises and the opportunity to use natural language (see e.g. Dulay and Burt, 1975b), while clear presentation of grammatical rules and selective error correction may be effective for those in class who are "Monitor-users."

References

Bailey, N., Madden, C., and Krashen, S. 1974. Is there a "natural sequence" in adult second language learning? *Language Learning* 24:235–243.

Braine, M. 1971. On two types of models of the internalization of grammars. In D. Slobin (ed.) *The Ontogenesis of Language*. New York: Academic Press, 153–186.

Brown, R. 1973. *A first language*. Cambridge, Mass.: Harvard University Press.

Burt, M., Dulay, H., and Hernández-Chávez, E. 1973. *Bilingual syntax measure* (Field Test Edition). New York: Harcourt Brace Jovanovich.

---

[3] Chastain's finding (Chastain, 1975) that both attitude and aptitude variables (reserved versus outgoing personality type and verbal SAT respectively) were related to high school foreign language grades supports this, as do Gardner's findings (Gardner, 1966; in Gardner and Lambert, 1972) that "school French achievement" subtests given to English speaking Montreal high school students relate to both aptitude (Carroll-Sapon Foreign Language Aptitude Battery) and attitude (integrative motivation) measures.

Buteau, M. 1970. Students' errors and the learning of French as a second language: a pilot study. *International Review of Applied Linguistics* 8:133–145.

Chastain, K. 1975. Affective and ability factors in second language learning. *Language Learning* 25:153–161.

Cohen, A. and Robbins, M. 1976. Toward assessing interlanguage performance: The relationship between selected errors, learners' characteristics, and learners' explanations. *Language Learning* 26, 45–66.

Covitt, G. and Stafford, C. 1976. An Investigation of the Monitor Theory. Presentation at the USC-UCLA Second Language Acquisition Forum, May 1976.

Dulay, H. and Burt, M. 1973. Should we teach children syntax? *Language Learning* 23, 245–258.

————. 1974a. Natural sequences in child second language acquisition. *Language Learning* 24, 37–53.

————. 1974b. A new perspective on the creative construction process in child second language acquisition. *Language Learning* 24, 253–278.

————. 1975a. A new approach to discovering universal strategies of child second language acquisition. In D. Dato (ed.), GURT 1975: *Developmental Psycholinguistics: Theory and Application*. Washington, D.C.: Georgetown University Press, 209–233.

————. 1975b. Creative construction in second language learning and teaching. In M. Burt and H. Dulay (eds.) *New Directions in Second Language Learning, Teaching, and Bilingual Education*. Washington, D.C.: TESOL.

Ervin-Tripp, S. 1973. Some strategies for the first two years. In A. Dil (ed.) *Language Acquisition and Communicative Choice*. Stanford: Stanford University Press, 204–238.

Fathman, A. 1975. Age, language background, and the order of acquisition of English structures. In M. Burt and H. Dulay (eds.) *New Directions in Second Language Learning, Teaching, and Bilingual Education*. Washington, D.C.: TESOL, 33–43.

Gardner, R. and Lambert, W. 1972. *Attitudes and motivation in second language learning*. Rowley, Mass.: Newbury House.

Klima, E. and Bellugi, U. 1966. Syntactic regularities in the speech of children. In J. Lyons and R. Wales (eds.) *Psycholinguistic Papers*. Edinburgh: Edinburgh University Press.

Krashen, S. 1975. A Model of Adult Second Language Performance. Paper presented at the Winter meeting of the Linguistic Society of America. December 1975.

Krashen, S., Madden, C., and Bailey, N. 1975. Theoretical aspects of mal instruction in adult second language learning. *TESOL Quarterly* 9, 173–183.

Krashen, S. and Pon, P. 1975. An error analysis of an advanced ESL learner: The importance of the monitor. *Working Papers on Bilingualism* 7, 125–129.

Krashen, S., Madden, C., and Bailey, N. 1975. Theoretical aspects of grammatical sequencing. In M. Burt and H. Dulay (eds.) *New Directions in Second Language Learning, Teaching, and Bilingual Education.* Washington, D.C.: TESOL, 44–54.

Krashen, S., Sferlazza, V., Feldman, L., and Fathman, A. 1976. Adult performance on the SLOPE test: More evidence for a natural sequence in adult second language acquisition. *Language Learning* 26, 145–152.

Labov, W. 1970. *The study of nonstandard English.* Urbana, Illinois: National Council of Teachers of English.

Larsen-Freeman, D. 1975. The acquisition of grammatical morphemes by adult ESL students. *TESOL Quarterly* 9, 409–420.

Lenneberg, E. 1967. *Biological foundations of language.* New York: Wiley.

Newmark, L. 1971. A minimal language teaching program. In P. Pimsleur and T. Quinn (eds.) *The Psychology of Second Language Learning.* Cambridge, Mass.: Harvard University Press, 11–18.

Pimsleur, P. 1966. Testing foreign language learning. In A. Valdman (ed.) *Trends in Language Teaching.* New York: McGraw-Hill, 175–214.

Richards, J. 1971. Error analysis and second language strategies. *Language Sciences* 17, 12–22.

Schumann, J. 1975. Second Language Acquisition: The Pidginization Hypothesis. Doctoral Dissertation, Harvard University.

Selinker, L. 1972. Interlanguage. *International Review of Applied Linguistics* 10, 209–231.

Slobin, D. 1973. Cognitive prerequisites for the development of grammar. In C. Ferguson and D. Slobin (eds), *Studies of Child Language Development.* New York: Holt, Rinehart and Winston, 175–208.

Wakefield, J., Doughtie, E., and Yom, B. 1974. The identification of structural components of an unknown language. *Journal of Psycholinguistic Research* 3, 261–269.

If Only I Could Remember It All! Facts and Fiction about Memory in Language Learning.

Wilga M. Rivers
Bernice S. Melvin

At times, it seems that we don't need to remember things any more. We have computers to do it for us. We have all these information retrieval systems which store everything we need to know—if we could only remember what it is we need to know. Our computers are insatiable and seem to have infinite memory banks. But they too have problems remembering many things— such as who has already paid what to whom. These problems with retrieval of relevant information and identification of correct relationships make our computers seem exasperatingly human. A memory bank of itself is not sufficient to simulate a "good memory." It is the way the computer moves through various procedures and routines that counts, that is, its memory in action—sorting, selecting, and interrelating.

Just "remembering it all" can actually be a curse rather than a blessing. Luria, the Soviet psychologist, tells the pathetic story of a man who could remember everything (1968). He was not a happy man. He had difficulties functioning efficiently from the intellectual point of view, because "remembering it all" made forgetting impossible. As a result, all kinds of material which might be quite irrelevant at the time remained vividly present in his mind, making it, in Bruner's words, "a kind of junk heap of impressions."[1]

---

[1] J. Bruner in Foreword to Luria, 1968, p. viii.

On first acquaintance, Luria's subject "struck one as a disorganized and rather dull-witted person" (1968, p. 65). He became very confused, for instance, when details of a story came at him at a fairly rapid pace, because for him each word called up images which, as he put it, "collide with one another, and the result is chaos." Because he remembered specific images for each word, he was never able to single out the key points in a passage. When he later gave performances as a mnemonist, for which he had to remember long lists of numbers that had been written on a blackboard, lists from previous performances, although already erased, would appear before his eyes as he studied the board (1968, pp. 68–69). It seems, then, we can be thankful that we can't remember it all.

When we talk about having a good memory, a bad memory, or a memory like a sieve, we are talking as though memory were an object: some part of us of a certain size, shape, and state of health, that can be precisely located and into which we can stuff things to be withdrawn as we require them. Neuropsychologists tried for years to locate "the memory." (Phrenologists thought they had found it.) Aphasics who are injured in various areas of the brain "forget" some things, but certainly not all. They forget the strangest things: one language, but not another; the ability to write but not to read; the ability to read letters but not numbers. With aphasics, some parts of the brain seem to pick up where other parts have left off, especially with young children.

We begin to understand this failure to locate a "memory" when we consider Miller's statement: "many psychologists prefer to speak of memory as something a person *does*, rather than something he *has*" (1966). Or as Jenkins puts it, "The mind remembers what the mind *does*, not what the world does" (1973). The mind does not just register impressions (visual, auditory, tactile, or kinesthetic), storing perfect images of them somewhere, so that they may be conjured up anew at will at a later period. Rather, the mind takes what it experiences (not everything but only what fits its perceived purposes) and then processes these experiences in many different ways, not only while it is preparing them for storage but also while they are being held in store. (Here we may think of the ways different eyewitnesses recall what they saw and the ways in which their individual accounts may vary at a retrial.)

The interesting questions for us, then, concern what the mind does with the material it encounters and how to present new knowledge, particularly of a second language, in such a way that it will remain and be retrievable in a usable form. Without becoming technical, we can draw some interesting implications from recent research into memory processes and see what these imply for second language comprehension and production. For the purposes of this article we will draw mainly from information-processing and conceptual memory research.[2]

In second-language teaching, the main form in which "memory work" has entered the classroom has been as memorization, or as repetition with minimal, formal variation, as a means of storing in the memory potentially useful material from the new language. Phrases and complete utterances have been memorized (taken from dialogues or derived from classroom activity). Vocabulary has been memorized, often in lists with native-language "equivalents" or with pictures (a procedure which parallels the paired-associate list learning of early memory experiments in the Ebbinghaus tradition). Rules have been memorized in the form of paradigm tables or as verbal instructions like "put the indirect object before the direct object." Another form of rule-learning has been through practice with frames demonstrating rules, as in simple substitution drills where the frame is committed to memory through its repeated use, as minimal, cued changes are made in slots (e.g. he gave them the book: *her:* he gave her the book).

Each of these procedures reflects an associationist stimulus-response approach to learning: if a stimulus and a response occur frequently enough in association with each other in a reasonably satisfying (successful) activity, the bond between them will be strengthened and the stimulus, when it appears again, will tend to call forth the response. The repetition of the operation presumably strengthens the memory trace. This says something about a view of learning, but very little about the operation of

---

[2] The theoretical discussion underlying the practical recommendations in this article, with bibliographic references, will be found in B. S. Melvin and W. M. Rivers, In one ear and out the other: implications of memory studies for language learning, in J. Fanselow and R. Crymes, *On TESOL 1976* (Washington, D. C.: TESOL, 1976) and W. M. Rivers and B. S. Melvin, Memory and memorization in comprehension and production: contributions of IP theory," *Canadian Modern Language Review* (in press).

memory which here is clearly considered to be a passive register of impressions.

If the stimulus is simple enough and designed to elicit only one particular response, the results of such procedures will be as anticipated. Students given the practiced cue will produce the learned response. The native-language word or a picture of the object will evoke the vocabulary word in the new language. An instance of the frame accompanied by a cue will elicit the frame incorporating the cue. An instruction to recite the paradigm, or even the first item of the paradigm given as a cue, will call forth the paradigm. A situation cue (John Doe meets Jane in the supermarket) will precipitate recitation of the dialogue (*Good morning, Jane. How are you? Fine, thanks. I'm doing my shopping . . .*), since dialogues memorized verbatim purely for the sake of memorization are a form of list-learning. As a consequence, results on tests which reproduce the original material in the form in which it was learned will show commendable results.

There is some place for simple stimulus-response association of this type in early second-language learning, mainly for associating the sounds of the language with new writing systems or different spellings, or even new sound combinations with simple, unambiguous, concrete meanings like cat, book, or pencil (in the same way that we can learn to call a cat a fif, if that is what our social group likes to call it). The memorization procedures described above, however, have very little to do with learning a new language for use in unpredictable contexts and bear no relation to the active memory processes which enable language learners to express their intentions (meanings) in new language forms. It is what the mind is *doing* during language-learning activities that will determine what is stored, in what form, and whether it is retrievable and usable in new contexts.

One thing is clear, from both psychological and linguistic research: that language is an exceedingly complicated phenomenon which cannot be reduced to simple stimuli and responses without distorting its true nature and function. Each language utterance, no matter how small or seemingly unitary ("Stop!" for instance) has several layers of complexity: phonological (sounds, intonation, stress, duration), syntactic (its role as a complete utterance in a discourse or as an element in a complete utterance), and semantic (its meaning is not as simple as it ap-

pears: in the appropriate context, not only linguistic but social—
"Stop!" can really mean "I want you to continue, but I know
from my upbringing that I should make at least a token pro-
test"). These layers have complex interrelationships, as do the
individual sounds and, in a longer utterance, the syllables,
words, breath groups, and sentences. How we are able to understand and produce such complex responses, and infinite variations of them, in what are apparently widely differing physical
contexts is in no way explicable in a simplistic stimulus-response
framework.

Furthermore, the mind extracts for storage from each linguistic situation (no matter how apparently limited) abstract features. These it interrelates in complex networks in such a way
that they can be retrieved from the network with quite novel
associations whenever a key or cue is perceived (that is, recognized by the individual as relevant to his or her immediate or
long-term concerns). The word to note here is *perceived*. The
same cue can elicit vastly different responses from the same
individual at different moments and in different contexts. For
instance, a hand held out may elicit a hand in response and
"Good to see you," or a brusque "Get yourself a job!", a turning
away movement, or "A dollar forty, fifty, seventy-five, two.
Thank you. Have a good day."

Such is the complexity of the internal and external responses
to even an apparently simple cue such as "Do you know
Esther?" that any attempt to teach standard, prefabricated responses to such stimuli is like shadowboxing: useful for practicing stance and possible movements, or even as a warming-up
exercise, but only marginally related to the real business of antici-
pating and circumventing an opponent with these practiced
movements.

Real language use is *conceptual* at base. People must have
something to communicate. What they have to say, or what they
comprehend, in normal circumstances is related in some way to
the totality of their experience, which is a vast network of interrelated concepts composing their long-term memory, not just to
their minimal acquaintance with the forms and units of a second
language. What they are learning becomes intricately entwined
with what they already know and in this way it is stored in long-
term memory—that is, it is remembered. This is why we often

166

recall the oddest pieces of information at the oddest moments: unobserved or unexpected cues dredge them up through the interconnections of the semantic networks that we have built up.

Note that these networks are semantic or conceptual and therefore independent of the forms of any language. They are networks of primitive meanings connected by relations, not networks of words. Words of a specific language become linked with various interconnections of the networks when we find they evoke the meanings we intend for our listeners, or help us to interpret what is said to us. Every listening or speaking experience modifies, expands, or strengthens these networks. The second language learner has to connect new forms and new lexical items with known meanings and sometimes to register new meanings for which the first language has not yet established connections. Unfortunately, even for those word-related meanings which already exist in the student's semantic networks, derived for the most part from the first linguistic-cultural experience, there are only some that exactly parallel meanings associated with seemingly equivalent words in the second language. And this can be a trap. The more meaningful connections that are established for the second language, the more readily will the necessary linguistic clothing become available to us as we need it for the expression of our personal intentions.

Since it is experience or use which develops the necessary interconnections, it is experience in using the second language which permits the incorporation of second-language material in the long-term memory. For what we have learned to be usable in many contexts, it must be *experienced in meaningful discourse* (through both hearing and speaking) *in all kinds of novel combinations.* The student has to become uninhibited in extrapolating from one known use to other possible uses in analogous situations (and situations can be analogous in many different ways as perceived by the participant). Furthermore, it is the interrelationships of the conceptual networks that enable students to understand, in oral or graphic form, material which contains words new to them. These comprise the basis for projected expectancies and informed guessing. It is on this potential that inductive approaches to learning like the direct method, which require the student to hypothesize meanings, have always relied. From this point of view, stored experiences from use of a first language can no longer be considered a burden or a negative influence on second language learning; rather, they are a boon, facilitating in many ways the learning of a usable second, third, or fourth language.

"Meaningful" implies not only that all material used should have sequential significance beyond the phrase and the sentence, but also that its meaning, once the new-language code has been penetrated, should be accessible to the language-learner. What is meaningful to the teacher is not necessarily meaningful to the student. "A trapezoid is a quadrilateral having two parallel sides" is meaningful and comprehensible to those who already possess this concept, or who have the constituent concepts in their stored experience, but it is neither meaningful nor comprehensible to those for whom such knowledge is not available in their long-term memory. Second-language material must build on what students know and what arouses their curiosity and interest at their age and in their circumstances, if it is to be effectively integrated into stored experience. The mind will not process what is perceived to be of little account by the individual concerned and it is what the mind does that counts.

What about the rules in this approach? Rules are instructions to be tested in use. They may be given explicitly or understood implicitly through seeing language in action. They serve as a support that ceases to be useful once the procedures they describe can be performed without conscious attention and monitoring. Rules seen as instructions for action will be presented in whatever form is most helpful to a particular group of students, and at the time when, and for as long as, they are clearly useful. They have no importance in themselves, but only insofar as they facilitate the establishment of essential structural routines which make the expression of nuances of meaning possible in the new language.

Vocabulary acquisition also takes on a new coloring in the theoretical approach we have just described. With every word comes a set of possible relationships, so that a word learned out of context is for the most part a useless bauble. Syntactic relations are relations among concepts and cannot be learned apart from the concepts they relate. With every new word, then, we learn its use: words with which it can co-occur and relationships into which it can enter. Put simply: a bucket can tip over, but not buy a hat. This implies that new words and phrases must be learned in meaningful discourse and be used to convey meanings of the student's own creation. What is encountered in a dialogue or reading passage must be immediately put to use in some creative way—through innovative dramatizations, skits, games, the give-and-take of conversation, and discussion.[3]

Since syntactic rules are inextricably interwoven with the expression of specific meanings, they cannot, and should not, be learned in isolation, apart from attempts to convey these meanings. This implies that after introductory familiarization exercises (warming-up routines) practice in syntactic use must be through the expression of the student's own meanings. Any standard grammar drill or exercise can, with a little imagination, be transformed into an activity which requires students to produce their own meanings within the framework of what is being practiced.[4] Students must be actively involved in recreating the relationships into which the second-language elements can enter if they are to store them personally in retrievable form. This is not only the most effective way of practicing new grammatical relationships, but it is also more fun. Every element of the language class must have as its goal the development of confident creators of new meanings in the second language. This approach involves a different view of the class session from that to which many teachers are accustomed. It means encouraging and expecting student initiative and imagination in using the second language in the actual classroom for, as nearly as possible, normal communicative purposes,[5] with the teacher serving as support, informant, and yardstick.

---

[3] For ways to exploit dialogue material in a creative way, see Chapter 1: Structured interaction, in W.M. Rivers and M.S. Temperley, 1977.

[4] Ways of converting intensive practice exercises from Type A (manipulative) to Type B (creative) are discussed in Chapter 4: Oral drills for the learning of grammar, in Rivers and Temperley, 1977, and in From linguistic competence to communicative competence, *TESOL Quarterly* 7 (March, 1973), pp. 25-34, reprinted in W.M. Rivers, Speaking in Many Tongues, expanded 2d ed. (Rowley, Mass.: Newbury House, 1976).

[5] For normal purposes of language in communication, see Rivers and Temperley (1977), Chapter 2: Autonomous interaction, and W.M. Rivers, The natural and the normal in language learning, in H.D. Brown, ed., *Papers in Second Language Acquisition*, Special Issue No. 4, *Language Learning* (Jan., 1976).

Since we remember what the mind *does,* rather than what it encounters, importance must be given to listening to (and reading) the language as it is actually used. In this way, the mind has many opportunities to extract from the material it is perceiving features of various kinds which it attempts to interrelate within the bounds of its experience, hypothesizing meanings until further experience confirms or invalidates the hypotheses. In this way, it is building up abstract representations at the various levels which can later serve as the framework for more precise relationships. Carroll has proposed a two-stream system for this language-learning experience (Carroll, 1974). The first stream would consist of material just within the current capabilities of the students, so that it is meaningful to them: the working stock of regular learning experiences. The second stream would present unrestricted discourse of an authentic character of interest to the students. The latter stream would permit them to experience the full range of the syntactic, intonational, and lexical forms of normal discourse and provide them with essential opportunities to hypothesize, test out hypotheses, and "pretune" themselves to the perception of forms they would later learn to use. The material of this second stream would be enjoyed as experience, but not rigidly tested. Authentic material of this type is already provided in classrooms where students have frequent opportunities to listen to songs and poems for pure enjoyment or to hear unedited newscasts and watch films in order to see how much information they can derive from them, even before they can follow all that is said. In a second-language classroom, radio and television commercials are also useful in this regard. (If one wishes to avoid the impact of the selling pitch, these materials can be used for a study of methods of persuasion and ways of breaking down buyer resistance in the second culture.) Teachers should create more of these real-language opportunities by telling stories and recounting anecdotes freely during class lessons or by inviting interesting speakers of the second language into the classroom for free discussion with the teacher while students listen and try to participate when they can.

Blumenthal (1970) describes language as "the intellectual living space of those who use it." It is encouraging to those of us who teach a second language to see ourselves as vastly increasing the dimensions of this "intellectual living space" for our students. Are we deluding ourselves or do we see this goal being realized for the students in our care? Do we see exploration, experimentation and enthusiasm for using the language naturally and comfortably? Whether we achieve our goal or merely aspire to it will be decided largely by the opportunities we provide for our students to move around freely within the second language and make it their own.

References

Blumenthal, A.L. 1970. *Language and psychology.* New York: John Wiley and Sons, 243.

Carroll, J.B. 1974. Learning theory for the classroom teacher. In G.A. Jarvis (ed.) *The Challenge of Communication.* ACTFL Review of Foreign Language Education, vol., 6, Skokie, Ill.: National Textbook Company.

Jenkins, J.J. 1973. Language and memory. In G.A. Miller, *Communication, language, and meaning: psychological perspectives.* New York: Basic Books, 170.

Luria, A.R. 1968. *The mind of a mnemonist: a little book about a vast memory.* Trans. by L. Solotaroff. New York: Basic Books.

Miller, G.A. 1966. *Psychology: the science of mental life.* Harmonsworth, Middlesex, U.K.: Pelican Books, 192.

Rivers, W.M. and Temperley, M.S. 1977. *A practical guide to the teaching of English: as a second or foreign language.* New York: Oxford University Press.

Attitude Variables in Second Language Learning

John W. Oller, Jr.

Perhaps it is not inappropriate for a brief paper on the role of attitudes in second language acquisition to begin with a few words on attitudes toward research. There is probably no topic in sociolinguistics that is more elusive, abstract, and subjective in nature than the topic of attitudes and their effect on learning a second language. Therefore, it is important that the methods of investigation applied to such a subject be as sharp, impartial, and systematic as is possible.

Some years ago, John R. Platt offered the startling observation that not all science is equal, that "certain systematic methods of scientific thinking may produce much more rapid progress than others" (1964, p. 347). He argued that the astounding progress in some fields, as compared to the lack of it in others, was attributable not to the "tractability of the subject," nor to the "size of the research grants," nor yet to the "quality" of the people doing the work, but rather to a difference of intellectual approach. He referred to "the discoveries" that regularly "leap from the headlines" in fields like "molecular biology and high-energy physics" while there are "other areas of science that are sick by comparison because they have forgotten the necessity for alternative hypotheses and disproof" (p. 350).

Platt urged a return to the fundamentals of "the simple and old-fashioned method of inductive inference that goes back at least to Francis Bacon" (p. 347). Platt was speaking of a beefed-up version of the method for which he proposed the term "strong inference." It differs from the Baconian approach only in the inclusion of multiple working hypotheses (as advocated by T. C. Chamberlin as early as 1897) and in its systematic regular recycling through the well-known steps of (1) formulating clear alternative hypotheses, (2) devising crucial experiments to eliminate some of them, and (3) carrying out the experiments. By adding step (4), namely, recycling the procedure with subsequent hypotheses "to refine the possibilities that remain" (p. 347), Platt argued that the researcher almost guarantees a spiraling process of growth from theory to data to theory to data with greater explanatory power achieved in every cycle.

It is commonly believed that the subject matter of the social sciences is such that the method Platt was advocating is less applicable there than in the so-called hard sciences. Yet the criticisms he offered of some of the work in the hard sciences would be just as appropriate for some of the research in applied linguistics, sociolinguistics, and attitude research. Consider "The Frozen Method. The Eternal Surveyor. The Never Finished. The Great Man with a Single Hypothesis. The Little Club of Dependents. The Vendetta. The All-Encompassing Theory Which Can Never Be Falsified" (p. 350). Is there not a familiar ring here? Surely such criticisms are as applicable to linguistics and other social sciences as they are to fields like chemistry which happened to be the one that Platt was addressing. He said, "We are all sinners, and . . . in every field . . . we need to try to formulate multiple alternative hypotheses sharp enough to be capable of disproof" (p. 351).

Platt observed further that "disproof is a hard doctrine. If you have a hypothesis and I have another hypothesis, evidently one of them must be eliminated. The scientist seems to have no choice but to be either soft-headed or disputatious. Perhaps this is why so many tend to resist the strong analytical approach—and why some great scientists are so disputatious" (p. 350).

There does not seem to be any reason to expect the Eternal Surveyor method of sociolinguistics, (or the Great Man with a Single Hypothesis, or the Ruling Theory approach) to be any more successful in the social sciences than it has been in the hard sciences. Is there any reason to expect the method of strong inference not to afford an improvement in research in our own little corner of the social sciences? Can it be any less effective

173

than the Eternal Surveyor or the Ruling Theory which have, sad to say, been so characteristic of much of the work in our area? (And I say "our", for I too am numbered among the sinners doing research in applied linguistics and more recently in sociolinguistics and attitudes.)

It seems that now is a good time at least to try to apply the method of strong inference to some of the perplexing questions of sociolinguistics—in this case, to the questions about the sort of relationship that may exist between attitude variables and the learning of a second or foreign language. First, we might ask what plausible hypotheses can be (or have been) posited about the nature of the possible relationship? Second, what evidence exists or could be acquired experimentally which could be used to exclude (disprove) some of the plausible alternative hypotheses? And third, what avenues of investigation may be expected to clarify some of the remaining possibilities?

In 1949 W. R. Jones published a pioneering study on the topic of attitudes toward learning a second language and a year later he reported results showing a positive, though not strong, correlation between measures of attitude and attainment in Welsh studied as a second language. One of his conclusions was that attitudes tended to become less positive as the students progressed farther in their study, and another was that the strength of the correlation between attitude and attainment tended to increase. Interestingly, R. C. Gardner (1974) advanced a somewhat different view: " . . . in the initial phases of second language learning, motivational variables are relatively more important than are language aptitude and intelligence. As the student becomes more proficient, aptitude and intelligence take on greater significance" (Desrochers, Smythe, and Gardner, Abstract 105, 1975). Although Gardner refers to additional variables and their relative importance, it is possible to distill mutually contradictory hypotheses from his statement and from Jones's conclusions: to wit (H1)[1] the strength of the relationship between attitudes and achievement increases with increments of time versus (H2) the relationship becomes weaker under the same conditions. An-

---

[1] The system of numbering hypotheses is used merely for the sake of convenience. It is not intended to establish priorities, nor should they be inferred from it.

other possibility is (H3) that the relationship tends to remain unchanged. However, to focus attention on such questions leaves a fundamental question unanswered, namely, whether the relationship is strong enough in the first place to merit such attention.

If one is interested in explaining the variance in language acquisition, the crucial question becomes how much of that variability is contributed by attitude variables, and how much is contributed by other variables. In a paper in 1969, Spolsky suggested that among the factors believed to contribute to variance in second language learning were "method, age, aptitude, and attitude" (p. 404). This suggestion hints at the hub of the question, yet most of the research seems to be directed at the periphery. There are other factors besides the ones Spolsky mentions that might be expected to affect the rate and ultimate leveling off point of foreign or second language learning, but little research has been directed at determining the relative strengths of the contributions of just the four factors he suggests. Another important factor may be the type of learning context in which the language learning takes place. Given the availability of the right sorts of experiences outside of the classroom, it may make little difference what the second language teaching methods are, or what the ages of the learners are, or their aptitudes. Yet such questions can hardly be posed in a meaningful way until research is directed toward the relative strength of the contribution of a variety of factors to second language learning.

It is true that Gardner, Smythe, Clement, and Gliksman (1976) have argued that the strength of the relationship between attitude variables and attained language proficiency is at least as great as the relationship between aptitude and attained proficiency. In commenting on a number of studies, they say that "the various studies differed with respect to the nature and number of variables investigated, but the conclusion warranted from all the studies was that motivational variables were related to second language achievement, and where such comparisons were possible, that the motivational variables were as highly related to second-language achievement as were the indices of language aptitude" (p. 199). In another context, Gardner (1975) mentions the fact that several studies have shown "that measures of motivation and attitudes toward the second-language community (in that order) account for more of the variance in continuing versus dropping the course than does language aptitude" (Gardner, 1975, p. 24)

All of this suggests the hypothesis (H4) that the relationship between attitude variables and variance in second language learning is quite strong—we might expect that the variance in language learning which could be accounted for by attitude variables might be above say, 25%. Another possible alternative is (H5) that the variance which can be explained by measures of attitude variables might be much less—below 10%. And yet another plausible alternative is that the amount of predictable variance in language acquisition attributable to attitude variables might vary with the learning context. For instance, consider (H6) that the relationship may be substantially stronger in contexts where many opportunities to communicate with the target language group are available, and substantially weaker in contexts where a relatively artificial classroom experience is all that is available (cf. Gardner, 1975, p. 30).

Let us return to a further consideration of the evidence that already exists concerning the strength of the relationship. Supposedly it is about the same as the relationship between aptitude and attainment. In 1967 John B. Carroll reported some of the results on a large and extensive study entitled "Foreign language proficiency levels attained by language majors near graduation from college." Among the variables investigated were scores on the *Modern Language Aptitude Test* (Carroll and Sapon, 1958). This may well be the most widely used and most imitated language aptitude test in existence. Of the 2,172 subjects on whom appropriate scores were available, 1,039 were graduating majors in French, 289 in German, 80 in Russian, and 764 in Spanish. The numbers certainly ought to be sufficient to give a fair indication of the strength of the relationship between aptitude and attained proficiency even in the case of the relatively small group of Russian students. Although a variety of language proficiency measures were used, only correlations of the three available aptitude subtest scores with the MLA Listening scores are reported. The results are interpreted by Carroll as showing that "language aptitude is significantly associated with success in foreign language study," but he goes on to say that "the association is not very strong" (p. 139). In fact, an inspection of the only reported data

176

in Table 8 (Carroll, 1967, p. 149) reveals that in exactly half of the cases, the relationship is not even significant ($p> .05$), and in none of the significant cases does the reported beta coefficient (i.e. simple correlation) exceed .17. This can be interpreted roughly as meaning that no single subtest on the MLAT (short form) accounted for as much as 3% of the variance in the Listening proficiency scores. Perhaps the correlations with other proficiency measures might have been higher, but though other matrices were apparently computed (Carroll refers to the results in Table 8 as "typical"), they are not reported. Thus, if attitude variables usually account for about as much variance in language proficiency as do reputable measures of aptitude, they account for very little variance at all. All of this evidence would have to be taken as favoring H5 stated above, and there is more data supporting that hypothesis.

In an extensive and, it would appear, very thorough review of research with attitude and motivation measures of various sorts, Gardner (1975) summarizes relationships observed between 2 measures of language proficiency (one a French Vocabulary test, and the other a Free Speech sampling technique) and 17 other measures including 3 aptitude scores and 14 attitude variables. The reported correlations were computed averages from no less than 21 samples of data with an average number of 90 subjects (hence, none of the reported figures should have been derived from less than 1,890 cases). Of the 6 average correlations between aptitude subtests (Spelling Clues, Words in Sentences, and Paired Associates) and the two proficiency measures, the highest was .25, thus accounting for less than 6% of the variance in the language proficiency measure, and of the 28 correlations between attitude variables and the language proficiency criteria, the highest was .29 which accounts for about 9% of the variance on the language proficiency measure in question. All of this evidence too would tend to support H5 rather than H4 stated above.

This is not intended categorically to mean that the relationship between attitude variables and attained language proficiency must be weak, but it is to say that the alternative that it may well be weak has not been excluded. The alternative that it is always strong has been excluded many times, just as the alternative that the relation between aptitude and attained profi-

177

ciency is strong has been excluded several times with large samples of data. There are many remaining possibilities, however, and one of the interesting ones is that the measuring sticks could be improved both for assessing attitude variables and for assessing language proficiency. It is yet possible that Lambert's belief that "beliefs about foreign peoples and about one's own ethnicity are powerful factors in the learning of another group's language and in the maintenance of one's own language" (1974, p. 8) is correct. The trouble is that a number of competing alternatives have not yet been ruled out. What is more disturbing is that the hypothesis that the relationship must be a strong one has now been ruled out many times. It may, nonetheless, be significant and it may be considerably stronger in some situations than in others. It is to these latter possibilities that we now turn our attention.

Gardner (1975) says that "teachers often state that the outgoing, friendly, and talkative student is the more successful second language learner (cf. Valette, 1964), but few empirical studies have attempted to validate this claim" (p. 18). Following this line of thought, we might predict that (H7) the more a learner is self-confident, extroverted, friendly, and willing to take the social risks involved in conversing with speakers of a target language, the more rapid will be his or her progress and the higher will be the ultimate level of attainment of proficiency in that language. This hypothesis presupposes that there is a causal relation between attitudes toward self and members of the target language, and the attainment of proficiency in a target language.

As Nancy Bachman pointed out at a meeting of researchers at the TESOL Convention in New York, March 1976, it is often assumed that (H8) the direction of causation is from attitudes to learning and achievement, but it is certainly plausible that (H9) high levels of attainment or rapid rates of learning may cause positive attitudes, whereas low levels and slow rates might cause negative attitudes. Another possiblity is that (H10) the direction of causation (if in fact one exists) is both from attitudes to attainment and the reverse (cf. Burstall, Jamieson, Cohen, and Hargreaves, 1974).

In a recent, yet unpublished paper, Gardner and Smythe (1976) support a version of H8. They contend that attitude variables are among the factors that contribute to motivation to learn, which is among the factors that eventually produce attainment in the language. They claim that the relationship must be quite indirect. One source of evidence is the apparent weakness of the relationship between attitudes and attained proficiency as demonstrated in many previous studies. They do not mention this but they do show that little variance overlap between attitude measures and various other criteria (including proficiency in the target language) remains once the motivation variance is partialed out. However, H9 and H10 cannot yet be ruled out.

If we assume that a significant causal relationship exists, then one of the obvious factors that would have to be taken into account in testing H7 (that willingness to take social risks is positively correlated with attained levels of proficiency) would be the result obtained in any study of H6 (that the relationship will be stronger in contexts where there are more opportunities to communicate). The combined results of four studies recently completed at the University of New Mexico with two different populations of foreign language learners and two different populations of second language learners support H6 and simultaneously rule out the alternatives that (H11) the relationship will be the same in foreign and second language learning contexts, and (H12) the contrast will reveal a stronger relationship in foreign language contexts.

It is apparently the case that the correlation between attitude variables and attained proficiency tends to be stronger when the learners are in a social context where the density of opportunities to communicate with speakers of the target language is greater. For instance, Oller, Hudson, and Liu (in press) found a correlation of .52 between an attitude factor defined chiefly in terms of the traits "helpful, sincere, kind, reasonable, and friendly" referenced against Americans, and scores on an ESL proficiency test. The subjects were Chinese nationals studying for advanced degrees in Albuquerque or El Paso. For another population (a group of Mexican-American women studying in a Job Corps school in Albuquerque), Oller, Baca, and Vigil (1976) found a correlation of .49 between an attitude factor defined mainly in terms of the traits "calm, conservative, religious, shy, humble, and sincere" referenced against Mexicans, and scores on an ESL proficiency test. Hence, for these two groups of learners of English as a second language, no less than 24% of the variance in the criterion measure could be predicted on the basis of an attitude variable in each case. However, in two studies of

179

different populations of Japanese subjects studying English as a foreign language in Japan (Chihara and Oller, 1976; and Asakawa and Oller, 1976), the maximum amount of variance predicted in the EFL proficiency criterion by any of the attitude factors was less than 8%.

In one of the latter studies (Chihara and Oller, 1976) it was also possible to examine correlations between proficiency scores and a battery of aptitude tests modeled after the MLAT. The highest correlation between an aptitude measure and any one of four distinct proficiency criteria accounted for less than 10% of the variance in the proficiency scores. The next highest (of 12 in all) accounted for less than 5% of the variance in any of the proficiency measures.

Another interesting possibility that has been much discussed in the literature is that different kinds of motivations to learn a target language may produce different rates and ultimate levels of proficiency. In numerous publications and at many professional meetings it has been claimed that (H13) an *integrative* orientation will produce more efficient learning and a higher level of attainment than an *instrumental* orientation. The terms are familiar enough, but their definitions have sometimes been altered to fit the exigencies of a particular sociolinguistic context. Generally, though, an *integrative* orientation can be taken to mean "a high level of drive on the part of the individual to acquire the language of a valued second-language community in order to facilitate communication with that group" (Gardner, et al., 1976, p. 199). An *instrumental* orientation on the other hand can usually be construed as a desire to acquire someone else's language system in order to use that language to achieve other goals such as material advantages, a better job, or a better education.

Unfortunately, the case for the superiority of an integrative orientation over an instrumental one is not closed. A study by Lukmani (1972) showed that an instrumental orientation was as strongly correlated with achievement in English for Marathi-speaking high school students as was an integrative orientation. Moreover, in Gardner's own extensive research summarized in his 1975 review article, he notes, "ratings of integrativeness tend to correlate more highly with achievement than do ratings of instrumentality (. . .), though the differences in correlation often are not significant" (p. 27). One is inclined to seek a refine-

180

ment of H13 that will produce a better fit with the observed data.

The difficulties of interpreting correlations between instrumental and integrative motives for studying a second or foreign language are even more serious. The typical method of assessing a subject's orientation toward the target language or the target language culture has been to ask certain fairly straightforward questions concerning reasons for studying the target language, or the importance (to the respondent) of possible reasons for travel to a country where the language is spoken. One of the problems is that subjects may tend to answer such questions in terms of what they think the question writer wants to hear, or what seems to be a socially acceptable response (e.g., one that makes the respondent appear acceptable by some definition). Another well-known difficulty is that the same question may mean different things to different people, or worse yet, different things to the same person depending on what happens to be on his mind at the moment. For instance, as Gardner (1975) points out, "travel abroad" may be either an integrative or instrumental motive depending on its interpretation in a given study. This, however, is true not only for some cases, but is generally true even for the motives that are often used as examples to illustrate one or the other orientation type. For example, although "being an educated person" is often used to exemplify an instrumental motive, it could be an integrative motive if the learner perceived valued models of the target language culture as typically "educated persons" and wanted to be like them. A motive that is typically interpreted by researchers as integrative may in fact be instrumental to a particular group of subjects. For instance, "in order to live in the country where the language is spoken" could be instrumental if you happen to be a homeless refugee seeking a place of shelter, or if you feel the political situation is sufficiently unstable in the country of your native language.

Furthermore, in several recent studies, factors that are defined as either integrative or instrumental orientations, or perhaps both, may either fail to correlate at all with a proficiency criterion, or worse yet for the prevailing theoretical positions, they correlate negatively when the theories predict relationships. Oller, Hudson, and Liu (1976) found that a factor defined principally as a desire to stay permanently in the United States (on the part of Chinese-speaking graduate students in Albuquerque and

181

El Paso) was negatively correlated with attained proficiency in ESL. Chihara and Oller (1976) found that a general travel motive factor, and a factor defined principally by a desire to travel to an English-speaking country, were both negatively correlated with attained EFL proficiency for a population of Japanese adults. Asakawa and Oller (1976) found no significant correlations for factors distilled from direct questions concerning reasons for EFL study and possible reasons for travel to the United States for a population of Japanese high school students. And finally, Oller, Baca, and Vigil (1976) found a significant negative correlation between an instrumental attitude factor and an ESL proficiency criterion for a group of Mexican-Americans in Albuquerque. None of the other six factors distilled from a series of direct questions correlated significantly with the proficiency criterion at all.

Promising avenues of further study include focusing serious attention on the reliability and validity of the instruments used to acquire attitude information (cf. Gardner, Ginsberg, and Smythe, 1976), and on the measures of language proficiency. It seems possible that in spite of the fact that many studies have failed to reveal a very strong relationship between attitude variables and attained language proficiency, under certain conditions the relationship may in fact be quite strong (say above a 25% overlap in variance). Clearly, the investigation of attitudes and proficiency needs to be done concurrently with the study of other potential variables contributing to variance in attained language proficiency. It seems safe to say that the area is still wide open to enterprising researchers and that the best explanatory theories have yet to be invented. It also seems likely that our rate of progress in all of this work will be faster if we diligently employ the method of "strong inference" and systematically work our way forward by clearly stating the plausible alternatives, disproving some of them by crucial tests, and always continuing to refine the remaining possibilities.[2]

[2] I sincerely want to thank Robert C. Gardner and Wallace E. Lambert for providing much of the manuscript material that is referred to in the text. G. Richard Tucker also supplied helpful references. I also want to thank the Department of Linguistics and Center for English as a Second Language at Southern Illinois University for the research and teaching grant which made possible the completion of this paper and some of the collaborative research which is referred to in it.

The author is on a leave of absence from his regular appointment with the Department of Linguistics at the University of New Mexico.

References

Asakawa, Yoshio and Oller, Jr., J. W. 1976. Attitudes and attained proficiency in EFL: A sociolinguistic study of Japanese learners at the
secondary level. Mimeo. Department of Linguistics, University of
New Mexico.

Burstall, C., Jamieson M., Cohen, S., and Hargreaves, M. 1974. *Primary
French in the balance.* Windsor, England: NFER Publishing.

Carroll, John B. 1967. Foreign language proficiency levels attained by
language majors near graduation from college. *Foreign Language
Annals* 1, 131–51.

——— and Sapon, Stanley M. 1958. *Modern language aptitude test.* New
York: Psychological Corporation.

Chihara, Tetsuro and Oller, Jr., J. W. 1976. Attitudes and attained
proficiency in EFL: A sociolinguistic study of adult Japanese learners. Mimeo. Department of Linguistics, University of New Mexico.

Desrochers, Alain M., Smythe, P. C., and Gardner, R. C. 1975. *The
social psychology of second language acquisition and bilinguality: An anno-
tated bibliography.* Research Bulletin No. 340. London, Ontario, Canada: Department of Psychology, University of Western Ontario.

Gardner, Robert C. 1974. Motivational variables in second-language
learning. *Proceedings of the fifth symposium of the Canadian Association
of Applied Linguistics.* 45–73.

———. 1975. Social factors in second language acquisition and bilinguality. Paper presented at the invitation of the Canada Council's
Consultative Committee on the Individual, Language, and Society
for a conference held in Kingston, Ontario, November 29–December 5, 1975.

Gardner, Robert C. and Symthe, P. C. 1976. The role of attitudes in
acquiring the language of another ethnic group. Mimeo. Department of Psychology, University of Western Ontario.

Gardner, Robert C., Smythe, P.C., Clement, R., and Gliksman, L.
1976. Second language learning: A social psychological perspective. *Canadian Modern Language Review* 32, 198–213.

———, Ginsberg, R. E., and Smythe, P. C. 1976. Attitude and motivation in second language learning: Course related changes. *Canadian
Modern Language Review* 32, 243–66.

Jones, W. R. 1949. Attitude towards Welsh as a second language, a
preliminary investigation. *British Journal of Educational Psychology*
19, 44–52.

———. 1950. Attitude towards Welsh as a second language, a further
investigation. *British Journal of Educational Psychology* 20, 117–32.

Lambert, Wallace E. 1974. Culture and language as factors in learning and education. Paper presented at the ninth annual TESOL convention in Denver, Colorado, March 1974. Also read and discussed at the University of New Mexico, October 1974.

Oller, Jr., J.W., Hudson, Alan J., and Liu, P. F. 1976. Attitudes and attained proficiency in ESL: A sociolinguistic study of native speakers of Chinese in the United States. Mimeo. Department of Linguistics, University of New Mexico.

Oller, Jr., J.W., Baca, Lori, and Vigil, Fred. 1976. Attitudes and attained proficiency in ESL: A sociolinguistic study of Mexican Americans in the Southwest. Mimeo. Department of Linguistics, University of New Mexico.

Platt, John R. 1964. Strong inference. *Science* 146, 347–53.

Spolsky, Bernard. 1969. Attitudinal aspects of second language learning. *Language Learning* 19, 272–83. Reprinted in H. B. Allen and R. N. Campbell (eds.) *Teaching English as a second language: A book of readings.* New York: McGraw Hill, 403–14. (Page references in the text are to the latter source.)

Valette, Rebecca M. 1964. Some reflections on second language learning in young children. *Language Learning* 14, 91–8.

Motivation: An Historical Perspective

Maureen Concannon O'Brien

Traditional psychology propounded a number of conflicting theories of motivation. The Behavioral School, whose theories have most influenced techniques of language teaching, and the Biological School, which is concerned with explaining the physiological functioning of the human organism, have offered only the most limited explanations in their theories to define and interpret human attitudes and motivation. I wish to examine why this should be so, and why, on the other hand, personality theory derived from the psychoanalytic school seems today to offer promising insights into attitudes and motivation for second language learning.

Let us consider the behaviorists first. As we know, they investigated animal behavior, which led them to the conclusion that motivation stemmed from basic drives and that learning resulted from a system of rewards and punishments. The theory was called hedonism, or the *pleasure-pain principle*, and it was subscribed to by such eminent psychologists as Thorndike (1913), Woodworth, and Hull. McDougall (1908), another behaviorist who was conducting research during the same period, disagreed, and postulated that instincts were the source of motivation. Though the concept of "instinct" was, for many years after McDougall, not in good currency, psychologists such as Tinbergen (1951) and Hess (1962) have returned to "instinct" which they say must account for some aspects of animal behavior, including human behavior.

Approximately half a century after Thorndike's publication of *The Psychology of Learning*, another behaviorist, B. F. Skinner, the man most closely associated with the stimulus-response theory which has affected current pedagogical principles, made a major contribution to the area of teaching and learning. His work on the behavior of rats was applied to the teaching of human beings and had as one result the preparation of programmed texts and the establishment of language laboratory courses. (Incidentally, it was this very aspect of his work—the extrapolation of his findings about the behavior of rats to that of humans—which has made his theories suspect in the last decade.)

Skinner concluded that the pleasure-pain principle is basic to learning. The subject is "rewarded" for the correct response and "punished" for the wrong answer. As related to language learning, the procedures used in both programmed texts and language laboratory courses generally follow this sequence: model (teaching question or statement); cue followed by student's response; correct answer (supplied by the text or tape); and sometimes followed by the student's repetition of the correct answer. If the student's initial response is correct, the reward is confirmation of the correct answer from the textbook (or tape) which thus reinforces the correct response. If, on the other hand, the student's response to the cue is wrong, the correct answer, heard or read, is considered to be a sufficient punishment to motivate the learner to extinguish the incorrect response. In the language laboratory the student is often given a second opportunity to supply the correct response and is therefore motivated toward further learning. In the programmed text, the student is directed to find the confirmation either in the margin or on a later page, or in the case of an incorrect response, in exercises or activities designed to extinguish the error.

Today it is rather widely accepted that this reward-punishment or pleasure-pain principle plays an important role in the development of motivation for learning.

Without denigrating the major contribution made by the empirical techniques of the Skinnerian School to methodology, course content, and teaching techniques, we must acknowledge that the contribution of the behaviorists to the role of attitudes and motivation in learning is extremely limited. It cannot be denied that much of human behavior is similar to animal behavior, particularly at the level of basic instincts. But in seeking a more realistic, functional definition of human motivation, we cannot ignore other factors not available to those lower in the animal kingdom than homo sapiens. I shall return to these other factors after describing the theories of the Biological School.

As its name implies, the Biological School related motivation to biological survival, as noted, for instance, in the desire for food, water, or warmth. It isolated three characteristics of motivated behavior:

1. *Persistence:* If behavior persists in spite of obstacles, we can infer that there is an underlying state of agitation or tension, which continues to initiate new actions.

2. *Variation:* If tension is not relieved by one pattern of action, motivated behavior will lead to diversified actions to achieve the goal—for example, a hungry child will beg for food, cry, become aggressive, and so on.

3. *Emotional Overflow:* When there is a delay in reaching a goal, the individual who is strongly motivated will react emotionally with anger, tears, pleading, silence, and so on.

Tension, the Biological School insists, provides the persistent physiological basis underlying and determining the dynamics of motivation. If we interpret the words "tension" and "agitation" to mean a dynamic impulsion to action and extend the third characteristic of motivated behavior to include "emotionally-toned processes," that is, the intense feelings fostered by parental and community attitudes, self-concepts, and individual personality structure, we may be approaching a more acceptable definition of motivation.

The man whose name is most closely associated with the theory that, in the hierarchy of human needs, the satisfaction of physiological needs must precede cognitive, creative, or affective needs is A. H. Maslow. Maslow places the physiological levels of human needs in the first stage of this hierarchy. At the next level he considers these along with the higher psychological levels of human personality to the point that he is at times classified as a "spiritualist." Although Maslow's theory was developed more than a generation ago, it forms the core upon which present trends are being developed in the area of motivation for second language learning. Thus it may be useful to examine the steps in his hierarchy in greater detail:

1) Physiological needs: At the most basic level for survival—the need for air, food, and water.

2) Needs for security: The need for shelter, stability, protection; and freedom from fear.

3) Needs for belonging: The need for a sense of personal identity, to be able to occupy a respected place within a group.

4) Needs for esteem: The need to feel adequate, independent; to be appreciated and valued by others.

5) Needs for self-actualization: By this Maslow and others refer to the need of each individual to realize his or her intellectual and creative potential, and to achieve human relations and vocational goals in consonance with these capabilities.

There can be no doubt that these needs are essential components of human motivation which had been disregarded by both the Behaviorist and Biological Schools. Attitude and motivation at the human level must include the need to think rationally—the ability, for example, to consider alternatives in the choice of a long-term goal, and to pursue such a goal despite intervening obstacles and short-term failures. Maslow's explanation of human motivation is not only functional, but also appealing to those who wish to apply his hierarchy of needs to the learning situation. As we have seen, it accounts for human motivation on the physiological and the affective, as well as on the cognitive level.

The cognitive approach to learning underlies the outstanding contribution of Jean Piaget to developmental psychology. His observation of children has led him to the conclusion that learning is subject centered. By this he means that the child learns inductively, through all the senses, as a result of his or her personal experiences in the surrounding world.

Relating Piaget's theories to second language learning, Mary Finocchiaro and many other methodologists describe cognitivism in practical terms: the student, on the basis of model experiences with language and strategies for learning which he or she has

188

actively developed through previous learning experiences, forms concepts and restructures new learning in his or her own way. Intensive and extensive use of these concepts in a variety of communication situations enables the learner to store the knowledge acquired in his or her memory bank, and to call upon that stored memory when needed. It will be obvious to teachers that this recall is generally dependent upon and facilitated by the reintroduction of these concepts at appropriate intervals, generally along with material which has been acquired subsequently.

The spiral approach in the instructional; i. e., reintroducing concepts at broader, deeper levels and with increasingly complex forms in order to facilitate a restructuring of learning, was developed by Jerome Bruner (1960). Bruner further held that in order to stimulate the student's desire to learn, the student himself has to feel that the material is worth knowing and of use for his future life, beyond the immediate learning situation. While Bruner's theories contributed in a highly practical way to a theory of learning, an even more global approach to motivation was still needed. The foundation for this had been laid by the Psychoanalytic School, which consciously or unconsciously had influenced the thinking of the psychologists mentioned above.

I have left the consideration of the Psychoanalytic School until this stage because much of the most recent research in attitudes and motivation is based on the theories of this school of psychology. For Freud, the founder of the School, the dynamic laws governing the behavior of organisms are based on the pleasure principle which corresponds to the Id, and the reality principle corresponding to the Ego. The Id makes simple, direct, infantile demands for the gratification of innate desires, while the Ego corresponds to more adult behavior in its ability to postpone immediate gratification for the purpose of achieving a valuable long-term goal.

Mowrer (1950) has adopted Freud's theories of the Id in his explanation of first language acquisition. According to Mowrer, the infant gratifies its basic biological and social needs by emulating and interacting with its parents or other caretakers. The infant is totally dependent upon these adults in his or her environment to satisfy his or her physical and emotional needs. When it makes sounds and puts them together, first into words and then phrases, this behavior is rewarded through positive reinforce-

189

ments, such as praise, food, or displays of affection. The infant's basic emotional and social needs for love, affection, or understanding are satisfied by approval which will affect and foster his or her learning.

Chomsky's (1965) Language Acquisition Device (LAD), on the other hand, explains first language acquisition as a biological function, an innate development. Far from conflicting, both these theories of first language acquisition seem to be complementary to each other. Language is a function of the physiological organism of human beings, but it is developed and nurtured by the social and emotional environment in which the child grows. Without the stimulation of the environment, there is either retardation or complete atrophy of first language development. To take this to its most extreme form we need only recall cases such as that of the "Wolf Child," who had been adopted by wolves shortly after birth and had learned to communicate only in the language of animals. He never succeeded in learning more than a few human words after he was found, despite intensive efforts to teach him. More recently, the case history of Genie, a 19-year old who suffered extreme sensory deprivation the first 14 years of her life, reveals a still-developing language, less developed than that of 5-year-old normal children (cf. Curtiss, S., Fromkin, V., Rigler, D., Rigler, M., and Krashen, S., 1975).

General Theories of Motivation

Thus far in this paper we have focused on general theories of motivation, applying them to both first language acquisition and to second language learning. In their recent work *Attitudes and Motivation For Second Language Learning* (1972), Gardner and Lambert have encompassed all three levels of personality development posited by Freud and his followers when they make the following statement: "A process such as identification, which is extended to an entire ethnolinguistic community, combined with an inquisitiveness and sincere interest in the other group (the integrative motive) must underlie the long-term motivation needed to master a second language." This is the functioning of the superego, while the ego is represented by "instrumental motivation" which reflects practical utilitarian values such as achievement either in school or in one's occupation.

190

Many psychologists have long been aware that if a goal (or long-term motivation) is perceived as being of high value, it takes on a more dynamic quality. For example, the welfare of one's family, the service to humanity, or a sincere interest in another culture, can sustain the individual long enough to achieve his or her final goal.

Gardner and Lambert's findings underscore the basic psychological differences in the field of attitude and motivation for second language learning when they describe the "integrative motive" as complex behavior, embodying not only the emotions, but attitudes and rational deliberations.

I would like to cite one example of a case with which I am personally familiar—the Irish language revival. In this case, the absence of the integrative and often of the instrumental motive has resulted in the failure to establish a bilingual state in Ireland. This is highlighted in a recent report published by the Committee on Irish Language Attitudes Research. According to this report the majority of the Irish population view the Irish language (one of the oldest and richest in Europe) as antiquated, agricultural, and backward. Most of the people are not (as Gardner and Lambert phrased it) "psychologically prepared to adopt various aspects of behavior" which characterize members of the Irish-speaking population.

Joshua Fishman, who was consultant to the research committee on the Irish language, commented that although it is the best country study he has read, it is also the most inconclusive. The survey showed that the attitude of most people was that Irish should be preserved in its symbolic role. Only 6% of the population speak it and the majority of the remaining population are not sufficiently motivated either to learn it or to use it.

Until very recently Irish was a compulsory school subject. It was taught as a first language although often for both teacher and student it was a second or even foreign language. The teaching methods were far behind the times and the school classroom was the only domain in which Irish was used. Many of the same factors, which still persist today, contribute to the feelings of resentment toward the language, the teachers, and the government authorities who insisted upon its use. This negative motivation found expression in such organizations as The Language Freedom Movement which, in highly emotionally-charged debate, insisted that until the Irish language was made an elective subject in school, the language would not be used by the population.

As a result of the Report on Attitudes Research, the compulsory requirement has recently been removed in schools, and also in the Civil Service, which in the past required all of its employees to be fluent Irish speakers.

These changes may help to reverse negative motivation, and assist in building up positive attitudes. There is some hope that this trend may develop, as the Report on Language Attitudes revealed that, in addition to isolated Irish-speaking districts of the country, the language is best known, used most, and most favorably regarded by the 17- to 22-year olds. Nonetheless, if the Irish language is not to die entirely, more positive attitudes and motivation to learn it have to be generated within the population. But even this will not be sufficient without up-to-date teaching techniques and wider opportunities to learn and use the language.

These components would all interact in Ireland as anywhere else to increase motivation. For example, without the opportunity to use a language, the motivation to learn it would soon disappear. The whole personality must be activated through appropriate, nonthreatening methods and strategies of presenting new linguistic/cultural material, in order to elicit the dynamic participation of the whole person. All the levels of Maslow's hierarchy must be satisfied if learning is to take place.

An interesting experiment along these lines is that of "suggestopaedia" used by the Bulgarians and developed by psychiatrist Georgi Lozanov (1975). Hypnosis, psychoanalysis, and similar psychiatric techniques are not necessary, since the power of suggestion alone, he claims, is sufficient to motivate students to much greater learning. This is done primarily by increasing their expectations of their own potential for learning. Hypernesia, which is an extension of the ability of the memory to function, and improved creativity of the learner generally, are two results of this technique, for which teachers must be specially trained.

Lozanov believes that the learner must be freed from tension and must be placed in a relaxed, pleasurable atmosphere so that no psychological interferences can distract him or her from learning. Physical comforts, such as easy chairs, are used and classical music is played at various stages in the learning sequence, sometimes simultaneously with the teacher's introduction of learning material. Fictional identities are given to the learners, such as names and occupations typical of the people in the countries of the target language. For example, in English courses for adults, the role of banker, doctor, pop star, businessman or woman, or secretary might be designated for each student. The purpose of these false identities (the other students never learn the real identity of their fellow learners) is to free the learner from embarrassment. By acting out a role there is no direct affront to the learner's ego, as each individual student feels freed —temporarily at least—from his or her own personality problems (Stevick, 1976). Suggestopaedia has been adapted for use outside Bulgaria mainly by the Canadians and Russians.

However, the data on suggestopaedia, and on other programs based on psychotherapeutics and personality theory generally, are still inconclusive. We must remain skeptical of claims that any theory of learning can provide a panacea for removing all learning difficulties. Teachers know by hard experience that many theories are not always either practical or applicable to the classroom situation.

This is not to say that personality theory ought to be eliminated from our considerations of motivation and attitudes. On the contrary, it is currently one of the most fruitful sources for investigation. But the very nature of personality theory, with its concentration on the unique character and dynamic qualities— including attitudes and motivation—of each individual, makes it a difficult area to analyze scientifically.

While researchers continue to develop new theories generally based on the traditional schools of psychology, some of which have been outlined in this paper, language teaching methodologists have applied what is relevant from this research, in many cases with intuitive awareness of its appropriateness for improving attitudes and raising the levels of motivation. For example, in a talk given to the Foreign Language Teachers in Sacramento, California in 1965, Mary Finocchiaro described some of the cognitive and affective needs which must be satisfied if the learner is to be motivated to pursue language learning both as an immediate and as a long-term goal.

In examining the mnemonic below, teachers will undoubtedly think of many other examples. Only one or two examples and techniques for fostering motivation are given in this list.

F—*Freedom from fear:* e.g. Learners should not be embarrassed if they have not done their assignment, if they make errors in production, or if they cannot respond immediately.

U—*Understanding:* e.g. Teachers must consider the socioeconomic, cultural, and emotional background of the learners in order to help them maintain their pride in themselves.

E—*Experiences:* e.g. Learners must engage in a wide variety of activities in order to fulfill their need for thinking, learning, doing, or choosing.

L—*Love:* e.g. The teacher often has to take the role of a substitute parent and be aware of the hunger for affection of the learner who, rightly or wrongly, feels rejected by family or peers.

B—*Belonging:* e.g. Learners should participate with the class "community" in all facets of planning and decision-making during the learning process.

A—*Achievement and Actualization:* e.g. Learners should be helped to perfect today what they might have been able to do only haltingly yesterday. They should receive continuous feedback of their progress; they should be able to use what they have learned to communicate their own aspirations and ideas.

G—*Grouping and Individualization:* e.g. The teacher should be aware of the level at which each student is capable of operating at any moment in time, of his or her optimal way of learning, of the time he or she needs to learn and should gear classroom group and individual activities to take all these factors into account.

S—*Success:* e.g. The learner should experience numerous small intermediate successes and attain short-term goals which will then motivate him or her to continue working toward individual, school, community, or nation-wide goals (depending on his or her age level and learning) (Finocchiaro, 1965).

Finocchiaro's practical advice to teachers is summarized in her book *English as a Second Language: From Theory to Practice* (1964 and 1974) when she says:

> The teacher who can give each student the feeling that he is an important part of the group, that he is capable of learning and that he can achieve success; the teacher who can demonstrate an understanding of conflict—both environmental and linguistic; the teacher who, through his enthusiasm, his art, and his skill, makes language learning a subject to look forward to, will in the final analysis be the one who will forge ahead of his less perceptive colleagues in promoting the desirable habits and attitudes needed for language learning.

The expectations outlined in the above quotation must be included in any consideration of attitudes and motivation in second language learning. To extend motivation and improve attitudes demands a well-balanced combination of the teacher's art and skills. It is not enough for the teacher to make use of psychological principles of whatever school to motivate learners. The teacher can also foster motivation through his or her own sense of security resulting from adequate linguistic and methodological preparation.

Most of the theories outlined in this article have, to a greater or lesser degree, influenced second language learning. It will be evident that this overview is not a complete resume of all the psychologists and educators whose theories have contributed to our present knowledge about attitudes and motivation. John Dewey, an educator, and Gordon Allport, an eclecticist, as well as the Gestalt psychologists, are notable omissions. Yet many of their ideas have either overlapped or been adopted by others. This overview is meant to indicate where the mainstream of current thinking on attitudes and motivation is flowing.

We owe a great deal to the research of Robert Gardner and Wallace Lambert, who were amongst the first to study attitudes and motivation specifically in the second-language-learning situations. Their concept of instrumental and integrative motivation may help to explain the behavior of learners. We owe much also to the Biological School for their explanation of the physiological elements of motivation, to the cognitivists for the inductive approach, and to the psychoanalysts for the understanding of the role of affective, emotional, and instinctual factors. The behaviorists' stimulus/response theories have contributed to practical teaching techniques, and Maslow's hierarchy of human needs has provided an eclectic distillation of the various levels of motivation which can be applied to the language learning situation.

Yet, in concluding, we must admit that psychological research has not evolved a definitive encompassing theory of human attitudes and motivation. We cannot fully account for the complexities of individual personality structure and the behavior resulting from it. In the last analysis, the psychologist may have to accept what is obvious to teachers—that the structures of no two personalities are the same, and that each individual has a different set of habits, drives, needs, and impulses. Teachers have to make continuous discoveries of what these factors are in each learner in order to motivate each to attain both his or her immediate and long-term goals. It is an exciting, demanding role, yet one which reaps enormous satisfaction for the highly motivated teacher.

References

Allport, G.W. 1937. *Personality: A psychological interpretation.* New York: Holt.

———. 1968. *The person in psychology.* Boston, Mass.: Beacon Press.

Bruner, J.S. 1960. *The process of education.* Cambridge, Mass.: Harvard University Press.

———. 1961. The act of discovery. *Harvard Education Review.*

Committee on Irish Language Attitudes Research: Report as submitted to the Minister for the Gailtacht. 1975. Dublin.

Curtiss, S., Fromkin, V., Rigler, D., Rigler, M., and Krashen, S. 1975. An update on the linguistic development of Genie. In D. Dato (ed.) *Development Psycholinguistics: Theory and Applications.* Washington, D.C.: Georgetown University Press.

Fishman, Joshua. 1975. What the great language survey revealed. In article by John Armstrong, *Irish Times,* Dublin, August 15.

Finocchiaro, Mary. 1974. *English as a second language; from theory to practice.* New York: Regents Publishing Company.

Gardner, R.C. and Lambert, W.E. 1972. *Attitudes and motivation in second language learning.* Rowley, Mass.: Newbury House.

Lozanov, G. 1975. The technique of suggestopaedia in second language learning. *Second Language Acquisition and Maintenance,* ATESOL, Dublin.

Maslow, A.H. 1954, 1970. *Motivation and personality*. New York: Harper and Row.

McDougall, W. 1908. *An introduction to social psychology*. London: Methuen.

Mowrer, O.H. 1950. *Learning theory and personality dynamics*. New York: Ronald Press.

Piaget, J. 1965. *Readings in the psychology of cognition*. New York: Holt, Rinehart and Winston.

Skinner, B.J. 1954. The science of learning and the art of teaching. *Harvard Educational Review*, Cambridge.

Stevick, E.W. 1976. *Memory, meaning, and method*. Rowley, Mass.: Newbury House.

Thorndike, E.L. 1913. The psychology of learning. *Education Psychology*, vol. 2. New York: Teachers' College, Columbia University.

A Humanistic Approach to Language Behavior

Renzo Titone

Many language teachers and methodologists are dissatisfied with current methods of foreign language teaching. The "audio-lingual approach" has been severely criticized and pattern practice is being superseded by or integrated with a rationalistic or "cognitive-code theory," aiming at mastery of internal rules rather than at formation of habits. The historical pendulum seems to be swinging back again to the formal approach characterized by knowledge of grammar, although the newly-accepted notion of grammar is considerably different from the traditional view (Titone, 1975).

To my mind, however, the solution to this methodological issue does not consist in reviving old theories and assigning them new labels, but in furnishing a deeper and more comprehensive analysis of the dynamics of verbal behavior and of the process of language acquisition. Many of the shortcomings in the application of existing instructional models seem to be due to the lack of an integrated and sufficiently flexible teaching-learning model of language behavior and language learning.

Both technological implementation and research in language teaching lack an adequate methodological basis. The application of the new instructional technologies emphasizes passive indoctrination instead of active, personal learning experience. On the other hand, research on language-teaching methods and techniques lacks clarity and justification because the scope, the general framework, and the actual variables of the language-learning process are ill-defined and not clearly focused (Freedman, 1971).

The solution I propose consists of the development of a synthetic approach to language learning, namely, the *glossodynamic model*. [1]

---

[1] The term *Glossodynamics* was first used by A.A. Roback to mean a general *dynamic psychology* of language that would consider international, especially motivational, variables. (Cf. A.A. Roback, "Glossodynamics and the Present Status of Psycholinguistics,"

The starting point of the "glossodynamic model" (GDM) of language learning is the recognition that language behavior, far from being a linear series of one-level operations, is basically a *stratificational* and *hierarchical system of dynamic structures*. Such a unified multiplicity implies the simultaneous and overlapping involvement of very different operational levels. I believe that language behavior is a very important manifestation of personality dynamics viewed in specific contexts. As such it cannot be reduced to a mere system of verbal habits or even to a system of cognitive processes. Such a reduction would be tantamount to admitting the possibility of "speaking" without a "speaker" or of "hearing" without a "hearer." Language behavior, like all behavior, postulates an adequate concept of "personality" as the ultimate root and source of communicative input and output. A comprehensive view of personality structure implies the "intra-action" and "inter-action" of cognition and habits.

This integrated view of language behavior and learning includes the coexistence and cooperation of three distinct levels, namely: a) personality structure and dynamics in context; b) cognitive processes; and c) operant conditioning.

These three variables are in essence mutually dependent and dynamically integrated. In other words, integration is not a state but a continuous process, a dynamic equilibrium never entirely achieved, as is typically evident in the case of individual bilingualism. The three different levels as we will note later are not simply a juxtaposition of three theories; rather, all three levels are the essential constituents of one unified theory of language behavior and language learning.

1. A Personological View of Language and Speech

My views are closely related to those recently expressed by "humanistic psychologists." Consider these statements by Floyd W. Matson:

> This recognition of *man-in-person*, as opposed to *man-in-general*, goes to the heart of the difference between humanistic psychology, in any of its forms or schools, and scientific psychologies such as behaviorism. . . . This emphasis upon the human

in A.A. Roback (ed.), *Present-day Psychology.* New York: Philosophical Library, 1955, pp. 897–912.) Here the term is restricted to signify a multi-level operational model of language behavior.

person, upon the individual in his wholeness and uniqueness, is a central feature of the "psychology of humanism." But there is an important corollary without which this personalistic emphasis would be inadequate and distorted. That corollary is the recognition, to use a phrase of Rank, that "the self needs the other."[2]

The names of the spokesmen of psychological humanism are well known: Martin Buber and his philosophy of dialogue; Ludwig Binswanger's, Viktor Frankl's, and Rollo May's existential psychology; and Abraham Maslow, Gordon Allport, Carl Rogers, Erich Fromm, Henry A. Murray, Joseph Nuttin, and others.

Personality is the cornerstone of this psychological outlook. Personality as defined, among others, by Allport is ". . . the dynamic organization within the individual of those psychophysical systems that determine his characteristic behavior and thought."[3] And further: "The individuality of man, the future-pointed thrust of his living, and the systematic interlacing of his key qualities, are the central features of his personality."[4]

But personality is not reducible to mere individuality. Personality is an "open system," that is, a "relational system." For this emphasis on the essential "relational" nature of human personality, I am especially indebted to the Belgian psychologist Nuttin's idea of the structure of personality.[5]

The "relational theory of personality" starts from the assumption that the human being is not only internally structured, but also dependent on the world. "Personality," writes Nuttin, "is a mode of functioning involving essentially two poles: the *Ego* and the *World*. The Ego is the total of the individual's functions and psychological potentials; the world is the intrinsic object of the Ego. Indeed psychological functioning—i.e., perception and behavior in general, including motivation—necessarily implies an object as the intrinsic reference point of the process itself. This functioning, therefore, cannot but locate itself within a structure implying an intrinsic and active reference of the Ego to a world of objects. This world of people and objects is not only situated

---

[2] F.W. Matson, "Humanistic Theory: The Third Revolution in Psychology," *The Humanist*, March-April 1971, p. 9.

[3] G.W. Allport, *Pattern and Growth in Personality*, New York: Holt, 1965, p. 28.

[4] Ibid., p. 21.

[5] Cf. J. Nuttin, *La structure de la personnalité*, Paris: Presses Universitaires de France, 1968, and *Tâche, réussite et échec*, 1953, 1961.

in front of the Ego but constitutes the very *content* of personalized psychological life. This amounts to saying that, from a functional point of view, a personality cannot exist but within the framework of a structure transcending the physical-psychological organism, in other terms, within an *Ego-World structure."* [6]

Personality is then an *open system* in Bertalanffy's sense. [7]

This particular idea is, to my mind, the very source of *language as communication.* Human communication is the very marrow of personality, and language as a species-specific power (the *Sprachfähigkeit* mentioned by Humboldt) is essentially and operationally connected with human personality.

The "Glossodynamic Model" of language behavior is but a logical application and development of my thesis about individual personality and its relationship to the world through language.

2. An Integrated Analysis of Language Behavior and Language Learning: the Glossodynamic Model

Communicating is rooted in profound layers of the individual's personality. The existence of such layers might not be consistent with the Chomskyan dichotomy of competence and performance (Chafe, 1970). In other words, it is necessary to postulate a hierarchical structure of operational levels in human behavior and learning in order to account for all types and instances of language events. [8]

The following three levels seem to provide explanation for our purpose, viz.:

1. *The Tactic Level.* [9] This is the appropriate *ordering* of each single language act with respect to all verbal antecedents and consequents. "Ordering" is seen here as the actual result of

---

[6] J. Nuttin, *Structure de la personnalité,* op. cit. pp. 205–206.

[7] Cf. L. Von Bertalanffy, "The Theory of Open Systems in Physics and Biology," *Science,* 1950, no. 3, pp. 23–28.

[8] The present model should not be confused with the "cybernetic model," which shows a seeming resemblance to the author's, as laid down by Miller, G.A., Galanter, E., and Pribram, K., *Plans and the Structure of Behavior.* New York: Henry Holt & Co., 1960.

[9] The terms "strategy" and "tactics" are taken here in analogy with military parlance. "In military usage, a distinction is made between *strategy* and *tactics. Strategy* is the utilization, during both peace and war, of all of a nation's forces, through large-scale, long-range planning and development, to ensure security and victory. *Tactics* deals with the use and deployment of troops in actual combat." *The Random House Dictionary of the English Language:* v. *strategy.*

language programming, namely as the finished product or concrete verbal performance. The tactic level is by its very nature contextualized.

2. *The Strategic Level.* The ordered nature of single language performances requires the action of "ordering" or programming mechanisms which are not directly observable, but are strictly "mental" in their nature. The mind of the speaker/hearer is responsible for the meaningfulness and grammaticality of each speech act. Tactics, therefore, presupposes strategy.

3. *The Ego-Dynamic Level.* All psychological and linguistic activities ultimately stem from and return to the self of the communicating person. The subject of responsibility, the center of accountability in human behavior, is the individual *self* (or the "ego," and not in the psychoanalytic sense only).

To think that a behavioral model can be complete by simply restricting itself to a cybernetic structure (tactics and strategy) is to posit an acephalous organism, a beheaded body. In *human* communication the cybernetic concept needs to be subsumed into a personological concept. It is indispensable, therefore, to admit a conscious, directing and unifying agent, the individual speaker's self operating on a higher level and controlling all subordinate activities (tactics and strategy).

To sum up the essential features of the GDM, one could visualize the genetic order of language acquisition as following these steps:

1	2	3
EGO	STRATEGY	TACTICS
the will to communicate	the ability to communicate	the act of communication

The act of communication takes the form of an automatic chain of events due to the fact that the total process results from the coordination and integration of all intermediate steps and centers into a compact unified behavioral system, i.e., a linguistically operating structure. External coordination of vocal elements on the tactic level issues from the internal coordination of programming rules on the strategic level, and finally both levels are unified into vertical control exerted by the ego.

202

I believe that this large blueprint of a humanistic idea of language behavior is capable of furnishing a vantage point for the construction and evaluation of well-integrated and yet flexible language teaching methods.

Suggested Readings

Allport, G.W. 1965. *Pattern and growth in personality*. New York: Holt.

Carpenter, C.R. 1970. The commission on instructional technology and its report. *Educational Broadcasting Review*, 4, 4:3–10.

Chafe, W.L. 1970. *Meaning and the structure of language*. Chicago: University of Chicago Press.

Chomsky, N. 1965. *Aspects of the theory of syntax*. Cambridge, Mass.: MIT Press.

Dieuzeide, H. 1971. Educational technology and the development of education. *Educational Broadcasting Review*, 5, 4.

Freedman, E.S. 1971. The road from Pennsylvania: where next in language experimentation? *Audiovisual Language Journal*, 9 1:33–38.

Matson, F.W. March–April 1971. Humanistic theory: the third revolution in psychology. *The Humanist*, 9.

Miller, G.A., Galanter, E., and Pribam, K. 1960. *Plans and the structure of behavior*. New York: Henry Holt & Co.

Nuttin, J. 1968. *La structure de la personnalité*. Paris: Presses Universitaires de France, and 1953 and 1961. *Tâche, réussite et échec*.

Roback, A.A. 1955. Glossodynamics and the present status of linguistics. A.A. Roback (ed.), *Present-day Psychology*, New York: Philosophical Library, 897–912.

Slama-Cazacu, T. 1961. *Langage et contexte*. Mouton.

Titone, R. 1975. "Dalle grammatiche funzionali alla 'performance grammar'." Atti della Società de Linguistica Italiana, Roma.

To Improve Learning: A Report to the President and the Congress of the United States by the Commission on Instructional Technology. 1970. Washington, D.C.: U.S. Government Printing Office.

Von Bertalanffy, L. 1950. The theory of open systems in physics and biology. *Science*, 3, 23–28.

SOCIO-POLITICAL DIMENSIONS

Migration Today: Some Social and Educational Problems

Mary Finocchiaro
Lars Ekstrand[1]

Introduction

Ensuring the personal and social adjustment of immigrants either to another region in their native land or to a country whose geography, history, language, and culture may contrast markedly with their own is one of the most difficult tasks facing many areas of the world at the present time. The problem is not new. It is, in fact, as old as history; but there are differences today.

Whereas in the distant past the immigrants were either the conquerors or the conquered, in the more recent past the immigrants were generally ignored or exploited. They were the ones who did the menial jobs, working and living in appalling conditions; whose schooling was nobody's concern; whose integration into the society of the receiving country was not envisaged and certainly not encouraged; whose cultural identity was often not respected, if not actually scorned. If there was acknowledgment of the newcomers' existence—and this was true several decades ago in the United States—it was that *they* had to make the effort to rise out of the common melting pot and to become "Americans."

---

[1] The research studies reported in this article were done by Lars Ekstrand. The personal reminiscences and comments are those of Mary Finocchiaro.

The past two or three decades have brought about a marked change in this attitude. The social conscience of many citizens has been awakened.

In the United States, for example, linguists, sociologists, anthropologists, and educators have finally initiated numerous research studies designed to identify the social and educational problems of immigrants and to find possible solutions for them. The current concept of coexistence, far from being assimilationist, stresses cultural pluralism; and, what I consider most important, the immigrants themselves are being consulted about and asked to help resolve the problems which would lead to their fuller, more active participation in the communities in which they live.

It is gratifying to note that other countries—in Europe particularly—which for many years had berated the United States for its treatment of newcomers, are now consciously aware of the difficulties faced by receiving countries and by the migrants themselves. The economic and social changes wrought by World War II have brought Turks and Moroccans to France, Italians to Switzerland and Germany (as well as to the industrial cities of Northern Italy), Pakistanis and Jamaicans to Great Britain, to name only a few.[2] Daily, hundreds of people from many parts of the world leave their homes seeking that elusive rainbow of a new and better life for themselves and their children. They generally find, perhaps, a better paying job than they could have had at home, but unfortunately they live with the fear of rejection, misunderstanding, and failure that I and many others have known from firsthand experience. As a child of Sicilian immigrants, that experience has shaped my life and my thoughts about teachers, learners, empathy, "cultural immersion"; just as I know that they have influenced the lives of my peers. Whenever I hear the words "cultural immersion" as the panacea for language acquisition, I still mentally add "not if you're living in a ghetto." I can assure you that, as children, we recognized the teachers who were empathetic and whom we would want to imitate. On the other hand we sensed the scorn

---

[2] A Rome newspaper (August 17, 1976) reported that France has over four million immigrants at the present time. In Sweden, the number of immigrants registered by labor authorities as employed, increased from 61,000 in 1947 to 233,000 in 1974.

and apathy of teachers (who should never have entered the profession) whose only desire was that we would leave school at eleven in order to serve an apprenticeship as seamstresses (if we were females), or shoemakers or barbers. While the scars still remain, I have become optimistic in the last decade since I note many rays of hope and real effort from many sources. TESOL, CAL, FIPLV, IATEFL, UNESCO, The Council of Europe, as well as Ministries of Foreign Affairs in many countries are organizing world conferences to discuss the difficulties inherent in cross-cultural migration.

Despite the American experience of the last century, attendance at these conferences underscores the fact that the same questions are being raised and the same educational and social problems are plaguing immigrants and host countries. In this, as in other major issues, we seem to learn little or nothing from history. Nor has sufficient research been carried out within and across countries. Crucial variables, which would permit schools and other social agencies to formulate and implement productive programs, have not as yet been isolated. Nor can effective school and social programs be deferred until valid and replicable studies are carried out. Immigrants have urgent needs to function immediately in host countries and to avoid exploitation (often by their compatriots who had preceded them!).

Before discussing these issues further, allow me to digress for a moment to mention a recent incident in which I was involved. I was asked to give the keynote address at an international conference on migration several months ago. I started congratulating the sponsors and participants and expressing my delight that the problems of immigrants were finally receiving the attention they deserved. I mentioned that my delight was indeed great because as the child of Sicilian immigrants I had suffered discrimination in school. I added that the English I was speaking was my third language.

After the talk, the chairman asked for comments and questions but there was dead silence. The "refusal" to discuss my paper continued embarrassingly throughout the afternoon and the next morning. During the coffee break, I walked over to a man who had smiled timidly once or twice in my direction and asked what the matter was. "Did I say something wrong?" "I'm afraid you did," was his answer. "What did I say?" "Well, you said you were Sicilian and that the English you speak was your third language." "That's true. What's wrong with that?" "Madam, you don't seem to realize that the immigrants who are giving all of us around the table the worst problems are the Sicilians! And most of them don't *want* their children to go to school to learn *any* language!"

So although many decades had elapsed since my personal experience, I realized not only that "plus ça change, plus c'est la même chose," but also that research reports on prejudice, stereotypes, and the period needed for adjustment to a new culture were unfortunately true.

Permit us, therefore, before discussing the educational pitfalls of programs for migrants, to give the briefest overview of some research studies which focus on the complexity of the task facing host countries. Several sections from Ekstrand's summaries of previous research follow.

Some Research Findings

Immigrants or Ethnics?

The North American continent is unsurpassed as an immigration area. With the onset of modern migration in Europe, a similar situation has arisen. There are several things to be learned from the history of American immigration. One is the "shortlivedness" of the immigrant. As a rule, after some years, the immigrant is no longer an immigrant, but a member of an ethnic group. In any case, members of the second generation are no longer immigrants.

This shift of conceptualization is discussed by Vecoli (1972) in his paper "European Americans: From Immigrants to Ethnics." Another interesting concept in Vecoli's paper is the following description, which may be seen as a forecast of the situation in Europe, perhaps twenty years from now (1974):

> Ethnicity has exercised a persistent and pervasive influence upon American history. Americans have traditionally defined themselves and others as members of ethnocultural groups. On the basis of their origins—national, racial, religious, and regional —they have shared with "their own kind" a sense of common heritage and collective destiny.

The American "Melting Pot theory" assumed that foreigners were transformed into real Americans in one generation, or two at the most. Later, sociologists put forward the three-generation theory. The assumption today is that it takes considerably longer before all traces of the origin have disappeared if, indeed, they ever do. Hall (personal communication) has pointed out that the Navajos, the Spanish, and the Americans have lived together in New Mexico for three hundred years, without assimilation. They work together in the cities, they often speak each other's languages, but they keep their cultures apart.

The present situation in the United States, as far as research is concerned, is summarized by Vecoli (1972) in the following way:

These assimilationist assumptions have been called into question by the "rediscovery of ethnicity" in recent years. White ethnic groups, as well as Blacks, Indians, and Hispanic Americans, have demonstrated an unanticipated longevity. The "New Pluralism" has inspired historians and others to explore the ethnic dimension of American life in the past as well as in the present. As a consequence we are in the midst of a renaissance of immigration history. A rich and growing literature awaits the student of European American ethnic groups, one which is enlivened by divergent interpretations and differing methodologies.

Not only do historians like Vecoli hold this view, but also members of other disciplines, including psychologists and anthropologists. Thus the anthropologist Edward T. Hall (1966) writes:

For, contrary to common belief, the many diverse groups that make up our country have proved to be surprisingly persistent in maintaining their separate identities. Superficially, these groups may all look alike and sound somewhat alike, but beneath the surface there lie manifold unstated, unformulated differences in the structuring of time, space, materials, and relationships.

We may conclude, then, that assimilation is a very slow process, stretching over many generations. Even when complete assimilation seems to have taken place, it may be only superficial. This is one area in which Europe may learn from the United States.

Attitudes and Stereotypes

Allport (1958) points out that there are at least a dozen classes of groups against which prejudice is known to exist: race, sex, age, ethnicity, language, region, religion, nation, ideology, caste, social class, occupation, education, interest (labor unions, professional societies, etc.), and, undoubtedly, others.

Immigrants are likely to differ from others in their new social environment in many of these respects. They are by definition from another region or from another nation. They differ linguistically, and are likely to differ in a number of other aspects as well. It is not surprising, therefore, that immigrants and their children often belong to "outgroups" which are particularly subject to unfounded prejudice. Prejudice is often the result of misinformation or ignorance. Thus, one would expect less prejudice (if any at all) among well-informed people. This hypothesis was borne out in a recent study by Trankell.

Trankell (1974) studied the attitudes toward and concepts about immigrants in Sweden in a representative sample of the total population. The items of a questionnaire were grouped under the headings Fear (7 items concerning the socio-economic consequences of immigration), Dislike (7 items concerning the desirability of assimilation), and Generosity (4 items concerning rights and supporting action for immigrants). These 18 items were chosen, on semantic grounds, from 32 statements concerning immigrants, 18 of which were negatively worded and 14 positively worded. Afterwards there was a statistical check to determine if these groupings could act as scales. After a few alterations, 14 negatively worded and 4 positively worded statements remained as "scales." Furthermore, 6 statements concerning facts about immigrants were grouped under the heading "Knowledge" and 4 questions concerning interaction with immigrants were grouped under the heading "Involvement."

These item groups were then compared with 9 background variables like sex, age, education, income, social class, and a few more.

The direction of the association was such that individuals with higher education and social class, more interaction with immigrants, more experience traveling abroad, higher income, and lower age had more positive and fewer negative attitudes toward immigrants. This finding—that the more informed people are about immigrants, the more favorable the attitudes toward them tend to be—is also borne out by studies of children's attitudes.

Zeligs (1953) studied children's stereotypes of ten groups. After comparing results of 200 children in 1931 with a similar group of twelve-year-old children in 1944, she concluded that the less children know about races or nationalities, the fewer favorable concepts they have about them.

In summary, a negative stereotype is typically based on scant and erroneous information. Crucial variables for the development of positive stereotypes seem to be the degree of general education and the amount of specific knowledge, preferably through direct contact, of the culture and people of a certain ethnic group or nation. Children's stereotypes are in part determined by the attitudes of the parents.

Factors Affecting Educational Programs

Having looked briefly at some research findings in this area, let us turn to some of the problems faced daily by learners, teachers, and other school personnel. I would be the first to admit that better answers are needed desperately to help us meet one of the most complex responsibilities facing society today—that of ensuring the successful and rapid integration of immigrant children and adults into the full life of the school and communities in which they live. While all of us would agree that *any* sound educational program for *any* person should be predicated on an intimate knowledge of the learner's background, needs, learning style, and goals (as perceived by the learner), we must be frank to admit that there may be factors in the background of immigrant children and adults which make it essential to adapt existing social and educational programs or to provide different ones.

Only with carefully designed programs can we hope to reduce the high failure and drop-out rate of students in the schools. Further, we cannot ignore the fact that in a school, the program for students whose dominant language and culture are not those of the host country will affect the program for all the other children in the school. It seems to us that schools and social agencies have four primary responsibilities:

211

1. They must help immigrant students to acquire and use the knowledge, skills, processes, and attitudes which would not only enable them to function in the schools, but also to develop their potential to assume social and civic responsibilities to the fullest extent.
2. They must ensure that the intensive, special programs for these newcomers will not curtail educational opportunities for the native population.
3. They must build into the program subject areas in the learners native tongue so that: a) they will retain pride in *their* language and culture; b) the native tongue may serve as a vehicle for immediate learning of other disciplines; and c) the learners may "go home again" and find a niche in their native schools or world of work if they so desire.
4. They must make provision for the continuous interaction of the immigrants and their native-speaking peers in a variety of respect-ensuring, prejudice-reducing, and mutually enriching activities both within the school and in the community.

Using the new language *only* in a classroom setting will never promote full use of the language nor will it foster "integrative" motivation.

What are some of the factors that may stand in the way of school and community integration of immigrants and established residents? I shall gloss lightly over the urgent provisions that sending and receiving countries or regions should take *before* migrants move into a new community: the immigrants need information about the culture of the peoples they will live and work with; about climate; housing, employment, basic laws and regulations; and they need to reassure the receiving communities that they will not lose their jobs or their homes because of the influx of foreigners. These are so obvious as not to warrant further discussion.

The educational problems are more complex, however, and must be thoroughly understood by the receiving schools. Much frustration on the part of school authorities and failure on the part of newcomers could be mitigated with straightforward information about schooling in sending countries and about attitudes toward education in these countries, particularly where women are concerned.

To begin with, what different school backgrounds may immigrant youngsters bring with them? As is well known, some of the newcomers of school age may never have attended school. Some may have attended school for a few hours a day in a rural area and may still be considered functionally illiterate in their native tongue. Some may lack the basic skills in their native language, despite several years of schooling. Others may lack basic concepts in the curriculum areas offered in the new schools. What we must realize is that despite valiant efforts of many sending countries, and a generally increased budgetary allotment for education, there are still inadequate facilities and personnel for children of school age in many developing regions and countries.

In addition, poverty and other circumstances beyond their control often force youngsters not to attend school or to leave at the end of the fourth grade. Although there may exist a compulsory education law, it is not always enforced because of inadequate facilities and lack of personnel. Thus, attendance officers, official letters, or lists of rules and regulations in schools within the receiving countries generally are quite new and therefore frightening to newcomers and their parents.

Let us look more closely at two examples with which I have had extensive firsthand experience: Puerto Rico and Italy. We will start with Puerto Rico. Even children who attended school in Puerto Rico for several years will seldom speak and understand English immediately upon their arrival. Their linguistic competence and performance will be influenced by such factors as the length of English study in Puerto Rico; the natural timidity of persons who find themselves in unfamiliar, strange surroundings; the fact that this is the first time they will be using English in an *all-English-speaking* community; the difference in sounds and melody of English spoken here and that heard and learned in Puerto Rico. (Let me say parenthetically that although English is now taught as a second language in every school in Puerto Rico from the first grade, the language program has been planned to bring about systematic, progressive growth of communication abilities over a twelve-year period. Thus a child whose record may indicate four years of English study may know only several hundred words and some elementary verbs and sentence patterns. Moreover, many teachers in the elementary schools in Puerto Rico, themselves products of an unfortunate school policy mandated by the United States, where the medium of instruction kept shifting from Spanish to English, represent a wide spectrum of ability in the English language.)

It is not surprising, therefore, to find that children entering schools with several years of instruction in the schools of Puerto Rico are on different curriculum levels in the English language arts. In general, it would do children an injustice to equate the years of English study in Puerto Rico with comparable years spent on a language arts program here.

And what about the Puerto Rican youngsters born in the continental United States or those who may have lived in the continental United States for several years? Some of these too may enter school with little or no knowledge of English.

Because of the sense of security which comes from sharing a common language and common culture, Puerto Rican immigrants, like all other immigrants to the United States before them, generally make their first homes with or near relatives and friends in the numerous Spanish-speaking enclaves which abound in every section of large cities. In most instances they zealously guard their language and their traditions and seek to instill in their offspring a pride in the Spanish language and culture. Moreover, some parents, especially those who know little English, may not always encourage the learning of English since they fear the gap which will widen between them and their children as they learn the new language.

A very similar situation exists in Italy, where migration is generally from the underdeveloped South to the industrial cities of Northern Italy or to countries such as Switzerland and Germany. People in the South still retain their dialects and seldom use standard Italian in social relationships or even in school; motivation for schooling is extremely low. Even youngsters who move within Italy to Northern Italy find themselves at a tremendous disadvantage and quickly drop out of school, as teachers in the northern schools have not yet received the necessary information and training which could help these youngsters.

We might add that the children of Mexican migrant workers in the United States fare little better. The many moves that parents are forced to make in order to be where they will find seasonal work make it impossible for schools to receive records or

214

to provide any adequate continuity of instruction. We could mention other groups even within the continental United States, but it is sufficient to say that the circumstances are distressingly similar nearly everywhere and that viable solutions have either not been sought, not been found, or not been implemented (viz., the absolute ban in the United States, until recently, on the use of Spanish in the classrooms or playgrounds).

But the problems, in nearly all host countries, go deeper than those of school and language. We are dealing with children and their families who may have come from a land and a culture quite different from those they find in new regions and countries. Generally, from small, agricultural communities, they have come into large, industrial, crowded areas. From a land where they may have experienced little or no discrimination based on skin color, they have come to a country where they are a minority group. (Many Puerto Ricans, for example, prefer to retain their Spanish in the continental United States in the hopes of avoiding racial discrimination.) From a land where they never suffered the extremes of heat and cold, they may have come to a region where the rigors of climate necessitate changes of clothing and worries about heating. From a land where rivalry for economic betterment is seldom part of the value system, they may find themselves in a country where competition and rivalry are considered acceptable forms of behavior. From a land where there is generally continuous interaction between the parents and the teachers who live in the same area and where the activities of the school and community often flow into each other, they come to a land where a language barrier makes such interaction difficult, if not impossible.

While these cultural conflicts cannot help but affect the attitudes of the children and their parents, we must also take a hard look at some educational policies which in the past may have militated against the more rapid admission of pupils into the mainstream of the school.

Fearing the stigma that might be attached to even a temporary segregation, many administrators have been reluctant to place these pupils in homogeneous classes with other language learners where they may have been given an intensive program in the new language. Thus within the same classroom, many teachers have had to prepare instructional programs not only for

215

linguistically different pupils at varying levels of linguistic ability and conceptual knowledge, but also for native pupils who may themselves be reading at two or three different levels.

Because of the widespread policy of placing pupils in classes with their age peers, youngsters with little or no previous schooling may find themselves in an eighth or ninth grade class without the concepts, skills, or language needed to function even minimally.

The practice in many school systems of placing all responsibility in the hands of the special "Language for Foreigners" teacher has been a deterrent to the solution of a problem that is school-wide and city-wide, and that demands *cooperative* efforts of all personnel. *All* teachers in schools with linguistically different children should be helped not only to develop attitudes of acceptance but also skill in adapting their teaching to the needs of these learners. One other problem that plagues administrators, particularly in the junior and senior high schools, is that of deciding which "department" should assume the major responsibility of the foreign teaching program. It has not always been recognized that although we are teaching the native language of the country, the methodology used is primarily that of foreign language teaching!

The community, too, is responsible for a large share of the difficulty which these newcomers experience. Established residents of the community fear that these create housing and employment problems. The old and new members of the community fail to accept each other because of the barriers of language and culture, as well as ignorance or misinformation about each other. Many host country parents feel that their children are deprived of full educational opportunities because of the time teachers must devote to the newcomers. In addition, many of the agencies best qualified to alleviate community problems have found themselves unprepared to handle the unexpected numbers of immigrants, who may enter the country at any time during the year and, in countries of the European Economic Community, even without special passports.

It would require one or more volumes to enumerate and explain the myriad interacting personal and social factors which hinder even willing and enthusiastic teachers from doing what they themselves would consider an acceptable job.

Since space is limited, let me simply list some of the variables which would determine the nature of an instructional program for immigrants:

1. Types of classroom organization available.
2. Number of language learners represented.
3. Variety of native languages represented.
4. Linguistic distinctions between L_1 and L_2.
5. Cultural background of learners.
6. Literacy in L_1.
7. Previous schooling in native country.
8. Schooling in host country (e.g. curriculum areas taught in L_1 and provision for maintenance of L_1).
9. Availability of qualified bilingual personnel.
10. Community (resources, interest, involvement, dominant language spoken, urban or rural, etc.).
11. Time of entry into class.
12. Age of entry into L_2 program.

These are obviously a bare minimum. Nevertheless, if school personnel obtained such information, it would become possible to develop a more meaningful program for newcomers. The program, of course, would include five major aspects:

C—Curriculum
O—Objectives
M—Methods and materials
E—Evaluation
T—Teachers (preparation and skills)

The COMET must, moreover, be tailored to the different needs of various age groups. For example, an illiterate newcomer of six *may* sometimes learn to function in a regular classroom with a minimum of special help, whereas a functional illiterate of fourteen should be placed in a special class, where the objectives are reordered, where the curriculum will differ from that of literate fourteen-year-olds, and where the materials and methods, for example, will have to take into consideration the two languages of the student. In conclusion, the COMET will have to reflect both the information regarding the variables listed and the various age levels of the newcomers.

It is a herculean task that teachers face—one requiring not only knowledge and special skill but also enthusiasm, devotion, dedication, and love. But, if we think for a moment of the contributions to the new society that newcomers can and will make, if given even half a chance, the advantages to host countries will far outweigh the time, effort, and money which productive programs may cost. Moreover, workers of the world will no longer accept the "ostrich in the sand" attitude which was tragically characteristic of host countries in the past. More and more, workers are seeking a fuller partnership in the host society—one designed to give them the rights and dignity that they have earned through their work and one to which every human being should have access.

References

Allport, G. W. 1958. *The nature of prejudice*. New York: Doubleday.

Ekstrand, L. January 1975. Migrant adaptation: A cross-cultural problem. Presented at FIPLV-UNESCO Symposium, Munich.

———. 1975. Age and length of residence as variables to the adjustment of migrant children. Presented at AILA Congress, Stuttgart.

Finocchiaro, M. December 1975. *Chart* in Learning Varieties. Presented at IATEFL and APLV Conference. St. Malo.

———. January 1975. Migration: problems and practices. Presented at FIPLV-UNESCO Symposium, Munich.

———. 1974. *The foreign language learner: a guide for teachers*. New York: Regents Publishing Company.

Hall, E. T. 1966. *The hidden dimension*. New York: Doubleday.

Trankell, A. 1974. *The Swede's prejudice toward immigrants*. Stockholm: Arbetsmarknadsdepartmentet.

Vecoli, R. J. 1972. European Americans: from immigrants to ethnics. *International Migration Review* 6, 403–434.

Zeligs, R. 1953. Children's concepts and stereotypes. *Genetic Psychology* 83, 171–178.

Educational Implications of the <u>Lau</u> v. <u>Nichols</u> Decision

Patricia J. Nakano

As a result of the *Lau* v. *Nichols* Supreme Court decision in January 1974, school districts throughout the United States are faced with the ominous and often perplexing task of reviewing educational policies and practices affecting students whose primary, home, or dominant language is other than English. The *Lau* decision has raised legal and educational issues which affect the obligation of school districts to provide effective educational services for these students. Of greatest legal and educational significance is the comment by the Court that if a child can neither speak nor understand the English language, that child is foreclosed from a meaningful and therefore equal educational opportunity. Beyond the legal consideration, educators are faced with the serious educational challenge of providing services that are designed to meet the needs of "linguistically and culturally different" students, i.e., choosing available instructional alternatives within the framework of legal requirements of both the Federal and state governments while instituting sound educational practices that can be implemented in the face of declining enrollments and dwindling personnel and fiscal resources.

The purpose of this paper is to attempt 1) to provide information regarding the evolution of the laws leading to the *Lau* decision; 2) to provide information regarding the role of the BABEL/Lau Technical Assistance Center, including a brief explanation of the process by which one of the nine national Lau Centers works cooperatively with school districts to achieve sound educational alternatives which meet the needs of students with different language backgrounds; and 3) to provide information regarding compliance requirements set forth in the Civil Rights Act of 1964 and subsequent Department of Health, Education, and Welfare regulations governing services to non- and limited-English-speaking students. Within this framework, the paper will address the controversial Lau Remedies, the role of the Office for Civil Rights and the legal compliance process, as well as the role of the BABEL/Lau Center.

Legal Developments Leading to the Lau Decision

It is not only helpful, but essential, to review the legal developments leading to the *Lau* decision because an historical perspective will provide a context for what often appears to be a rather arbitrary and capricious action of the Court.

There are two dominant themes that emerge and parallel each other in the course of legal developments: 1) an increased willingness on the part of the courts to intervene in educational policy making when students are denied access to facilities and services on the basis of race, and 2) an extension of the Fourteenth Amendment to the Constitution making provision to protect "linguistic minorities" who are entitled to equal protection under the law.

In tracing the first theme, we can demonstrate the willingness of the courts to intervene in educational policy-making in the *Brown* v. *Board of Education* [1] decision in 1954. In this decision, the Supreme Court ruled that a *de jure* [2] system of segregated schools is unconstitutional if students are denied access to school facilities on the basis of race. In this case, a family filed a class action suit against the Topeka, Kansas School Board for discrimination on the basis of race by allowing for and maintaining a dual school system, i.e., one school system for Blacks and one for Whites. The court found that such a system, based upon the tenets of "separate, but equal" was inherently unconstitutional. In effect, this decision overturned *Plessy* v. *Ferguson* [3] of

---

[1] *Brown* v. *Board of Education*, 347 U.S.483,74S. Ct. 686,98L. Ed. 873.

[2] *De jure* is defined as that which is based upon statute or law.

[3] *Plessy* v. *Ferguson*, 163, U.S. 537,16S. Ct. 1138,41L Ed. 256,1886.

1886, which permitted "separate but equal" facilities on the basis of race. Although in *Brown* v. *Board of Education*, the Court found a violation of the Fourteenth Amendment, it did not require that any specific affirmative steps be taken by the School Board.

As a further extension of the *Brown* decision, we can turn to the *Swann* v. *Charlotte Meckienberg* [4] decision in 1971. *Swann* demonstrates the increased willingness of the courts to intervene in educational policy-making by demanding that affirmative steps be taken to correct past discriminatory policies and practices which contributed to racially identifiable schools. In this case, a school district in North Carolina was sued in a class action suit on the basis of a *de facto* [5] segregated school system. The school district argued that the racial segregation of schools was the result of housing patterns which were determined by a Housing Authority rather than by a statute or policy of the school district. Consequently, the district contended that they had not willfully discriminated against Black students. Moreover, the district argued that the schools had no control over housing patterns and thus could not be held accountable for the racially segregated schools. In this instance, the Supreme Court ordered the district to desegregate its schools by using noncontiguous zoning rather than the previous "neighborhood schools" zoning patterns. Thus, the courts not only reviewed the educational policy of the schools, but also ordered the district to take specific affirmative steps to correct racially discriminatory practices. This decision, in fact, stated that a *de facto* segregated system was tantamount to a *de jure* system in that both resulted in the exclusion of Black students on the basis of race. Moreover, the Court went beyond the issue of access to that of quality, stating that characteristics of the students themselves affect the quality of educational services.

In the *Larry P.* v. *Wilson Riles* [6] (1972) decision, the courts once again demonstrated their willingness to intervene in educational policy making by demanding that affirmative steps be taken to correct discrimination against students. In this case, a Black stu-

---

[4] *Swann* v. *Charlotte Meckienberg*, 402 U.S. 1,91S. Ct. 1267,1971.

[5] *De facto* is defined as that which is based upon a factual situation rather than upon statute or law.

[6] *Larry P.* v. *Wilson Riles*, C-71-2270 RFP Dist. Ct.

dent, joined by the Bay Area Black Psychological Association, filed a class action suit against the San Francisco Unified School District and the State Department of Education for using discriminatory policies to place students in classes for the educable mentally retarded (EMR). In this class action suit, the Supreme Court found it discriminatory (and therefore unconstitutional under the Fourteenth Amendment) to use culturally and socio-economically biased testing instruments to place students into special education classes. The Court ordered the District to retest the Black students who had been placed in EMR classes with a test that was culturally and socio-economically unbiased against Blacks. Upon retesting, at least two-thirds of the Black students previously assigned to EMR classes tested out of that program and were reassigned to regular classrooms for instruction.

In summary, since 1954, we can trace the extent to which the courts have demonstrated a willingness to review educational policies and practices and to demand that action be taken to correct past discrimination on the basis of race, thereby ensuring individuals equal protection under the law.

A review of case law reveals the extension of equal protection under the Fourteenth Amendment to "linguistic minorities" as well. In the *Castro* v. *State of California* [7] decision in 1970, the California Supreme Court found it unconstitutional for the State to impose an English language test as a measure of literacy to determine whether someone could vote or not. Before the *Castro* decision, an individual who could not pass an English language literacy test was prohibited from voting by California law. The State argued that such a requirement was necessary to promote an intelligent electorate in the State. Since this was a reasonable goal, they argued, such a requirement did not discriminate against a person on the basis of language. The Supreme Court disagreed and found that the statute was discriminatory because such a provision effectively excluded persons with different language backgrounds from voting. The Court ruled that the use of English language literacy tests was not a proper measure to ensure that an intelligent electorate would ensue as a result of such a statutory requirement.

---

[7] *Castro* v. *State of California* 85 CR 20, 1970.

The *Diana* v. *State Board of Education*[8] (1970) decision further established equal protection to "linguistic minorities." In this case, a family filed a class action suit against the State for discriminatory policies and practices affecting the placement of non- and/or limited-English-speaking students in classes for the educable mentally retarded (EMR). The California Supreme Court found that non- or limited-English-speaking students were tested unfairly with English language intelligence tests administered by English-speaking testers. As a result of such testing, students were classified as mentally retarded or educationally handicapped and were placed into special education classes. The California Supreme Court ruled that the State Board of Education would have to take affirmative steps to correct the past discrimination against these students by retesting them in a language understood and spoken by the students, and required that the test administrator be proficient in the language of the students being tested. As a result of the *Diana* case, there were massive reforms in California State educational policy and practices affecting testing, classification, and placement of students with different linguistic and cultural backgrounds in special education classes.

Thus, we find that well before the *Lau* v. *Nichols* decision, the courts had been willing to extend protection to those individuals with a language other than English and to require corrective action to eliminate past discrimination.

In addition to the court rulings, there have been historical developments in statutory law and governmental regulations which affect educational services accorded to students who speak languages other than English by school districts receiving federal financial assistance. In 1964, one decade after the landmark decision of *Brown* v. *Board of Education,* the Civil Rights Act (CRA)[9] was passed. Title VI, Section 601 of the Act prohibits discrimination on the basis of race, color, or national origin in programs receiving federal financial assistance. This particular title is enforced by the Office for Civil Rights, the enforcement agency within the Department of Health, Education and Welfare.

---

[8] *Diana* v. *State Board of Education* C70,37 RFP California, 1970.

[9] *Civil Rights Act* 42 U.S.C. 2000d, Washington, D.C., 1964.

In an attempt to clarify "national origin" discrimination cited in Section 601, CRA 1964, the Department of Health, Education and Welfare issued revised regulations in 1968.[10] These stated that "school systems are responsible for assuring that students of a particular race, color, or national origin are not denied the opportunity to obtain the education generally obtained by other students in the system."

As further clarification, the Office for Civil Rights issued a memorandum in May 1970 to all school districts advising them of their obligations under Title VI of the Civil Rights Act, namely, to ensure provision of equal educational services to students of national origin minority backgrounds. The May 25 Memorandum[11] was sent to "school districts with more than five per cent national minority group children" regarding "identification of discrimination and denial of services on the basis of national origin." This memorandum was published in July 1970 in the Federal Register and served as an elaboration of Section 601 and the 1968 Departmental regulations. The "national origin" memorandum outlined the affirmative steps that a school district must take to ensure equal access and effective participation in the educational programs offered by the district in order to ensure the provision of equal educational opportunities. The major points of the memorandum are:

(1) Where inability to speak and understand the English language excludes national origin minority group children from effective participation in the educational program offered by a school district, the district must take affirmative steps to rectify the language deficiency in order to open its instructional program to these students. (2) School districts must not assign national origin minority group students to classes for the mentally retarded on the basis of criteria which essentially measure or evaluate English language skills. (3) Any ability grouping or tracking system employed by a school system to deal with the special language skill needs of national origin minority group children must be designed to meet such language skill needs

---

[10] U.S. Department of Health, Education and Welfare, 33 FR. 4956, Washington, D.C., 1968.

[11] Department of Health, Education and Welfare, 35CR F. Reg. 11595, Washington, D.C., 1970.

as soon as possible and must not operate as an educational dead end or permanent track. (4) School districts have the responsibility to adequately notify national origin minority group parents of school activities which are called to the attention of other parents. Such notice in order to be adequate may have to be provided in a language other than English. [12]

It is critical that there be a sound understanding of the above statutory provisions and governmental regulations pertaining to students whose primary, home, or dominant language is other than English because the Supreme Court ultimately based the *Lau* decision upon previously cited statutes and regulations enforced by the Department of Health, Education, and Welfare and the Office for Civil Rights, rather than upon the Fourteenth Amendment.

The Lau v. Nichols Decision

With this background in mind, it is appropriate to discuss the *Lau* v. *Nichols* [13] decision of 1974 and the factual situation surrounding the case. The family of Kinney Kinmon Lau filed a class action suit on behalf of 1,800 Chinese-speaking students against the San Francisco Board of Education for its alleged failure to provide equal educational opportunities to these students. This failure to provide services was deemed to be in violation of the Fourteenth Amendment. The School Board argued that: 1) it was not discriminating against these students because they were afforded the same opportunities, services, teachers, and facilities as all students in the School District; 2) it was not the fault of the schools that these students brought a handicap to school in that they did not speak or understand the English language; 3) the Board certainly had not caused this handicap and therefore could not be held culpable for the characteristic; and 4) the Board was only following State policy by providing instruction in the official language of instruction, i.e., English. The Ninth Circuit Court of Appeals decided in favor of the San Francisco School District. It decided that there had been no discrimination against

---

[12] *Ibid.*

[13] *Lau* v. *Nichols,* 414 U.S. 563 (1974)

these students, and that, therefore, the School Board was not in violation of the Fourteenth Amendment. The Court argued that if one is a resident of the United States, one should learn to speak the language of America.

The only dissenting opinion, written by District Judge Irving Hill, stated that:

> The majority describe the plight of these children as being the "result of deficiencies created by themselves in failing to learn the English language." To ascribe some fault to a grade school child because of his "failing to learn the English language" seems both callous and inaccurate. (*Lau* v. *Nichols*, 483 2d 791, Ninth Circuit Ct., Calif. 1973 p. 805)

Upon appeal to the U.S. Supreme Court, the decision of the lower court was reversed. The Supreme Court found that the "English only" policy of the School Board was denying students a meaningful opportunity to participate in a public educational program and constituted a violation of the Civil Rights Act of 1964 and subsequent governmental regulations. Justice Douglas in the majority opinion stated:

> Under these state (California State Education Code Sections 71, 8573 & 12101) imposed standards there is no equality of treatment by providing students with the same facilities, textbooks, teachers, and curriculum; for students who do not understand English are effectively foreclosed from any meaningful education. . . . Imposition of a requirement that, before a child can effectively participate in the educational program, he must already have acquired those basic (English) skills is to make a mockery of public education. (*Lau* v. *Nichols*, 414 U.S. 563, 1974)

The Supreme Court remanded to the lower court the responsibility to ensure that the San Francisco School District develop a comprehensive educational plan to remedy the past practices of discrimination against the students on the basis of linguistic characteristics.[14]

---

[14] For further discussion of litigation and case law, including *Aspira of New York* v. *Board of Education of the City of New York* (1974), *Keyes* v. *Denver School District No. 1* (1975) and *Otero* v. *Mesa County School District No. 51* (1975) as it affects the law and education for students with different language backgrounds, please refer to a paper by Herbert Teitelbaum and Richard J. Hiller, *"Trends in Bilingual Education and the Law"* presented at a national conference sponsored by the National Institute of Education in June 1976 in Austin, Texas.

As a result of the court order, the Department of Justice requested that the Office for Civil Rights convene a group of educators, attorneys, and equal opportunity specialists to develop guidelines to assist school districts in meeting the compliance standards set forth by the *Lau* decision, and respond to the implementation of "affirmative steps" under Title VI of the Civil Rights Act and its subsequent regulations, most notably the May 25, 1970 Memorandum. In October 1975 the group issued a document commonly known as the "OCR/Lau Remedies." These will be discussed later. As the result of the *Lau* decision and its implications for school districts throughout the U.S., the Congress recognized the need to provide districts with General Assistance Centers that focused upon the educational needs of non- and limited-English-speaking students. It seems appropriate, then, for us to turn to a discussion of these Centers and their role in assisting school districts in shaping "educational relief" to respond to the *Lau* decision.

The Role of the "General Assistance Centers"

The BABEL/Lau Center is one of the nine General Assistance Centers funded under an annual contract pursuant to Title IV of the Civil Rights Act, administered by the U.S. Office of Education in the Department of Health, Education, and Welfare. The legislative intent in funding General Assistance Centers was founded upon the need to provide school districts with technical assistance in areas pertaining to the needs of limited- and non-English-speaking students and the *Lau* v. *Nichols* decision. The legislative mandate includes the following areas of technical assistance provided by General Assistance Centers (GAC): 1) identification and assessment of student language needs related to instructional services and programs for students who are non- or limited-English-speaking; 2) educational program planning and selection; 3) fiscal and administrative management; 4) community education programs and services; and 5) information relative to regulations governing educational treatment and services to non- and limited-English-speaking students. The nine GAC areas are: Area A, serving the northeastern U.S. and Puerto Rico; Area B, serving parts of the Northeast, Central, and Southeastern U.S.; Area C, serving the Midwestern U.S.; Area D, serving the

Southwest U.S. (Texas, Arkansas, and Louisiana); Area E, serving the Mountain States; Area F, serving Southwestern U.S. (New Mexico, Arizona and Nevada); Area G, serving 10 counties in Southern California; Area H, serving 48 counties in Northern California; and Area I, serving the Pacific Northwest, Hawaii, the Trust Territories, and Samoa.

Within the broad legislative mandate and regulations governing the General Assistance Centers, there is provision within each contractual agreement for variations in delivery systems for each GAC. The BABEL/Lau Center, which serves Area H, uses a "Three Phase Approach" which calls for 1) Needs Assessment; 2) Needs Analysis, Program Planning, and Development; and 3) Implementation of Services. This approach is outlined in the diagram on p. 229. It may be adopted by any school district, whether it has been found in noncompliance or not.

The major goals of the BABEL/Lau Center are to encourage school districts, through their respective decision-making bodies, parents and community members, instructional personnel, etc., to recognize the educational merit of utilizing the dominant language for instruction with the purpose of developing skills mastery while developing linguistic skills in a second language, i.e., English. The objective of the Center is to provide current and factual data regarding bilingualism, methods and approaches, etc. for meeting the educational needs of students whose primary, home, or dominant language is other than English. As a corollary objective, the Center attempts to provide guidelines and interpretations of past and current programs providing services to students in addition to interpretations of compliance procedures followed by the enforcement agency, the Office for Civil Rights.

It is the ultimate goal of the Center to assist school districts in initiating, improving, and expanding instructional programs that will significantly enhance the *educational* opportunities and experiences of all students. Ideally, programs will reflect the spirit of the *Lau* v. *Nichols* decision in addition to satisfying the legal obligations. Most importantly, the BABEL/Lau effort is an attempt to affect the quality of the educational processes and products of the educational system and to facilitate institutional changes that would ensure that students with other language backgrounds are effectively participating in a meaningful education.

228

THE DEVELOPMENT OF A COMPREHENSIVE EDUCATION PLAN

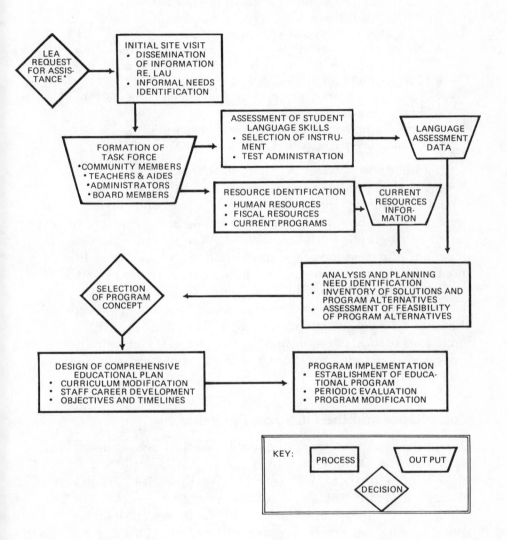

As a means of achieving the Center goals, services and information in the following areas are made available to school districts:

1. Legal and educational aspects of the *Lau* decision
2. Primary and home language identification
3. Language dominance assessment
4. Needs assessment of district human and fiscal resources
5. School-community Task Force organization and procedures
6. Bilingual education models and the role of ESL
7. Language acquisition theory and instructional models
8. Evaluation design
9. Professional growth development frameworks
10. Community participation and education

In addition to services provided to school districts, the Center is developing products in response to concerns expressed by school-community members, administrative and instructional personnel, and Board of Education members; for example, a series of monographs on bilingual education, second language acquisition, and first language maintenance and loss, and instruments to determine primary and home language usage patterns.

In summary, the BABEL/Lau Center seeks to bring together the legal and educational imperatives in meeting the needs of students who speak languages other than English, within the limitations of local decision-making frameworks, community concerns and demands, and human and fiscal resources in a given school district.

Compliance and the OCR/Lau Remedies

One of the questions most frequently asked by school districts is related to the OCR (Office for Civil Rights) compliance effort. Most school districts are confused by the term "legal compliance" and are not aware of the role and functions of the Office for Civil Rights. Those individuals responsible for responding to compliance requirements of the Office for Civil Rights are perplexed by the web of bureaucratic language and requirements. It is important to distinguish between the role and function of the Office for Civil Rights on one hand, and that of the General Assistance Centers on the other. First of all, the role of the Office for Civil Rights is to enforce the Civil Rights Act of

1964 to ensure that no program receiving federal financial assistance discriminate against students because of race, color, or national origin. The General Assistance Centers function as an objective party capable of rendering technical assistance to school districts when they respond to legal and educational obligations regardless of whether or not the school district has been found in noncompliance under Title VI, (or the May 25 Memorandum) by the Office for Civil Rights. The General Assistance Centers do not have any enforcement authority and do not review and/or monitor school districts to ensure compliance.

As the civil rights enforcement agency, the Office for Civil Rights (OCR) assumed the awesome responsibility of devising an internal document establishing a uniform set of guidelines to measure the efforts of school districts in taking affirmative steps to provide services to non- and limited-English-speaking students. The document, widely known as the "OCR/Lau Remedies" [15] sets forth parameters for the components of a comprehensive educational plan submitted by a school district. In summary, the major components of a comprehensive educational plan are:

1. Identification of the students' primary and home language, as well as language dominance testing;
2. Utilization of diagnostic and prescriptive measures;
3. Educational program selection for elementary and secondary levels based upon linguistic characteristics and academic achievement;
4. Assurances that required and elective courses do not encourage racially or ethnically identifiable tracking or ability grouping practices, that course content include the role and contributions of various groups, and that counseling practices are impartial and "open";
5. Assurances that teachers are linguistically proficient and culturally sensitive and that staffing patterns include provision for teachers possessing such skills;
6. Prohibition of racially or ethnically identifiable schools and classes;

---

[15] U.S. Department of Health, Education and Welfare, "Task Force Findings Specifying Remedies Available for Elimination of Past Educational Practices Ruled Unlawful Under *Lau* v. *Nichols*," Washington, D.C., October 1975.

7. Provision for notification of school activities in languages other than English;
8. Provision for an evaluation design with timelines for projected completion and actual completion activities contained in the comprehensive educational plan; and
9. Submission of progress reports 60 days after the beginning of school and 30 days after the last day of school for a three-year period.

As referred to earlier, these OCR/Lau Remedies have become the center of a heated controversy and have fueled a professional rivalry between bilingual education and English as a second language practitioners. The controversy revolves around two questions: 1) the legal status of the OCR/Lau Remedies and 2) the appropriateness of ESL.

Both of these qualify as "red herrings" that tend to obfuscate the central issue of providing services to non- and limited-English-speaking students. The essential spirit of the *Lau* decision does not have to deal fundamentally with whether the Lau Remedies have been published in the Federal Register or not.

Perhaps the single most inflammatory and injudicious statement made in the OCR Remedies pertains to the role of English as a Second Language. To wit, the statement that:

> Since an ESL program does not consider the affective nor cognitive development of the students in this category and the time and maturation variables are different here than for students at secondary levels, an ESL program *is not* appropriate. (Items III 1.A. and 2.A.)

Much of the furor surrounding the statement can be attributed to the historical pattern of misinformation that has been perpetuated about bilingual education and ESL, i.e., that in bilingual education programs English is not taught or that students become linguistically confused; and conversely, that ESL classes ignore or denigrate the student's language and culture. In addition, bilingual education is often defined and implemented by school districts and others as teaching students a second language without the utilization of the dominant language of the students.

Fundamentally, English as a Second Language (ESL) is an integral part of a bilingual education program, although it may also be used as part of a monolingual program. The goals of the program may vary in terms of the importance placed upon maintaining the students' home language and culture, but teaching students English as a second language remains a constant variable.

A maintenance model of bilingual education (as the name suggests) seeks to maintain the student's home language by using it to teach certain basic subject matter. At the same time, of course, instruction in English as a second language is provided, so that the students become and remain proficient in both languages. A transitional model of bilingual education, on the other hand, does NOT seek to maintain the students' home language and, therefore, uses it as a medium of instruction only until the students become proficient enough in English to function in an English-speaking classroom. When there are only a few non- or limited-English-speaking students in a district, representing different language backgrounds, it may be impractical to do more than provide them with an ESL class in the context of a monolingual English program. However, cross-age or parent tutoring in the dominant language(s) should be used whenever possible.

In addition to selecting instructional programs for non- and limited-English-speaking students, school districts must give serious consideration to measuring the impact upon student learning of the specific instructional programs or models selected for implementation. Regardless of legal obligations, a school district must know what specific ways the instructional methods, materials, and personnel affect students' educational performance.

As a direct means of addressing the points raised about the options prescribed in the Lau Remedies, the BABEL/Lau Center has urged districts to consider a number of recommended instructional models that rely on the results of language dominance testing as well as identification of the primary and/or home language of the students.[16]

Some of the recommended instructional models go beyond the options outlined in the Remedies but they are justified on the basis of sound linguistic and pedagogical principles. This flexibility is in harmony with the ruling of the U.S. Supreme

---

[16] For further information, please contact the author at the BABEL/Lau Center, 2168 Shattuck Avenue, Berkeley, California 94704.

Court; specifically, Justice Douglas stated in the *Lau* v. *Nichols* majority opinion that:

No specific remedy is urged upon us. Teaching English to the students of Chinese ancestry who do not speak the language is one choice. Giving instruction to this group in Chinese is another. *There may be others* (emphasis added). Petitioners ask only that the Board of Education be directed to apply its expertise to the problem and rectify the situation.[17]

Unwittingly, bilingual education and ESL practitioners have taken opposing sides in an imaginary battle, one that creates artificial impediments to effective student learning. This serves only to undermine the essence of second language teaching and bilingual education, that essence being the philosophy and means whereby individuals will encourage and embrace educational goals recognizing diverse languages and cultures within our society.

As a tribute to Dr. James Alatis, to whom this text is dedicated, I wish to conclude with a quote from his address before the 1975 TESOL Convention in Los Angeles, because it reminds us of our need to bear in mind the children that we serve and the society in which we live:

What we need is more cooperation between, and a coalition of teachers of English as a second language and specialists in bilingual education who would work together toward a common purpose, and that purpose is to help thousands of children throughout the United States to reach their full potential as citizens of our increasingly complex and troubled society. Such cooperation will contribute to the solution of our most pressing national problems. . . .[18]

---

[17] *Op. cit.*, 414 U.S. S.Ct., 1974, pp. 564.

[18] Alatis, James E. 1975. "The Compatibility of TESOL and Bilingual Education." In M.K. Burt, and H.C. Dulay (eds.), *New Directions in Second Language Learning, Teaching, and Bilingual Education*. Washington, D.C.: TESOL, 10.

Bilingual Education: A Viable Resource for Cross-cultural Enrichment

José A. Vázquez

Looking back into the educational history of the United States, let us consider two occurrences of significance for bilingual education, private as well as public.

The first of these took place in 1840 in Cincinnati, Ohio, where a large group of German immigrants found the public schools to be inferior to those in Germany and proceeded to establish their own schools. After these German schools managed to compete successfully with the existing public schools, the already "assimilated Americans" became overly concerned that these newcomers might not adapt to join the English-speaking majority. This concern caused the state of Ohio to pass a law that year which required the teaching of English as well as German in the German schools. Additionally, the city of Cincinnati introduced the teaching of German in its public schools as an optional language. It should be noted that this episode did not happen in one of the cosmopolitan centers of the nineteenth century, where the effects of immigration were most profound, but rather in the primarily rural Middle West, where new language pockets were being formed.

The law of 1840 stated:

> It shall be the duty of the Board of Trustees of Common Schools and Visitors of the Common Schools to provide a number of German schools under some duly qualified teachers for the instruction of such youth as they desire to learn the German and English languages together. (Kloss, 1940–42.)

Preference was given to bilingual schools, for which Cincinnati became famous. These bilingual schools existed until 1917, when, because of World War I, anti-German sentiment forced their closing. German was not one of the languages of the colonial powers in America;[1] but that fact and the number of non-standard and non-prestige variants of the language spoken here notwithstanding, the German bilingual schools constitute a trend in education in the United States.

It would be far too complex to present historical data on all efforts that were initiated during the nineteenth and the first half of the twentieth centuries to promote bilingual schooling among other language groups in this country. Because of socio-economic and political pressures, however, the bilingual schools of these eras developed language programs within the public schools, without their philosophy being incorporated into the practice of either the institution or the society it served.

The other movement we shall consider started in 1963 in the public schools of Dade County, Florida; this resurgence resulted directly from the influx of Cuban political refugees into Miami. To expedite the assimilation of this group into the United States' system, a bilingual education program was initiated. Significantly, the Cuban students were not isolated in projects designed exclusively to teach them English. The fact that this Spanish-speaking population had suddenly been incorporated into the schools was capitalized upon, so that English-speaking children might be provided with second language instruction as well.

Among the Dade County Public Schools, Coral Way became the prime recipient of national attention and interest. The bilingual approach utilized there was seen as a possible means of combating a legion of academic ills which had plagued students of other linguistic groups in various parts of the country. The largest of these groups were the Mexican-American and Puerto Rican. However, in the vast majority of bilingual experiments triggered by the Coral Way accomplishments, English monolin-

---

[1] Other than English, languages spoken in the continental United States are commonly divided into three groups: (a) indigenous or native languages; (b) colonial languages; and (c) immigrant languages (Haugen, 1946). Accordingly, German would be classified as belonging to the immigrant group.

gual students were not included as they had been in the Coral Way Elementary School. Whatever the reasons for these exclusions, the programs developed into one-way channels, utilizing the students' native tongues as vehicles for assimilation.

What could have been a golden opportunity was missed; the true concept of bilingual education was distorted. In 1963, the scenario was ready for educational enrichment through modern foreign languages; why did this not come about? The critical situation of educational failure affecting speakers of languages other than English obscured the full potential of the bilingual approach. By no means am I implying that the transitional aspect should have been subordinated, but the consequences of the neglect of the enrichment aspect have been profound.

In evaluating the situation from 1963 onward, one might well look back to 1958. In that year, Congressional action resulted in the National Defense Education Act, which regarded the teaching of science and modern foreign languages as vital to national security. Yet over the past decade, there has been an accelerating decline in the teaching of foreign languages at all levels of schooling; even those other languages most widely represented in our national community have been affected.

This trend is one of the strongest and most pervasive in American education today. In our elementary schools, the teaching of foreign languages (FLES) is a thing of the past. Since 1968, only a fifth of the high school graduates have had even superficial exposure to any language other than English. Language requirements for admission to colleges and universities in the United States have been dropped in 90 percent of these institutions, and the number which do not require foreign language credits for graduation has quadrupled since 1966. Barely half of those receiving doctoral degrees must demonstrate even a reading knowledge of a language other than English. These changes reflect and reinforce the ever-increasing attitude that, since everything an educated American needs to know is available in English, a facility in English alone is sufficient to survive, even to excel. This is a purely isolationist stance, based on the overly optimistic belief that, because English prevails, the acquisition of other languages is no longer relevant.

The decade of the 1960s marked a new involvement of the federal government in the field of education. The 88th Congress, often referred to as the Education Congress, acted upon concerns mainly pertaining to the disadvantaged, so often masked by the camouflage of inaccurate labels such as "culturally deprived," "linguistically handicapped," and many others. The Civil Rights Act of 1964 created an atmosphere supportive of non-English speaking minorities (another pejorative label: who wants to be identified as a non-something?). Four years later, the Elementary and Secondary Education Act was amended to include Title VII: the Bilingual Education Act.

Prior to the implementation of this amendment, federal policy- and decision-makers heard the testimony of parents, educators, and scholars in favor of bilingual education. Concordant with the pleas, available data, and research, Title VII funding guidelines were written, prescribing bilingual education as a panacea to cure the ills of all students of limited English-language skills. However well-intentioned, these guidelines made no provision to assure the propagation of the enrichment aspects of bilingual education.

Having federal monies available, as insignificant as the amount was, led many educators down the path of opportunistic planning, the results of which are always unpredictable. Speculation is a poor substitute for a rational model. This resurgence of public bilingual schooling came about in response to a critical situation; consequently, it assumed a compensatory role. Community pressures notwithstanding, most programmatic activity in bilingual education ranked among the lowest district-level priorities for the improvement of the total functioning of the schools. Most federally-funded programs were limited to short-term commitments, the precedent for which was, inappropriately, Title I, in which funding had not been competitive. Today, after a few visible results, we encounter similar conditions.

Public bilingual education is basically bound to a fundamental network of decisions on social integration of different ethnolinguistic groups, on immigration, and on national expansion. As promulgated today, it is more a political effort than the institutionalized educational process it should be. If languages other than English are viewed as diseases of the poor or disadvantaged, it is futile to use as treatment superficial exposure to these languages, as in the process of building a natural immunity.

This ultimately leads to the eradication of these languages, and, realistically, there are other more drastic but less expensive treatments to cure the use of a native tongue. If the goal is to be an English-only policy, one should never refer to the means by which it is achieved as bilingual education.

The situation being as it is, may we still hope to institute a genuine system of bilingual education in our public schools? Or must we now move to private institutions if this is to be accomplished?

At present in the United States, private English/Spanish bilingual schools are virtually nonexistent. A few examples may be found in extracontinental territory. Puerto Rico, since the American intervention, has had several models of private bilingual schools. These have been mainly sectarian, with a strong emphasis upon the acquisition of English. Today a few nonsectarian private schools (for example, Monte Olimpo in Caimito, nursery to third grade) are employing both Spanish and English as media of instruction.

In order to consider the establishment of private English/Spanish bilingual schools in the United States, one must realize that the value of acquiring a second language is often assessed in proportion to its prestige. The case is different in an English/French situation, in which the second language carries prestige equal to or greater than that of the first.

Two of the most successful private schools in New York City have English/French bilingual curricula. At the Lycée Français de New York, with a French-speaking enrollment of approximately 50 percent, all areas are taught in French, including mathematics and science. At the United Nations International School, a French/English bilingual program involves the teaching of social studies and mathematics in a language other than the main medium of instruction. It has been determined that graduates of the Lycée and the UNIS do well in math and science courses they subsequently take at American universities. Moreover, they acquire different approaches to study and problem solving which may be used to advantage in other areas. But of all the implica-

239

tions which may be drawn, perhaps the following is most important: if one examines the difference between a student in a bilingual program and one in a regular language program,[2] it is usually found that the student in the former program develops an interest growing year after year in both languages; whereas for the student in the latter program, the interest in the second language will in many cases lapse after a few years, regardless of the teachers or methodology employed.

These two private English/French bilingual schools have clienteles comprised of middle- and upper-income-level parents; they have chosen these programs not for reasons of enthno-linguistic background but because they have been convinced that a bilingual curriculum provides a better way for their children to learn two languages. Unfortunately, the attitude toward English/Spanish bilingual education is not parallel in the minds of the populace: Spanish in the United States lacks the aura of prestige that French carries. This country's ten million speakers of Spanish are generally viewed by the English-speaking majority as using an inferior language. They have been adjudged as guilty of speaking too loud or too fast or too slow; of speaking with their hands; and most assuredly of not speaking a "pure" form of Spanish.

As if discrimination from the English-speaking majority against speakers of Spanish were not enough of a handicap, this country's Spanish speakers have developed partisan attitudes for their particular dialects bordering on chauvinism. Specifically among the practitioners in public bilingual schools, one encounters discriminatory practices against dialectal variations. Alternate intonation patterns and a few lexical differences should not be factors working against the maintenance and enhancement of a language; yet this has been most prevalent in the creation and selection of printed materials for the bilingual classroom. How often one has heard "These materials are not appropriate for Puerto Ricans because they are for Mexicans" or " . . . not appropriate for Mexicans because they are for Cubans" or " . . . not appropriate for Cubans" because they are for another group.

---

[2] Such an example may be drawn from the United Nations International School, where both programs exist.

And so it goes: vicious circles are easily formed. Unification among Spanish speakers in the United States cannot come about until the different groups realize that their language variants must cross-pollinate to produce a hardy strain for nationwide communication. This calls for further exploration in the area of dialect geography, as is being done by specialists in American English.

A generative force for the creation of private English/Spanish bilingual schools is the fact that our Spanish-speaking community is steadily achieving a higher educational level, which enables the maintenance of an intellectual life encompassing literary, theatrical, journalistic, and other cultural manifestations of the language. These will be further expanded, and concurrently so will be the common use of the language. The time must come when English/Spanish bilingual schooling can be discussed in Spanish as well as English. Until then, the concept will be something of a misnomer.

Not to underestimate the promise of the private school, it is within the public schools that the greatest potential remains. These institutions can provide the largest arena in which the English speaker and the Spanish speaker may interact in both languages, the goal of the total educational process. Emphasis should be placed upon the early years of schooling, since it is accepted that second language learning changes with age and that younger second language learners more closely resemble first language learners than older ones do. This primary instruction will form a basis for a continuum traversing all levels. Cultures are learned through the language of communication and interaction. The relationship between language and culture, if fully appreciated, will strengthen linguistic abilities. Only by making bilingual education readily available to all will we see it survive.

It is axiomatic that school boards and educators respond more readily to what they see as the needs of individual students than they do to national needs. Yet it is in this respect that bilingual schooling has the most to offer. The multiple problems with the English language, faced by the vast majority of English monolingual students, will not be corrected until such students gain a sense of the language as such. They may gain this sense

241

in many ways, one of the most intellectually expanding from exposure to a language other than English.

An ongoing problem is the misconception of what bilingual education really is and what it can do for us as a nation. As an example of a distorted view of this approach, one may consider the following passage from a publication of the National Education Association, "Bilingual/Bicultural Education: Why you should know about it" (Stock number 051-02262):

"What is Bilingual/Bicultural Education?"

> In bilingual/bicultural education, the teacher encourages children who are not from an English-speaking, middle-class background and respects their culture. The teacher teaches in the children's native language and in English all the skills the children will need to compete successfully with people from the English-speaking middle class. The aim of bilingual/bicultural education is to give every student the chance to choose between competing in the white Anglo world and living comfortably in her or his own culture.

What this publication describes is not bilingual education: it is advocacy for societal insulation, and it impedes the implementation of the genuine concept.

How then may the true goal of bilingual education be achieved?

—By convincing the English monolingual parents and students of this country that bilingualism provides unique intellectual, social, and commercial advantages.
—By transforming public schools into fully operational bilingual models within their districts.
—By creating a national network of these schools for the purpose of exchanging developed curricula and research findings on all aspects of the teaching/learning process, so as to avoid geographical isolation and duplication of effort.

But in order to facilitate the aforementioned process, there must be established among national organizations and institutions, specifically those involved in language teaching, and decision-makers at the national, state, and local levels, a consensus that bilingual education as enrichment is of universal value.

242

Quality in Bilingual Education

Albar A. Peña

As one looks at bilingual education programs being implemented throughout the United States today, one of their major objectives is "to enable children whose dominant language is other than English to develop competitive proficiency in English so that they can function successfully in the educational and occupational institutions of the larger society."[1] That this should be one of the primary objectives, no one would disagree. Unfortunately, many of these so-called bilingual education programs today focus only on this primary objective as the most expedient way of "curing the potential bilingual child" of his "linguistic problem" and getting him ready to be assimilated into the regular monolingual, monocultural program. Provisions to utilize his native language are allowed only until the student has gained the desired proficiency in English. When this objective has been reached, this so-called bilingual program is discontinued as being patently no longer necessary.[2] In short, what happens is that such programs now become compensatory bilingual education programs. The full potential of bilingual education is again neglected and students are still denied the benefits that could be derived if the programs were allowed to continue. At the recent International Bilingual/Bicultural Education Confer-

---

[1] From a letter by Commissioner of Education Terrell H. Bell, dated November 15, 1974, to Senator Joseph Montoya of New Mexico. Source: *Defensa*, 1976, No. 1, p. 18.

[2] Joshua A. Fishman, "Bilingual Education: The State of Social Science Inquiry," (Paper prepared for the Institute for Advanced Study, Princeton, New Jersey.)

ence held in San Antonio, Texas, Joshua Fishman made the following statement:

> . . . if bilingual education is to survive in this country it cannot continue to be treated as compensatory . . . a kind of a public health program to stamp out disease. . . . Those poor people out there are bilingual. We had better give them a bilingual program to help them get over it.[3]

It is inconceivable that the proponents of bilingual/bicultural education today continue to stand by apathetically and allow this type of bilingual education to ruin whatever chances were available to make this a truly viable educational approach. What, then, are our alternatives? The obvious one should be the establishment of bilingual programs as language maintenance or enrichment programs. However, in order to make an intelligent choice, let us first examine what both of these modes of bilingual education have to offer.

Compensatory (Transitional) vs. Maintenance (Enrichment) Bilingual Education Programs

It is now history that the rebirth of bilingual education in the United States occurred in 1963 with the waves of thousands of Cuban refugees coming into this country whose children needed special attention to their educational needs. However, it was the enactment of the Bilingual Education Act in 1968 that gave this important educational movement the impetus it deserved.

As important as this legislation has been in helping school districts throughout the country to wake up from their apathy and really provide the viable alternatives in education that are necessary to educate all children, it has had its detrimental effects. The Federal Government, cautiously avoiding a dictatorial role in the area of education, was fully aware that in enacting such legislation monetary concerns would be a key factor as to whether or not the identified number of children (over 5 million) in the United States would all be served. Since the intent of the legislation was only to provide "seed money" for demonstration

---

[3] Joshua A. Fishman, "Bilingual Education: An International Sociological Perspective," (Keynote address delivered at the Fifth Annual International Bilingual/Bicultural Education Conference, San Antonio, Texas, May 1976.)

projects in bilingual education that could be easily replicated by interested school districts, the monies available for this purpose were rather restricted. What ensued was that priorities had to be established in order to have an equitable distribution of funds among the many states that had high concentrations of non-English-speaking children. As a consequence, not only does the legislation specify that the primary eligible applicants were to be school districts with high concentrations of non-English-speaking children but it also adds that these children had to come from homes in which parents were earning $3,000 or less. Provisions are also made to allow English-speaking children to participate in the program but in a limited number—ergo, its relegation to a compensatory status. Therefore, this important educational movement is now being considered to be purely compensatory and only "good" for the non-English-speaking minorities in the United States, rather than the landmark it should be in the annals of education.

It follows, then, that skeptical school districts, forced to implement bilingual education programs in order to appease the vocal communities demanding quality education for their children, have now chosen the least effective alternative to bilingual education, e.g., the transitional approach.

It is folly to think that bilingual education is only suitable for those non-English-speaking children who are doing poorly in school. Bilingual education, in its full implementation, is quality education for all, be they non-English-speaking or English-speaking. To allow bilingual education programs to utilize the native language of the child only as a "crutch" (transitional) until such time as the child gains proficiency in English is pedagogically and psychologically unsound. For the non-English-speaking child it means the native language (and all cultural, sociological, and psychological implications involved) is only important until the second language is acquired. Such a policy again relegates the child's native language to an inferior status. For the English-speaking child this reinforces the tacit assumption that English is superior, and it denies these children the opportunity to acquire a second language and its related benefits.

It is unfortunate that non-English-speaking children are not allowed to develop fully their native language (nor are English-speaking children given the opportunity to learn a second one) at an age when they are physiologically and mentally ready to do so. Often, around three to six years later they are forced to pick up the language as a college entrance requirement at an age which research has shown to be troublesome and traumatic. If, indeed, the native language is important for a learner's academic development, it follows that it should be maintained and fully developed throughout one's educational career. This does not lessen the opportunity for the student to gain the proficiency required in English. On the contrary, having been given the opportunity to do so, one's native language will supplement and complement the second one to the point that the learner becomes a better English-speaker and a more well-rounded person, not to speak of the advantages that will be gained from having a true cultural understanding of one's fellow human beings.

Bilingual education as a *maintenance* program provides the student ample opportunities not only to become a bilingual/bicultural person but also biliterate in every sense of the word. This approach favors no ethnic or linguistic minority *per se*, but in essence upholds the true meaning of bilingual education—that every child has an inalienable right to develop to his or her fullest potential, through the educational process.

Summary

If bilingual education is to become an integral part of American education, care must be taken not to allow it to become one of the compensatory programs that are in vogue today for the so-called "disadvantaged." It must be viewed as the *enrichment* program that children need in order to survive in this shrinking world. It must be viewed as a program that can provide more than just an ethnocentric perspective to life's complexities but one that fosters cross-cultural and cross-linguistic understanding and respect.

In retrospect, let us not forget that the Bilingual Education Act, even with its shortcomings, gave us a beginning in our quest for quality education for all children. However, complacency cannot be allowed to set in to the point that we allow this educational movement to be as poorly implemented as it has been recently; for this would certainly mean its demise. Let us insure that bilingual education be continued only as quality education and not as a poor excuse for mediocrity.

The Edinburg Experience in Bilingual Education—1966 to 1976

Alfonso Ramírez

Whether non-English speakers in our schools succeed or fail in their effort to acquire English language skills often depends more upon the "language mix" in the classroom than upon instructional strategies. A single Spanish speaker in a class of thirty English speakers has a much better chance of acquiring English than if the entire class speaks no English. In the Southwest, particularly along the Mexican border, much of the population speaks Spanish at home and must learn English in school, usually a free public school, designed for monolingual English-speaking pupils and run by monolingual English-speaking teachers and administrators. What happens in that school to adjust to the needs of the non-English speakers will determine whether or not this segment of our population is participating in the American dream of universal education.

Prior to 1966 very little was happening to improve the educational opportunities of non-English-speaking beginners in the United States. With the exception of New York and Miami in the East, and San Antonio and Laredo in the Southwest, there was little evidence that school districts were responding to the growing need for changes in the curriculum offered children who spoke little or no English. If there was a recognition of the need

247

for change, each school district was on its own to pursue the matter, and three formidable obstacles faced any innovator:

1. No desire to change on the part of the policy makers.
2. No money to support a major change.
3. No experienced personnel to direct the change.

Since 1966 at least one ESL curriculum revision project succeeded in overcoming all of those barriers, but it took the Russians, the President of the United States, and the Congress to make the breakthrough possible. This report necessarily begins with the background and the context in which the experiment developed.

There is something curiously contradictory about our system of free compulsory education. The law of the land guarantees each child equal access to tax-supported schooling, but the fulfillment of this promise is left to the taxing agencies—the state and local boards of education. While there are only fifty state educational systems, each one has from one (Hawaii) to 1404 (Nebraska) school districts. In 1975 there were 16,960 such local education agencies in the United States, each with its own school board and superintendent to make decisions on curriculum, zoning, busing, hiring, taxing, spending, and so on. Expenditures per pupil, one measurable factor indicating relative ability and willingness to provide free education, ranged from $790 per year in Alabama to $2102 in Alaska in 1974, with a national average of $1281. Thus, while our society claims a commitment to quality education for all, the disparities from state to state and from district to district indicate that we do not have a system of education that necessarily serves the national interest. It is as though the defense of the country were dependent upon the actions of 17,000 autonomous military units. The analogy may be inappropriate, yet our expenditures suggest that our two biggest concerns are domestic ignorance and foreign oppression. We fought ignorance with $108 billion in 1974 and spent $87.5 billion on defense. The federal share of all education costs is about twenty percent and, of course, the full military budget is federally supported.

There was a time, however, in the first half of the twentieth century when federal participation in public education was almost negligible. Special programs for the culturally and linguistically different were rare. Then on October 4, 1957, the Russians

248

launched the world's first known man-made satellite. Before Sputnik had completed its first orbit America's two major fears emerged in full force. Were our idealogical foes smarter and stronger? Were we neglecting to educate our children for the technological revolution? Our total expenditures for education the year before were $16.8 billion, representing 4.2 percent of the gross national product. The defense budget in 1955-1956 was $36 billion. Twenty years later our commitment to education is six times greater in total dollars spent and approximately 8 percent of the gross national product. Military spending in that period grew only two and a half times.

Without the impetus of the rockets developed by the German and Russian scientists, American education might still be slumbering and clinging to its parochial purposes. For it was the National Defense Education Act of 1958, a reaction to that space shot, that provided the money needed to strengthen instruction in foreign languages, as well as science and mathematics. Six years later in the summer of 1964, the first English as a Second Language NDEA institutes were held. This marked the beginning of renewed interest in and support for modifications in the curricula being offered to non-English speakers. The following year, Congress passed the Elementary and Secondary Education Act of 1965, providing, among other things, grants to schools serving children from low-income families. In a commendable display of unanimity and cooperation, forty school districts in the extreme southern tip of Texas chose to pool their grants under the provisions of Title III of the bill and gave their cooperative, The Valley Association for Superior Education, the mandate to develop an adequate ESL curriculum for the primary grades. Planning for the experiment began in 1966. The base of the instruction was to be a two-year course of carefully sequenced, linguistically sound oral language lessons developed at UCLA under a federal grant. The Texas staff, experienced in teaching young Spanish monolinguals but only slightly aware of linguistic analysis, made no changes in the content of the lessons. The realia and illustrations, the songs, games, stories, and other enrichment and reinforcement activities were carefully selected. But probably the greatest contribution to the new course was the introduction of "language experience" attitudes and activities. Throughout the teaching manual and in all of the train-

249

ing sessions, the emphasis was upon the acceptance of and respect for every pupil. The traditional role of the teacher as the arbiter of speech, dress, taste, and talent was to be discarded. The assumption was that while six-year-old children need direction and instruction, they first need acceptance and affection.

This was to be the most difficult training task of all. Project staff members sometimes were unable to accept and respect the teachers they were training, thereby invalidating the prime concept. In time, however, thanks to intensive orientation conducted by Spanish-speaking professionals and community members, trainers as "corrective agents" were transformed into "friendly helpers."

We could observe other changes resulting from the new attitudes. Children "blossomed" as a result of having their opinions valued, their work displayed, and their individuality preserved. Parents attributed the early reading successes to a fortunate distribution of genes. "This is the smartest of all our kids," was the usual manner of expressing it. Gone were the feelings of doubt and inferiority. School was fun and finishing the writing of a story was often more fun than playing on the slides on the playground. There was a new spirit—a challenging but non-threatening environment that contrasted with the non-project classrooms next door.

As children and teachers responded to the new style, enthusiasm for the new program began growing. At the end of the first year, the experimental class had a significantly higher attendance record than the control class in the same school. The scores in oral language achievement were also gratifying, indicating that the emphasis on grammatical proficiency and communication skills within a variety of real-life situations, as opposed to mere vocabulary and pronunciation development, was having the desired results. The percentage of correct responses by Spanish speakers to an oral test devised to measure proficiency in comparison to native speakers of English is shown below.

Test Component	Experimental	Control
Communication	96%	67%
Structure	47%	18%
Vocabulary	83%	79%
Pronunciation	74%	74%

Hawthorne effects and personal biases undoubtedly affected the decision to replicate the experiment and to mass produce the materials, but the demand for a beginning course in ESL was so great in those years that the evaluation was probably not even a consideration. Three hundred kits were prepared for migrant classrooms in Texas in 1968, and the second year's lessons went through the same testing process as the first.

And during this period, what was happening to the need to read? In Texas, as in most states, literacy training was thought of only in terms of English reading. The related activities of the oral English course, by then known as The Region One Curriculum Kit (ROCK), included pre-reading practice, principally in the form of a daily show-and-tell session called "sharing time." While the children's statements were written on a reading-experience chart in the language they themselves used to express them, the practice exercises were in English since instruction in Spanish was then a violation of state law.

Two developments in education legislation in the late 1960s changed the entire perspective of the new curriculum. One was the addition of the kindergarten year for Texas children of limited English ability and the other was the amendment to the Federal Elementary and Secondary Education Act providing for experimentation in Bilingual Education. Once the Texas law prohibiting the use of Spanish was rescinded, the children's language resources could be fully exploited. The effect of the following educational practices could then be determined:

1. Children who spoke only Spanish would receive an extra year (from age 5 to 6) to begin oral English practice.

2. Reading instruction in Spanish could begin in kindergarten because the children had the oral language skills needed to succeed and because Spanish reading is relatively easy to learn at that age.

3. Language experience activities, including creative writing, could begin in Spanish and then be done bilingually as the pupils were ready.

251

4. The transition into English reading instruction would be planned as a natural development of Spanish reading and oral English skills.

5. Traditional English basal reading instruction would begin in second grade, after two years of oral English and of Spanish reading, and after a year of transitional English and creative writing.

Details of this experimentation, which ended in 1975, are recorded in the evaluation reports filed with the Title VII and Right to Read Offices in the Office of Education in Washington.

(1) Students who received instruction in the bilingual curriculum reached achievement levels in vocabulary, comprehension, total reading, language usage and structure, and spelling that were equal to or better than the achievement levels reached by their older siblings who received instruction in the traditional school curriculum.

(2) Bilingual instruction was significantly better in producing educational gain in the subject areas of comprehension, total reading, language usage and structure, and spelling.

Another type of test was devised by the project staff in an effort to measure gains in creative writing. A short non-verbal film is shown to the subjects and immediately afterwards sheets of blank paper and pencils are distributed for the pupils to use in writing, in English, their immediate impressions of the film. After a short break the writing task is repeated in Spanish. The essays are scored on the basis of the number of words and sentence units produced and on the correctness of spelling. Comparisons are made with control groups who were not taught by the language experience approach and who were not taught in their native language. Two such comparisons were made, one in 1973 and the other in 1975. The first was between 155 children from one school district in Texas, taught in kindergarten and first grade with the experimental materials and methods, and 120 children of similar background in another school district fifty miles away who received conventional instruction. The following means were obtained:

	English Exp.	Writing Control	Spanish Exp.	Writing Control
Number of words	32	23.5	29	.7
Words spelled correctly	19.5	17.5	19.9	.3
Recognizable words	12.4	6.0	9.5	.3
Length of sentence units	10.5	6.9	11.7	7.0

When compared on the basis of scores on the Metropolitan Achievement Test, the differences are slight and in favor of the control group.

	MEAN GRADE EQUIVALENT	
SUBTEST	Exp.	Control
Word knowledge	1.7	1.8
Word analysis	1.9	1.9
Reading	1.6	1.8

The report of this study, prepared by D. G. Ellson of Indiana University on the basis of material supplied by the project, includes this summary:

By 1976 the two-year ESL course, The Region One Curriculum Kit (ROCK), and the Spanish and English Region One Literacy Lessons (ROLL) were on the state adopted lists in Texas and California. The materials were also in use in several hundred classrooms in other states and in Mexico.

Other attempts have been made to evaluate these materials and methods by means of standardized English reading tests. The most detailed and carefully controlled study is Larry Dean Hord's unpublished doctoral dissertation at Texas A&M, *A Longitudinal Evaluation of the Edinburg Bilingual Reading Project*. Hord's conclusions, based on results from the California Achievement Test scores of experimental subjects and their older siblings are:

In a comparison of the performance of primarily Spanish-speaking children taught by the Region I 'creative writing' method in kindergarten and first grade with that of similar children taught by conventional methods:

a) performance in reading comprehension as measured by a standardized test favored the conventionally taught group, but

b) in writing a descriptive essay in English, the creative writing group wrote much more and used longer sentences than the conventionally taught group, and

c) in writing a similar essay in Spanish, the creative writing group wrote almost as much and as meaningfully as they had written in English, while the conventionally taught group wrote almost nothing.

In a second study, involving over 1,000 children in each group, the comparison was between second graders in seven school districts. The control group attended K, 1, and 2 from 1971 to 1973, receiving no bilingual or creative writing instruction. The experimental group attended the same schools and the same grades but from 1973 to 1975, and those pupils were taught with the experimental methods and materials.

The results, which are too numerous to list here, favor the experimental group in English writing in all of the schools. No analysis was made of Spanish writing because the control group was unable to write in that language. The scores on standardized tests yielded inconclusive results. In four school districts the experimental group gained from one to six months in mean grade equivalents; in two schools there were losses of two to five months; and in the seventh there were no differences.

On the basis of these studies, what conclusions can be reached concerning the experiment after spending nine years and almost two million dollars on development, production, implementation, and training?

1. That the "establishment" came through and responded to a long-recognized need for quality education for Spanish-speaking children;

2. That tangible products are on the market and in use in hundreds of classrooms with similar needs;

3. That we still are not able to quantify many of the positive results accruing from bilingual education programs; and most importantly

4. That we pioneered in the right direction—towards dignity for both learner and teacher and away from fear of failure on the part of both learner and teacher.

References

Digest of Educational Statistics. 1974. National Center for Educational Statistics, U. S. Department of Health, Education and Welfare.

Ellson, D. 1974. Statistical comparison of two non-English speaking groups of students. Study commissioned by Region One Service Center, Edinburg, Texas.

Hord, Larry D. 1976. A Longitudinal Evaluation of the Edinburg Bilingual Reading Project. Unpublished doctoral dissertation, Texas A & M University, College Station, Texas.

Region One Curriculum Kit (ROCK) and Region One Literacy Lesson (ROLL). 1970. Dallas, Texas: Melton Book Company.

ABOUT THE
AUTHORS

J. Donald Bowen is Professor of English at the University of California, Los Angeles; Visiting Professor of English Language Teaching, the American University in Cairo; and Visiting Professor, Faculty of Education, Ain Shams University. He was formerly Scientific Linguist in the Foreign Service Institute, the United States Department of State. Professor Bowen is author of *Patterns of English Pronunciation* (Newbury House, 1975), coauthor of *The Grammatical Structures of English and Spanish* (University of Chicago Press, 1965), and has written numerous articles on language teaching and English and Spanish linguistics. He has also been Co-Director, Philippine Center for Language Study, 1958–1962; Field Director, Survey of Language Use and Language Teaching, Eastern Africa, 1968–1970.

Marina Burt is Consultant in Educational Psycholinguistics at the BABEL/Lau Center, Berkeley, California, and has been Senior Research Associate at the State University of New York at Albany, an instructor in Linguistics at the Massachusetts Institute of Technology, and Lecturer in Linguistics at Stanford University. She is author of *From Deep to Surface Structure: An Introduction to Transformational Grammar* (Harper & Row, 1971), and coauthor of the *Bilingual Syntax Measure*, English, Spanish, and Filipino Editions (Harcourt Brace Jovanovich, 1975) and of *The Gooficon: A Repair Manual for English* (Newbury House, 1972). She has coauthored and coedited several other major publications and written numerous articles on second language acquisition, language testing, and error analysis. She was TESOL Second Vice-President and Co-Chairperson of the 1975 TESOL Convention, and faculty member at the 1976 Linguistics Institute of the Linguistic Society of America.

257

John B. Carroll is Kenan Professor of Psychology, University of North Carolina, Chapel Hill. He was formerly Senior Research Psychologist at Educational Testing Service and Professor of Educational Psychology at Harvard University. Professor Carroll is author of *Language and Thought* (Prentice-Hall, 1964), editor (with Jeanne Chall) of *Toward a Literate Society* (McGraw-Hill, 1975), and author of *The Teaching of French as a Foreign Language in Eight Countries* (NY: Halsted Press, 1975). Professor Carroll has also written numerous articles on the psychology of language, language testing, and applications of linguistics to education. He is a Founding Member of the National Academy of Education.

Heidi Dulay is Consultant in Educational Psycholinguistics at the BABEL/Lau Center, Berkeley, California, and has been Assistant Professor of Puerto Rican Studies and Education at the State University of New York at Albany, Lecturer in Linguistics at Stanford University, and Instructor in Bilingual Education at Harvard University. She was formerly Assistant Director of Research for Bilingual Children's Television, the producers of *Villa Allegre*, a national bilingual television series for young children. She is coauthor of the *Bilingual Syntax Measure*, English, Spanish, and Filipino Editions (Harcourt Brace Jovanovich, 1975), *Why Bilingual Education? A Review of Research* (BABEL/Lau Center, 1977), and coeditor of *New Directions in Second Language Learning, Teaching, and Bilingual Education* (TESOL, 1975). Dr. Dulay has also written numerous articles on psycholinguistic factors in the process of becoming bilingual. She has been Co-Chairperson of the 1975 TESOL Convention and faculty member at the 1976 Linguistics Institute of the Linguistic Society of America.

Lars Henric Ekstrand is Lecturer in Education at the School of Education, Malmö, Sweden. He was formerly psychologist at the National Board of Education in Sweden. Mr. Ekstrand is coauthor of *Vi lär oss svenska (Learning Swedish)*, Stockholm: SÖ-förlaget, 1966; *Fallet Heimo (The case of Heimo): Practical methods for the socio-emotional development of immigrant children*, Stockholm: Skandinaviska Testförlaget, 1973, and is author of *DPI: Diagnotiska prov för invandrarelever (Diagnostic Tests for Immigrant Pupils)*,

Stockholm: Skandinaviska Testförlaget, 1974. He has also written numerous articles on migrant adaptation, adjustment of migrant children, second language acquisition, and linguistic and socio-emotional adjustment and their interrelations.

Mary Finocchiaro is Professor Emeritus, Hunter College of the City University of New York and Special Assistant, Cultural Office of the American Embassy, Rome, Italy. She was formerly Professor of Applied Linguistics, University of Rome; Specialist in Linguistics and Language Teaching, U.S. Department of State; and Coordinator, Fulbright Professorship Program, Italy and Spain. Professor Finocchiaro is the author of many texts, among which are *The Foreign Language Learner* (Regents, 1973), *Teaching Children Foreign Languages* (McGraw-Hill, 1964), *English as a Second Language: From Theory to Practice* (Regents, 1974), *Teaching English as a Second Language* (Harper and Row, 1969), *Let's Talk* (Regents, 1970), to name just a few. She has been President of TESOL (1970–1971) and has received three Fulbright Professorships, a Medal from the Government of Poland (1974), and the USIA Outstanding Achievement Award (1976).

Reinhold Freudenstein is Professor at Marburg University and Director of the Foreign Language Research Information Center (IFS) at Marburg, Federal Republic of Germany. He formerly taught German at Manchester College, North Manchester, Indiana, and English as a second language at a German high school. He is author of *Unterrichtsmittel Sprachlabor* (Bochum: Kamp[4] 1975), and editor of *Praxis des Neusprachlichen Unterrichts*, a quarterly for teachers of foreign languages, (Dortmund: Lensing), and has written numerous articles on methodology of foreign language teaching and educational technology. Professor Freudenstein is also Secretary General of the World Federation of Foreign Language Teachers' Associations (FIPLV) 1971–1977.

Charles R. Hancock is Assistant Professor at the State University of New York at Albany. He was formerly Assistant Professor at Teachers College, Columbia University. Professor Hancock has written numerous articles on attitudes and motivation and teacher education. He is a member of the Executive Council of ACTFL, a member of the Board of Directors of the New York

State Association of FL Teachers, and a member of the Teacher Training Commission at the AATF.

Eduardo Hernández-Chávez currently teaches in the Linguistics Department, Stanford University. He was previously Coordinator of the Chicano Studies Program at the University of California, Berkeley. He is coauthor of the *Bilingual Syntax Measure* (Harcourt Brace Jovanovich, 1975) and coeditor of *El Lenguaje de los Chicanos: Regional and Social Characteristics of Language Use of Mexican-Americans* (Center for Applied Linguistics, 1975). He has also written on both phonological and syntactic aspects of language acquisition, on code-switching in Spanish and English, and on sociolinguistic aspects of bilingual education.

Kenneth Johnson is Associate Professor of Education, University of California, Berkeley. He was formerly Associate Professor of Education, University of Illinois, Chicago Circle Campus. He is a contributing author of *Teaching Culturally Disadvantaged: A Rational Approach* (Chicago: SRA, 1970) and has written articles on Black dialect and its effects on learning.

Stephen D. Krashen is Associate Professor in the Department of Linguistics at the University of Southern California. He was formerly Director of ESL, Queens College of the City University of New York and Postdoctoral Fellow at the Neuropsychiatric Institute, UCLA. Professor Krashen is coauthor of *The Human Brain* (Prentice-Hall, forthcoming) and has written numerous articles on neurolinguistics and adult second language acquisition.

Robert Lado is Professor of Linguistics, Georgetown University. He was formerly Dean, School of Languages and Linguistics, Georgetown University; Director, English Language Institute, University of Michigan; and Fulbright Professor, University of Madrid, Spain. Professor Lado is author of *Linguistics Across Cultures* (University of Michigan Press, 1957), *Language Testing* (Longmans, 1961. McGraw-Hill, 1964), *Language Teaching* (McGraw-Hill, 1964), and has also written numerous articles on language teaching, language testing, applied linguistics, and early reading. He is former President of the Michigan Linguistic Society, the Washington Linguistics Club, ALFAL (asociación de linguística y filología de América Latina), and is Numerary member of the "Academia Norteamericana de la Lengua Española."

William Francis Mackey is Research Professor in the International Center for Research on Bilingualism, Quebec, Canada. He was formerly Federal Commissioner of Bilingual Districts, Professor of English Philology and Linguistics at Laval University and Senior Lecturer in the Division of Language Teaching of the Institute of Education at the University of London. He is author of *Language Teaching Analysis,* (London: Longmans, 1965), (Bloomington: Indiana University Press, 1967), (Paris: Didier, 1972), *Bilinguisme et contact des langues,* (Paris: Klincksieck, 1976), and *Bilingual Education in a Binational School,* (Rowley, Mass.: Newbury House, 1972). He has also written numerous articles on bilingualism, language didactics, vectorial phonology, geolinguistics, interlingual distance, language policy analysis, componential semantics, language behavior, and research methods for the study of language contact. He has been a member of the Permanent International Committee of Linguists (CIPL) since 1957. He was the 1966 Adair Memorial Lecturer at McGill University, and received the 1974 Jubilee Medal (Institute of Linguists) "for distinguished service to the profession."

Bernice Melvin is Assistant Professor in the Department of French-Italian, University of Texas at Austin. She has written articles on the role of memory and second language learning and teaching.

Patricia J. Nakano is Manager of the BABEL/Lau Center, Berkeley, California. She was formerly Confidential Assistant to the Under Secretary of the United States Department of Health, Education, and Welfare; Member, Task Force for the Development of the May 25th Memorandum; Consultant to the Office for Civil Rights (OCR) in rendering technical assistance to school districts in the United States; and Special Assistant for Special Groups to the Director of OCR. She is presently a member of the California Joint Legislative Steering Committee on Educational Evaluation for Coordination of Bilingual Education Support Services.

Maureen Concannon O'Brien is President of Dublin College and Secretary General, ATESOL (The Association of Teachers of English as a Second or Other Language) in Ireland. She was formerly Registrar at Dublin College, and Founder/Director of The English Language Institute, Dublin. She is editor of two monographs on language learning and testing and has written articles on bilingualism in Ireland and psychology and language teaching.

John W. Oller, Jr. is Associate Professor of Linguistics at Southern Illinois University, Carbondale, Illinois. (He is on leave from the University of New Mexico.) He was formerly Associate Professor of Psycholinguistics (English Department—TESL) at the University of California, Los Angeles. Professor Oller is co-editor of *Focus on the Learner: Pragmatic Perspectives for the Language Teacher* (Newbury House, 1973) and author of *Coding Information in Natural Languages* (Mouton, 1971). He has also written many articles on linguistic theory, language testing, and pragmatics. Professor Oller served for four years as a member of the TOEFL Examiner's Committee for Educational Testing Service and directed the placement of foreign students in ESL classes at UCLA for three years.

Albar A. Peña is Director of the Division of Bicultural/Bilingual Studies at the University of Texas, San Antonio. He was formerly National Director of Title VII, ESEA, the Bilingual Education Program U.S.O.E., Washington, D.C. and President (1975 –76) of the National Association for Bilingual Education. Professor Peña is contributing author of *Reading for the Disadvantaged* (Harcourt, Brace & World, Inc., 1970) and of *Mexican-American and Educational Change* (U.S.O.E. publication, 1971), along with numerous articles on bicultural/bilingual education and English as a second language. He was U.S. Representative in the International Colloquium in Bilingualism and Biculturalism, Paris, France and attended the invitational White House Conference on Bilingual Education. Listed in *Who's Who in Government*, Professor Peña is a member of the Prominent Mexican-American Educators in the United States.

On June 22, 1976, **Paul Pimsleur** suffered a fatal heart attack in Paris. Only a week before, he had submitted this article for inclusion in this volume. Paul was serving as Professor Associé at the Sorbonne, while on leave from the State University of New York at Albany where he was Professor of French and Education. Formerly, he had been Director of the Listening Center at Ohio State University, had taught at UCLA, and had served as visiting professor in universities and NDEA institutes in the United States and Europe.

Among his many major publications are those with which many in foreign languages and ESL are familiar: *Pimsleur Foreign Language Tests* (French, Spanish and German); *Le pont sonore: Une méthode pour comprendre le français parlé;* and *Encounters: A Basic Reader,* all major publications in the field. His latest undertaking was basic research in French second language acquisition which was to have served as the basis for the development of a French edition of the *Bilingual Syntax Measure.*

Although we have already benefited immensely from his work, Paul Pimsleur's death is a profound loss to us and to all those who are interested in language research and teaching.

M.B., H.D., M.F.

Valerian A. Postovsky is Curriculum Developer and Researcher, Concepts and Systems Division, Defense Language Institute, Foreign Language Learning Center, Presidio of Monterey, California. He was formerly Chief of the Slavic Language Group and Chairman of the Russian Department at the Institute. He has written numerous articles on language learning and methods of foreign language teaching.

Alfonso Ramírez is Coordinator of Instructional Development at the Pan American University, Edinburg, Texas. Director of the Bilingual Division of Region One Service Center for ten years, he is principal author of *Region One Literacy Lessons* (Melton Book Company, 1971) and contributing author of *Open Highways* (Scott Foresman, 1973). He served as President of TESOL, 1972–73.

Wilga M. Rivers is Professor of Romance Languages, and Coordinator of Language Instruction in the Department of Romance Languages at Harvard University. She was formerly Professor of French at the University of Illinois at Urbana-Champaign and Visiting Professor at Teachers College, Columbia University. Professor Rivers is author of *Teaching Foreign Language Skills* (University of Chicago Press, 1968), *The Psychologist and the Foreign Language Teacher* (University of Chicago Press, 1964), *Practical Guide to the Teaching of French* (Oxford University Press, 1975) as well as *Practical Guide to the Teaching of German* (1975), *Spanish* (1976), and *English as a Second Language* (1977). In addition, she has written numerous articles on the applications of psychology and linguistics to language teaching and language teaching methodology. Professor Rivers received the National Distinguished Foreign Language Leadership Award (New York State Teachers), served as Consultant Panelist to National Endowment to the Humanities, was a Rockefeller Foundation Consultant in Bangkok (1971), and taught at linguistics institutes in Cairo (1974) and Oswego, New York (1976).

Betty Wallace Robinett is Professor of Linguistics and Director of the Program in English as a Second Language, University of Minnesota, Minneapolis, Minnesota. She was formerly a faculty member at the University of Michigan, the University of Puerto Rico, and the Inter-American University, Puerto Rico. Professor Robinett has coauthored the *Manual of American English Pronunciation* (Holt, Rinehart and Winston, 1972), and *Lado-Fries English Pronunciation: Exercises in Sound Segments, Intonation and Rhythm* (University of Michigan Press, 1954). She has also written numerous articles on pronunciation of American English and teacher training in English as a Second Language. Professor Robinett has been President of TESOL, 1973–74; Chairman of ATESL of NAFSA, 1976–77; and Chairman, Advisory Screening Committee for Linguistics and EFL/ESL for Fulbright Awards. She was a member of the English Teaching Advisory Panel of UCLA, 1961–63.

Renzo Titone is Professor of Educational Psychology and Applied Psycholinguistics at the University of Rome, Italy. He was formerly Professor of Methodology at Salesian University,

Rome, and Professor of Applied Linguistics and Psycholinguistics at Georgetown University, Washington, D.C. He is author of forty books in applied linguistics and psycholinguistics, and of about 200 articles published in several languages. His latest books are *Psicolinguistica Applicata* (1971: translated into Spanish and Serbo-Croatian); *Bilinguismo Precoce e Educazione Bilingue* (1972: translated into French and Spanish); and *Problems in Educational Psychology* (1975). He is also editor of the *Italian Review of Applied Linguistics,* Director of the Italian Center for Applied Linguistics, and President of the Association of Teachers of English to Speakers of Italian (A.T.E.S.I.).

José A. Vázquez is Chief, Multicultural/Bilingual Division Educational Equity Group of the National Institute of Education, Department of Health, Education, and Welfare, on leave from Hunter College, CUNY, where he was Associate Professor of Education. He was also Director of the Bilingual Program in School and Community, New York City Board of Education; Chairman, New York State Commissioners of Education Council on Bilingual Education (1976); Chairman, Center for Applied Research in Bilingual Education in Affiliation with the Puerto Rican Institute on Social Research (1975); and has written numerous articles on bilingual education, teacher training, and comprehensive planning for bilingual programs.